Publisher's note:
This modern version has been updated from the original text. Words, expressions, and sentence structure have been revised for clarity and readability.

All rights are reserved. No part of this revised text may be reproduced or distributed without the publisher's explicit written consent.

AbidingInk.org

Version: 2025-08-10

DYING THOUGHTS

RICHARD BAXTER (1688)
REVISED TO MODERN ENGLISH (2025)

1.	Preface to the Reader	1
2.	Introduction	3
3.	What Is Desirable in the Present Life	15
4.	Departing to Be with Christ	85
5.	Why Being with Christ Is Far Better	123
6.	The Final Reasons	133
7.	Reasons Arising from My Intellect	141
8.	Reasons Arising from My Will	166
9.	Reasons Drawn from Heavenly Living	195
10.	How God Makes Us Willing to Depart	203
11.	Divine Revelation and the Truth of Christianity	253

1. Preface to the Reader

Reader, I have no other purpose in a preface to this book than to give a plain reason for its publication. I wrote it for myself, uncertain whether anyone would ever see it. In the end I resolved to leave the decision to my executors, who could publish or suppress it after my death as they thought fit.

As my circumstances worsened, my goods were seized and sold by constables, and I was driven from my home because of my preaching in London. I had long kept many manuscripts laid by, but with no house to return to and only a small room hired among strangers, I could not carry everything. I was forced to throw away entire volumes — controversies, practical letters, and cases of conscience — that I could not take with me.

After weeks of nephritic and colic pains and other long afflictions, I resolved to take this little book with me when I moved, for my own use during my sickness. Three weeks later I suffered another violent fit and, thinking death near, had no friend at hand to whom I could safely leave my papers. Fearing they might be lost, I judged it best to commit this one to the printer. I hold that everyone ought to make safe and comfortable preparation for death, and that other people may need the same meditations as I do. If any dislike the title because it seems to imply that the author is dead, let them know that I die daily, and that which will shortly happen is near at hand. The title suits my present case; those who find it unsuitable can simply pass it by. If those now engaged in destructive contests, warring and tearing a distracted land, would spend their lives in serious thoughts of death, they would spare themselves much sorrowful repentance.

The exercise of three sorts of love—toward God, toward others, and toward myself—gives me a threefold contentment, and so makes me willing to depart. I am sure that my departing will satisfy the law of love itself, to which I am chiefly bound to conform and please. That love is the beginning, rule, and end of all things. Even Antonine (Emperor Marcus Aurelius) might draw sober thoughts of death from that notion.

The world is not at an end with my death, nor the church, nor the praise and glory of God; He will be honored from this world to the end. If I love others as myself, I shall carry their lives and comforts in my thoughts as if I lived in them. God will be praised by those who live after me. Even if I were utterly annihilated, that consideration would now afford me solace, provided I live and die in perfect love.

But a fairer and more glorious world lies before me, to which I hope to be translated by death. All three loves should take in the desires of my rising soul: love of myself, that I may be fully happy; love of the triumphant church, of Christ, angels, and glorified men; and love of the glory of the whole creation, which I shall behold. Above all is the love of the most glorious God, the infinite fountain of life, light, and love— the chief and most fitting object of human affection. To be perfectly content in Him, and perfectly acceptable to Him forever, is my chief end and the end of the highest, wisest, and best creatures. Amen.

RICHARD BAXTER

2. Introduction

For I am hard-pressed between the two (Philippians 1:23). I write chiefly for myself, and so I will apply the text to what may profit my own heart and practice.

It was a happy condition into which grace had brought this apostle, who saw much that was both tolerable and desirable in living and in dying. For him, to live is Christ, and to die is gain, the former signifying Christ's interest and work, the latter his own advantage and reward. His difficulty was not whether it was good to live or to depart—both were good—but which was the more desirable.

Was there any doubt between Christ's interest and his own? No, not if the contest were full and absolute. By "Christ" or "Christ's interest" he means his service for the church's good in this world. Yet he knew Christ had an interest in his saints above, and that more might be raised up to serve Him here. But judging by what he saw, there was a scarcity of such servants on earth, and that influenced his choice. For the sake of Christ's work and the church's welfare, he was more willing to delay his reward by self-denial, knowing that such delay would promote their good. I note this to caution against the extreme of thinking only heaven worthy of our regard, and so making an unsound contempt of the world under the pretense of mortification and a heavenly life.

I set this down to avoid being led into the excess of imagining that only heaven deserves our care, and so rejecting the world sinfully under the plea of mortification and a heavenly spirit and life.

By this I do not mean that anything on earth is better than heaven, or should be preferred to it in itself. The end is better than the means, and perfection is better than imperfection.

However, the present use of the means may sometimes be preferred to the present enjoyment of the end. Using means for a higher end may also be preferred to possessing a lower end. Everything has its season. Planting, sowing, and building are not as good as reaping, gathering fruit, and dwelling, but they must be done first, in their season.

But what is so desirable in this life? While it continues, it accomplishes the will of God, who wills that we remain here; and what God wills is best.

The life to come depends on this, just as a man's life in the world depends on his generation in the womb; as reward depends on work; as a runner's or soldier's prize depends on his race or fighting; and as a merchant's gain depends on his voyage. Heaven is won or lost on earth. The possession is there, but the preparation is here.

Christ will judge all men according to their works on earth. "Well done, good and faithful servant;" must precede "Enter into the joy of your lord." "I have fought the good fight, I have finished the race," comes before "the crown of righteousness, which the Lord, the righteous Judge, will give." Everything that must be done for our salvation must be done here. It was on earth that Christ Himself accomplished the work of our redemption, fulfilled all righteousness, became our ransom, and paid the price of our salvation; it is here that our part must be completed.

The granting of the reward is God's work, and we are sure He will never fail. There is no room for the slightest suspicion or fear that He will fail in any of His undertakings. The danger lies in our own shortcomings, lest we be found unworthy of receiving what God will certainly give to all who are prepared to receive it. To distrust God is a grievous sin and folly; but we have good reason to distrust ourselves. Therefore, if we would secure our place in heaven, we must diligently make our title, calling, and election sure here on earth. If we fear hell, we must fear being unprepared for heaven.

This is a great and difficult task that must be accomplished here. Here we must be cured of all damning sin; we must be regenerated and born again; we must be pardoned and justified by faith. Here we must be united to Christ, made wise unto salvation, renewed by His Spirit, and conformed to His likeness. Here we must overcome the temptations of the devil, the world, and the flesh, and perform the duties toward God and men that will be rewarded.

Here Christ must be believed on in the heart unto righteousness, and confessed with the mouth unto salvation. Here we must suffer with Him that we may also reign with Him; and be faithful unto death that we may receive the crown of life. Here we must run in such a way that we may obtain it.

We have greater work to do here than merely secure our own salvation. We are members both of the world and of the church, and we must labor to do good to many. We are entrusted with our Master's talents for His service. In our several places we must do our utmost to propagate His truth and grace, to strengthen His church, to bring souls to Him, to honor His cause, to edify His flock, and to further the salvation of as many as we can. All this must be done on earth if we would secure the end that is in heaven.

It is an error—though I believe only a few fall into it—to think that all religion lies in focusing solely on the life to come while disregarding everything in this present life. True Christians must seriously consider both the end and the way of reaching it. If they do not mind the end with faith, they will never be faithful in the use of means. If they do not diligently use the means, they will not obtain the end.

No one can use the earth well who does not prefer heaven, and none can reach heaven at life's end without being prepared by rightly using the earth. Heaven must hold our highest esteem, habitual love, desire, and joy; but the earth must occupy most of our daily thoughts for present practice. A man traveling to the most desirable home longs for it all the way, yet his immediate business is the journey; the horse, companions, inns, roads, and weariness may occupy more of his present thoughts and actions than his home does.

I have often marveled that David, in the Psalms, and other saints before Christ's coming expressed so strong a sense of the things of this present life while saying so little about the next. They made much of prosperity, dominions, and victories on the one hand, and of enemies, defeats, and persecution on the other. Yet I do not think this arose from mere carnal interest. They cared for the church of God, and for His honor, Word, and worship.

They knew that if things go well with us on earth, they will go well in heaven. If the militant church prospers in holiness, it will certainly triumph in glory. God will do His part to receive souls if they are prepared here. Satan does much of his damning work through men; if we escape the snares of men, we escape much danger. When idolaters prosper, Israel is tempted to idolatry. The Greek church suffers from Turkish prosperity and dominion. Most people follow the powerful and prosperous side. Therefore, for God's cause and for our everlasting interest, we must greatly regard our own state, but regard the state of the church here on earth even more.

If the earth is desired only for its own sake, and prosperity is loved solely for the present welfare of the flesh, that marks damning carnality and an earthly mind. But to desire peace, prosperity, and power to be in the hands of wise and faithful men for the sake of souls, the increase of the church, and the honor of God—so that His name may be hallowed, His kingdom come, and His will be done on earth as it is in heaven—this ought to be chief among our prayers to God.

Therefore, do not be ungrateful, O my soul, for the mercies of this present life—for those granted to your body, to your friends, to the land of your nativity, and especially to the church of God.

This body is so closely united to you that it must be either a great help or a great hindrance. Had it been more afflicted, it might have been a discouraging burden—like a tired horse on a journey, a poor tool for a workman, or an untuned instrument in music. A sick or bad servant in a house is a great trouble, and a bad wife is often worse; but your body is nearer to you than either, and will be more of your concern.

Yet if it had been stronger and healthier, sense and appetite would likely have been stronger, and lust would have been stronger as well. Therefore the danger would have been greater, and victory and salvation much more difficult. Even weak senses and temptations have often prevailed. How do you know what stronger temptations might have done? When I see a thirsty man suffering from fever or dropsy, and especially when I see strong, healthy youths raised in abundance and amid temptations—how mad they are in sin, how violently they are carried away, disregarding God's rebukes, conscience, parents, friends, and all regard for their salvation—it reminds me how great a mercy I had, even in a body not subject to their condition.

Many bodily deliverances have greatly benefited my soul, renewing my time, opportunity, and strength for service, and bringing frequent and fresh proofs of the love of God.

If bodily mercies were not of great use to the soul, Christ would not have shown His saving love by healing all manner of diseases, as He did. Nor would God promise us a resurrection of the body if a suitable body did not further the welfare of the soul.

I am obliged to great thankfulness to God for the mercies of this life that He has shown to my friends; that which furthers their joy should increase mine. "Rejoice with those who rejoice." Nature and grace teach us to be glad when our friends are well and prospering, even though all is in order to better things than bodily welfare.

The mercies of this life to the land of our habitation must not be undervalued. The lack of them is part of God's threatened curse; and godliness is profitable for all things, having promise for the present life and the life to come. When God sends upon a land the plagues of famine, pestilence, war, and persecution, especially a famine of the word of God, it is a great sin to be insensible to it. If anyone says, "While heaven is sure, we have no cause to accuse God or to abandon comfort, hope, or duty," they speak well; but if they say, "Because heaven is all, we must make light of all that befalls us on earth," they are mistaken.

Good princes, magistrates, and public-spirited individuals who promote the safety, peace, and true prosperity of the commonwealth greatly benefit religion and men's salvation; they are to be loved and honored by all. If the civil state, known as the commonwealth, fails or falls into ruin and calamity, the church will suffer as well, just as the soul suffers from the ruin of the body. The Turkish, Muscovite, and other such empires show us how the church diminishes and falls into contempt, or withered ceremony and formality, where tyranny brings slavery, beggary, or prolonged persecution upon the subjects. Certainly, various passages in the Revelations contain the church's glorification of God for their power and prosperity on earth when emperors became Christians. What else can be meant by Revelation 9:10, "And have made us kings and priests to our God; And we shall reign on the earth"? This means that Christians shall be freed from heathen persecution and have rule and sacred honor in the world, some of them being princes, some honored church leaders, and all a peculiar, honored people. If Satan had not found that cursed way of placing wicked men, who hate true godliness and peace, into the sacred offices of princes and pastors to do his work against Christ, in Christ's name, surely no good Christians would have begrudged the power of rulers of state or church. I am sure that many, called fifth-monarchy men, seem to make it their great hope that rule shall be in the hands of righteous men; and I believe most religious groups would rejoice if those they consider to be the best and most trustworthy men held great power, which shows that it is not the greatness of power in most princes or sound bishops that they dislike, but the badness, real or perceived, of those whose power they oppose. Who would blame power to do good?

Surely the first three great petitions of the Lord's Prayer include some temporal welfare of the world and the church, without which the spiritual rarely prospers extensively, although it may prosper intensively in a few, since miracles have ceased.

Therefore, be thankful for all the church's mercies here on earth; for all the protection of magistrates; the abundance of preachers; the preservation from enemies; the restraint of persecution; the concord of Christians; and the increase of godliness, which in this land it has experienced in our ages, despite all of Satan's malignant rage and all the bloody wars that have interrupted our tranquility. How many psalms of joyful thanksgiving are there for Israel's deliverances, the preservation of Zion, and God's worship in His sanctuary: "Pray for the peace of Jerusalem: May they prosper who love you"; especially that the gospel continues while so many rage against it is a mercy not to be taken lightly.

Be especially thankful, O my soul, that God has made any use of you for the service of His church on earth. My soul magnifies the Lord, and my spirit has rejoiced in God my Savior. Oh! What am I, whom You took up from the dunghill or low obscurity, that I should live in the constant enjoyment of Your sweet and sacred truth, and with such encouraging success communicate it to others? Now that my public work seems to be ending, after forty-three or forty-four years, I have no reason to think that I ever labored in vain! O with what gratitude must I look upon all the places where I lived and labored; but above all, that place that had my strength. I bless You for the great numbers who have gone to heaven, and for the continuance of piety, humility, concord, and peace among them.

And for all those who, through my writings, have received any saving light and grace. O my God! Let not my own heart be barren while I labor in Your vineyard, bringing others to holy fruit. Let me not be a stranger to the life and power of that saving truth which I have done so much to communicate to others. O let not my own words and writings condemn me as void of that divine and heavenly nature and life, which I have proclaimed to the world.

Stir up, then, O my soul, your sincere desires and all your faculties to complete the remaining work of Christ appointed to you on earth, and then joyfully wait for the heavenly perfection in God's own time.

You can truly say, "For to me, to live is Christ." It is His work for which you live; you have no other business in the world. Yet you do His work with many oversights and imperfections, and you trouble your thoughts with doubts about God's part, who never fails. If your work is done, be thankful for what is past, and that you are so near the port of rest. If God will add any more days to your life, serve Him with double eagerness, now that you are so close to the end. The prize is almost within sight; time is swift and short. You have told others that there is no working in the grave, and that it must be now or never.

Though the idea of earning through commutative justice is no better than madness, do not dream that God will save the wicked, nor equally reward the slothful and the diligent, because Christ's righteousness was perfect. Paternal justice makes distinctions according to the worthiness defined by the law of grace; and as sin is its own punishment, holiness and obedience are much of their own reward. Whatever God appoints you to do, see that you do it sincerely and with all your might. If sin leads men to be angry because it is detected, disgraced, and resisted, if God is pleased, their wrath should be patiently borne, for they will soon be far more angry with themselves. If slander and reproach endure, so will the better effects on those who are converted; and there is no comparison between these. I shall not be harmed, when I am with Christ, by the calumnies of men on earth; but the saving benefit will be enjoyed eternally by converted sinners. Words and actions are transient things, and once past, they are nothing; but their effects on an immortal soul may be endless. All the sermons that I have preached are nothing now; but the grace of God on sanctified souls is the beginning of eternal life. It is unspeakable mercy to be sincerely thus employed with success; therefore, I had reason all this while to be in Paul's dilemma and make no haste in my desires to depart. The crown will come in its due time; and eternity is long enough to enjoy it, however long it may be delayed. But if I will do that which must obtain it for myself and others, it must be done quickly before my declining sun sets.

O that I had no worse reasons for my unwillingness to die than my desire to do the work of life for my own and others' salvation, and to finish my course with joy, and the ministry committed to me by the Lord.

And as it is on earth that I must do good to others, so it must be in a manner suited to their state on earth. Souls are here closely united to bodies, through which they must receive much good or harm. Do good to men's bodies if you wish to do good to their souls; do not say that physical things are worthless trifles, for which the receivers will never be better; they are things that nature easily senses, and sense is the passage to the mind and will. Do you not find what a help it is to yourself to have, at any time, any ease and cheerfulness of body? And what a burden and hindrance pains and cares are? Labor, then, to free others from such burdens and temptations, and do not disregard them. If you must rejoice with those who rejoice and mourn with those who mourn, further your own joy by furthering theirs; and avoid your own sorrows by alleviating or curing theirs.

But, alas! what power does selfishness have over most. How easily do we bear our brethren's pains, reproaches, wants, and afflictions in comparison to our own! How few thoughts, and how little cost or labor do we expend for their needs, in comparison to what we do for ourselves. Nature indeed teaches us to be most sensitive to our own condition; but grace tells us that we should not make such a great distinction as we do, but should love our neighbor as ourselves.

And now, O my soul, consider how mercifully God has dealt with you, that your dilemma should be between two such desirable conditions. I shall either die speedily or stay yet longer on earth; whichever it is, it will be a merciful and comfortable state. That it is desirable to depart and be with Christ, I must not doubt, and shall soon consider more fully. If my time on earth is extended, it is such a great mercy that it must be weighed against my current possession of heaven. Surely it is a state that obliges me to great thankfulness to God and comfortable acknowledgment; and it is not my pain, or sickness, or suffering from malicious men that should make this life on earth unacceptable while God continues it. Paul had a thorn in the flesh, a messenger of Satan to buffet him, and suffered more from men (though less in his health) than I have done; yet he gloried in such infirmities, rejoiced in his tribulations, and was in a strait between living and dying, indeed, he preferred to live yet longer.

Alas! it is another kind of dilemma that most of the world is in: the dilemma for many is between the desire for life for fleshly interest and the fear of death, which they see as ending their happiness. The dilemma for many is between a tiring world and body, which makes them weary of living, and the dreadful prospect of future danger, which makes them afraid of dying. If they live, it is in misery; if they must die, they are afraid of greater misery. Whichever way they look, behind or before them, to this world or the next, fear and trouble are their lot. Yes, many an upright Christian, through the weakness of their trust in God, lives in this perplexing dilemma; weary of living and afraid of dying; pressed continually between grief and fear. But Paul's dilemma was between two joys; which of them he should desire most. If that is my case, what should much interrupt my peace or pleasure? If I live, it is for Christ; for His work, and for His church; for preparation; for my own and others' everlasting happiness. Should any suffering, which does not render me unserviceable, make me impatient with such a work and such a life? If I die presently, it is my gain; God, who appoints my work, limits my time, and surely His glorious reward can never be unseasonable or come too soon if it is the time He appoints. When I first engaged myself to preach the gospel, I expected (as probable) only one or two years; and God has continued me for over forty-four years (with such interruptions as others in these times have had); and what reason do I have now to be unwilling, either to live or die? God's service has been so sweet to me that it has overcome the trouble of constant pains or weakness of the flesh, and all that men have said or done against me.

But the following crown exceeds this pleasure more than I am capable of conceiving. There is some trouble in all this pleasant work, from which the soul and flesh would rest; and blessed are the dead who die in the Lord; even so says the Spirit; for they rest from their labors, and their works follow them.

But, O my soul, what need do you have to be troubled in this kind of dilemma? It is not up to you to choose whether or when you will live or die. It is God who will determine it, who is infinitely more fit to choose than you. Therefore, leave His own work to Himself, and focus on what is yours; while you live, live for Christ; and when you die, you shall die for Christ; even into His blessed hands. Live in such a way that you can say, "It is Christ who lives in me, and the life that I live in the flesh, I live by faith in the Son of God, who loved me and gave Himself for me." Then, as you have lived in the comfort of hope, you shall die unto the comfort of vision and fruition. And when you can say, "He is the God whose I am, and whom I serve," you may boldly add, "and whom I trust, and to whom I commend my departing soul; and I know whom I have trusted."

3. What Is Desirable in the Present Life

For I am hard-pressed between the two, having a desire to depart and be with Christ, which is far better. (Philippians 1:23)

"Man who is born of woman
Is of few days and full of trouble.
He comes forth like a flower and fades away;
He flees like a shadow and does not continue.
And do You open Your eyes on such a one,
And bring me to judgment with Yourself?" (Job 14:1-3)

Just as a watch, when it is wound up, or a newly lit candle, so man — newly conceived or born — begins a motion that continually hastens to its appointed end. An action and its time once past are nothing. So vain would man be, and so vain his life, were it not for the hopes of a more durable life to come. Those hopes, and the means to attain them, not only distinguish a believer from an infidel but a man from a beast.

When Solomon describes the difference, with respect only to the time and things of this life, he truly tells us that "one thing befalls them: as the one dies, so dies the other... surely they all have one breath; man has no advantage over animals, for all is vanity." Thus the one end that befalls both shows that, viewed only in terms of this life, both are vanity—yet man's vexation exceeds that of beasts.

And Paul rightly says of Christians, "If in this life only we have hope in Christ, we are of all men the most pitiable." Though even in this life, as related to a better one, and as we are exercised about things of a higher nature than the concerns of temporal life, we are far happier than any worldly people.

Being to speak to myself, I shall pass by the rest of the exposition of this text. I will suppose its proper explanation and set before my soul only the doctrine and uses of the two propositions contained in it.

1. That the souls of believers, when departed from here, shall be with Christ.

2. That to be with Christ is far better for them than to be here in the body.

Concerning the first, my thoughts shall keep this order.

1. I shall consider the necessity of believing it.

2. Whether it is best to believe it, without consideration of the proofs or difficulties.

3. The certainty of it manifested for the exercise of faith.

Whether the words signify that we shall be in the same place with Christ (which Grotius groundlessly denies) or only in His hand, care, and love, I will not pause to dispute. Many other texts concur to assure us "where I am, there My servant will be also" (John 12:26; 17:24, etc.). At the very least, "with Him" can mean no less than a state of communion and a participation in happiness. To believe in such a state of happiness for departed souls is of manifold necessity and use.

If this is not soundly believed, a person must live beyond or below the true purpose of life. They must have a false end or be uncertain about what their end should be.

I know it may be objected that if I make it my aim to please God by obeying Him and doing all the good I can, yet trust Him with my soul and future while remaining utterly uncertain about what He will do with me, I still have an intended end that will make me godly, charitable, just, and happy, so far as I am made for happiness. Pleasing God is indeed the right end of all.

But, 1. Must I desire to please Him no better than I do in this imperfect state, in which I have done so much that is displeasing to Him? He who truly desires to please God must desire to please Him perfectly; our desire for our ultimate end must know no bounds. Am I capable of pleasing God no better than by such a sinful life as this?

God has made the desire for our own happiness so necessary to the soul that we cannot expect our desire to please Him to be separated from it. Therefore, both with respect to God as the end and our happiness as the secondary end, we must believe that He is a rewarder of those who diligently seek Him.

If we make such a poor estimate of God that He will turn our pleasing Him into our loss, or will not turn it into our gain and welfare, or if we are unsure whether He will do so, it will hinder our love, trust, and joy in Him. Those affections are the means by which we must please Him. Consequently, such doubts will blunt the eagerness, soundness, and constancy of our obedience.

It will also diminish that self-love which must motivate us, and it will rob us of part of our necessary end. I think objectors will agree that if they have no certainty about what God will do with them, they must at least have some probability or hope before they can sincerely devote themselves to pleasing Him.

If a person is uncertain about the purpose of their life, how can they choose a goal? If they waver to the point of having no goal, they cannot apply any means to attain one. When both goal and means are disregarded, a person no longer lives as a rational human being but rather like a brute.

What a torment for a thoughtful mind to be unsure of what to aim for and what actions to take through life! It is like stepping out the door without knowing where to go. The result is either standing still or moving aimlessly, driven only by immediate sensations—like a windmill or a weathercock—rather than by reason.

If someone settles on a wrong end, it may be worse than having no end at all; for they will only harm others or create the need for repentance. All the actions of such a life must be formally wrong, however good they may seem materially, if their ultimate end is wrong.

If I do not derive my actions from this proper end, and do not believe that God rewards His servants in a better life, what motives remain that will suffice—given our present difficulties—to make me live a holy or even truly honest life? Piety and honesty are good in themselves; but the goodness of a means lies in its suitability for the end.

We face many impediments, competitors, diversions, and temptations that anyone must overcome to live in piety or honesty. Our natures are often diseased and strongly inclined against plain duties. Will we ever fulfill those duties and conquer all these temptations if we lack the necessary motive? Duty to God and to man is often hard and costly to the flesh, though amiable in itself. It may cost us estates, liberty, even life. The world does not easily distinguish good men from bad, or encourage piety and virtue; it often opposes them. Who will abandon present welfare without some hope of better reward? People do not typically serve God for nothing, nor suppose it will be their loss to do so.

A life of sin will not be avoided by lower ends and motives; indeed, when pursued alone, those lower ends will themselves be a constant sin. Preferring vanity to glory, the creature to God, and setting our hearts on that which will never make us happy—when lust and appetite strongly and constantly incline people to various objects, what can restrain them except greater and more enduring delights or motives drawn from higher things? Lust and appetite do not distinguish between lawful and unlawful.

We see where such principles of infidelity lead in the brutish politics of Benedictus Spinosa, in his Tractatus Theologico-Politicus. If sin so pervades the earth that the whole world seems drowned in wickedness despite all hopes and fears of a life to come, what would it be like if there were no such hopes and fears at all?

No mercy can be truly known, valued, or rightly used by someone who does not see its tendency toward the end, who does not perceive that it leads to a better life, and who does not employ it for that purpose. God deals more bountifully with us than worldly people understand. He gives the mercies of this life as helps toward an immortal state of glory, and as earnest tokens of it.

Sensualists do not understand what a soul is, nor what soul-mercies are; therefore they do not grasp the essence of bodily mercies, but settle for the carcass, shell, or shadow. If a king were to give me a lordship and send a horse or coach to carry me to it, and I only rode about the fields for my pleasure without making any other use of it, would I not undervalue and lose the principal benefit of the horse or coach? It is no wonder unbelievers are ungrateful when they do not recognize that part of God's mercies which is the life and real excellence of them.

And, alas, how can I endure the sufferings of this wretched life with any comfort if I have no hope of a life with Christ? What would support and comfort me through physical ailments, weary hours, and the daily experience of the vanity and vexation of all things under the sun, if I had no prospect of a comforting end? I, who have lived among great and precious mercies, have often been tempted to wish I had never been born. I have overcome that temptation only through belief in a blessed life hereafter.

Solomon's sense of vanity and vexation long made all the business, wealth, honor, and pleasure of this world seem like a dream and a shadow to me. Were it not for the hope of the end, I could hardly distinguish between men's sleeping and waking thoughts, nor would I value the waking part of life more than sleeping; I might even count it a kind of happiness to have slept from birth to death.

Children cry when they enter the world, and I often feel regret when awakened from peaceful sleep—especially when called to face the troubles of a restless day. In a reflective state, one might be strongly tempted to complain against the Creator, thinking He deals with us more harshly than with the brutes. We must endure cares, griefs, and fears, know our lacks, face death and future evils that animals are spared, and yet lack the hope of future happiness to support us.

Seneca and the Stoics had little else to say to such complainers who denied a better life except to tell them that if this life had more evil than good and they thought God wronged them, they could remedy it by ending their lives whenever they pleased. But that answer does nothing to ease a nature that is weary of life's miseries yet afraid of death.

It is no wonder that many believed pre-existent souls were placed into these bodies as punishment for something done in a former life, since they did not see the hoped-for end of all our fears and sorrows. "Therefore I hated life because the work that was done under the sun was distressing to me, for all is vanity and grasping for the wind" (Ecclesiastes 2:17).

I have often pondered whether an implicit belief in future happiness—without inquiry into its nature or consideration of objections—is better than a searching, testing approach. On one hand, I have known many godly women who never disputed the matter but served God comfortably into very old age (between eighty and one hundred), living many years in cheerful readiness and desire for death—something few learned, studious men ever attain to in such degree. No doubt this was a divine reward for their long and faithful service to God and their trust in Him.

On the other hand, a studious person can hardly fend off all objections or secure their mind against the suggestions of difficulties and doubts. If such doubts arise, they must be addressed; otherwise we give them half a victory by dismissing them without answer. A faith not supported by evidence discernible to reason is often accompanied by much secret doubt. People may not express that doubt, but it does not therefore vanish, and its weakness can undermine the graces and duties that faith should strengthen. Who knows how soon a temptation from Satan, from infidels, or from our own dark hearts may assail us—temptations that cannot be overcome without such evidence and illuminating light? Yet many who reason and dispute most do not possess the strongest faith.

I have often wondered whether implicit faith in future happiness—without inquiry into its nature or consideration of opposing arguments—or a searching, testing faith is better. On one side, I have known godly women who never disputed the matter but served God comfortably into very old age (between eighty and one hundred), living many years in cheerful readiness and desire for death, a state few learned, studious men attain to in such degree. No doubt this was a divine reward for their long and faithful service to God and their trust in Him.

On the other side, a studious person can hardly keep off all objections or secure the mind against suggestions of difficulty and doubt. If such doubts arise, they must be answered, for dismissing them before we can answer gives them half a victory. A faith not supported by evidence that reason can discern and justify is often accompanied by much secret doubt—doubt people dare not express, yet which does not disappear. Its weakness may weaken all the graces and duties that faith should strengthen. Who knows how soon a temptation from Satan, from infidels, or from our own dark hearts may assault us—one not overcome without such evidence and resolving light? Yet many who debate most are not the strongest in faith.

Yet man, being a rational creature, is not taught by mere instinct and inspiration alone. God's effective teaching ordinarily presumes a rational, objective, and organized understanding. The unlearned Christians mentioned earlier are convinced, by good evidence, that God's Word is true and His rewards certain, even if they have only a vague awareness of that evidence and cannot articulate it in clear concepts.

To push those who have this fundamental evidence into hasty disputes, confusing them with words and artificial objections, only harms them. It sets the artificial, organized body of knowledge against the true light and perception of the matter, which functions like the soul. Just as carnal men set the creatures against God—what should lead us to God—so they oppose true perception with logical, artificial knowledge.

Those prepared for disputes and equipped with all artificial aids may use them to defend and clarify the truth for themselves and others, provided they use such tools as means to the proper end and do not set them against — or in place of — the real, effective light.

We must distinguish what is revealed and necessary from what is unrevealed and unnecessary. Studying until we clearly understand the certainty of future happiness — and what it consists of, namely the sight of God's glory, perfect holy mutual love, union with Christ, and all the blessed — is of great use for our holiness and peace. But when we seek to know more than God intends for us, it blinds us — as gazing at the sun does — and can make us doubt certainties because we cannot resolve uncertainties.

It is better to leave many questions unanswered: how souls exist and act outside the body, whether with organs or without, how they remain individual, where they will reside, and how they will be reunited with the body. If these matters were essential, they would have been revealed. Regarding such curiosities and unnecessary knowledge, a believer should implicitly entrust their soul to Christ, satisfied that He knows what we do not. Be wary of vain, vexatious inquisitiveness about good and evil; it is selfish, betrays distrust of God, and is itself a sin — the sort of thing the learned world fears too little.

That God is the rewarder of those who diligently seek Him, and that holy souls will be in blessedness with Christ — these following evidences, when combined, affirm the hopes of my soul.

The soul, an immortal spirit, must exist eternally in either a good or bad condition. Man's soul is an immortal spirit, and the good are not in a bad condition. Its immortality may be shown thus: a spiritual, most pure, invisible substance, naturally endowed with the power, virtue, or faculty of vital action, intellection, and volition; which is not annihilated or destroyed by separation of parts, nor ceases to exist or loses its power, species, individuation, or action, is an immortal spirit. Such is the soul of man, as will be demonstrated in parts.

The soul is a substance; for that which is nothing can do nothing. It moves, understands, and wills. No one can deny that these actions are performed by something within us, and that something is what we call the soul. It is not nothing; it exists within us.

As for those who claim it is the temperament of various parts combined, I have fully refuted them elsewhere and proved that: 1. There is one part that acts upon the others—what all who call it the material spirits or fiery part acknowledge. Bones and flesh do not understand; a purer substance does, as all agree. 2. Whatever part it may be, it cannot do more than it is capable of doing, and a combination of many parts, none of which possess the power of vitality, intellection, or volition, cannot perform those acts. There can be no more in the effect than is in the cause; otherwise it would not be an effect.

The objections that claim a lute, a watch, or a book perform actions through cooperation which no single part can achieve are vain, as I have demonstrated elsewhere.

Indeed, many strings produce various motions and effects on the ear and imagination, which we perceive as sound and harmony. But all of this is merely the vibration of air caused by the strings. If that motion were not received by a sensitive soul, it would not be music or melody. Thus nothing occurs that each part does not have the power to accomplish. However, intellection and volition are not merely the combined motions of all the body's parts. They receive their form from a nobler, intellective nature—just as the sound of strings produces melody in a person. If this were the case, that receptive nature would still be as excellent as the effect it produces.

A watch or clock moves only by the action of its spring or weight. That it serves as a sign and measure of time for humans is due to the human who ordered it for that purpose. There is nothing in the motion that the parts do not have the power to cause. That it signifies the hour of the day to us is not an action but an object utilized by a rational soul — much like the shadow of a tree or house, which itself does nothing.

Similarly, a book does nothing at all; it is merely a collection of passive signs arranged so that a person's active intellect can understand what the writer or organizer intended. Therefore nothing occurs beyond the power of the agent, nor is there anything in the effect that was not present in the cause, either formally or eminently. For a collection of atoms, none of which possess sense or reason, to become sensitive and rational through mere combined motion is an effect that exceeds the power of the supposed cause.

Yet while some think so poorly of our noblest acts as to believe that merely agitated atoms can perform them, others think so highly of those acts as to attribute them solely to God or to some universal soul within the body of man. They conclude there is no life, sense, or reason in the world except for God himself (or such a universal soul); thus either every man is God in terms of his soul, or the body alone is what we call man, distinct from God. This is the self-entangling and self-confounding folly of busy, bold, and arrogant minds that do not understand their own capacity and limitations. Following similar reasoning, they must ultimately assert that all passive matter is also God, and that God is the universe, consisting of an active soul and passive body. That implies God is no cause and can create nothing, or nothing with life, sense, or reason.

But why do we stray from certain matters with such presumptions? Is it not certain that there are lesser creatures in the world than men or angels? Is it not certain that one man is not another? Is it not certain that some men suffer torment of body and mind? Would it comfort a man in such torment to be told that he is God or part of a universal soul? Would not a man on the rack, or suffering from stones or other misery, say, "Call me by whatever name you wish; it does not alleviate my pain. If I am part of God or a universal soul, I am still a tormented, miserable part. If you could convince me that God has parts that are not serpents, toads, devils, or wicked or tormented men, you must give me other senses and perceptive powers before it will comfort me to hear that I am not such a part. If God has wicked and tormented parts on earth, why could He not have such parts, and I be one of them, hereafter? And if I am a holy and happy part of God, or of a universal soul on earth, why should I not hope to be such hereafter?"

We do not deny that God is the continuous, first cause of all being whatsoever, and that the branches and fruit depend not, as effects, so much on the causality of the stock and roots, as the creature does on God; and that it is an impious notion to believe that the world, or any part of it, exists independently and separately from God, or subsists without His continual causation. But can God not create, as a Creator, by making something that is not Himself? This yields the self-deceiver no other honor or happiness than what equally belongs to a devil, a fly, a worm, a dunghill, or the most miserable man!

Just as man's soul is a substance, it is also formally distinct from all inferior substances, characterized by an innate (indeed essential) power, virtue, or faculty of vital action, intellection, and free will. We observe all these acts performed by it, just as motion, light, and heat are observed in fire or the sun. If anyone were to argue that these actions are like those of a musician, resulting from the combined efforts of various parts (both principal and organic), even if they could prove it, that would only demonstrate that the lower powers (the sensitive or spirits) are passive organs receiving the operations of the higher. The intellectual soul has the power to cause intellection and volition through its action on the inferior parts, just as a man can create musical motions on his lute that produce melody—not for the lute itself, but—

for himself. Consequently, while music is a lower operation of man (whose proper acts of intellection and volition are higher), so too are intellection and volition in the body not the noblest acts of the soul; rather, they are performed by an eminent power that can accomplish greater things. If this could be proven, what would it contribute to the unbeliever's goals or disadvantage our hopes and comforts?

Even the atomists and Epicureans will concede that man's soul is not annihilated at death, for they believe that no atom in the universe is annihilated. We observe not only the sun and heavens continuing, but also every grain of matter, and that compounds are altered through the dissolution of parts, rarefaction, migration, etc., and not through annihilation. Therefore we have no reason to believe that God will annihilate a single soul (though He can do so if He wishes, and even annihilate the entire world); this is beyond rational expectation.

We need not fear the destruction of the soul through the dissolution of its parts. First, an intellectual spirit is either divisible and partible, or it is not. If it is not, then we have no reason to fear it. If it is divisible, then we must consider whether nature tends toward such division or not. It is evident that nature does not tend toward division.

There is a strong inclination toward unity and an aversion to separation in all things. Even earth and stones, which have no other known natural motion, exhibit an aggregate motion in their gravitation. If one attempts to separate the parts from the whole, it must be done by force. Water is even more resistant to partition without force and is more inclined to unite than earth is. Air is more inclined to union than water, and fire is more inclined to unity than air. Therefore anyone who tries to cut a sunbeam into pieces and create many from one must be an extraordinary agent.

Surely spirits—even intellectual spirits—would be as resistant to division and as inclined to preserve their unity as fire or a sunbeam. It is therefore not something to be feared that they would fall apart naturally.

Secondly, anyone who claims that the God who established nature will change and overcome the natures He created must produce solid evidence for that claim; otherwise it is not something to be feared. If God were to act so as a punishment, we should find such a penalty threatened somewhere in His natural or supernatural law — but we find no such threat. Therefore, we need not fear it.

Even if one feared that souls could be divided and broken into parts, that would not amount to their destruction in substance, powers, form, or action. It would simply be a division of one soul into many.

Souls are not made of heterogeneous parts; they are simple substances, comparable to the elements earth, water, air, and fire. Every atom of earth remains earth; every drop of sea-water is still water; every particle of air or fire remains air or fire, retaining the properties of its kind. The same would hold for every particle of an intellectual spirit.

But who can give a reason to fear such a division — something that God has never threatened?

We have good reason to believe that souls do not lose their formal powers or virtues, because those powers are their very essence. Souls exist as simple, not compound, substances.

Some imagine passive elements can be transformed into one another by thinning or thickening. Yet earth remains earth, water remains water, and air remains air. Such claims lack proof. Even if proved, they would only show that none of those elements is primary.

But what could an intellectual spirit be transformed into? How could it lose its formal power? Not by nature, since its nature does not tend toward deterioration, decay, or self-destruction. The sun does not decay through its admirable motion, light, and heat; why should spirits? Nor by God changing or destroying them, for although all things are in constant motion, God preserves the natures of simple beings and delights in constancy of operation. This is the view that led Aristotle to think the world eternal.

Moreover, God has given no law threatening such a transformation as a penalty. To imagine that intellectual spirits will be changed into other things and lose the essential powers that define them is contrary to sober reason. Let them first prove that the sun loses its motion, light, and heat and becomes air, water, or earth. Such changes are beyond rational fear.

Some suppose that souls will sleep and cease their activities while retaining their powers. That notion is even less reasonable than the previous one. We are not speaking of a merely passive power but of an active power that has as strong an inclination to act as passive natures have to refrain from action. If such a nature did not act, it must be because a stronger force prevents it. But who could impose such a hindrance?

God would not sustain an active power, force, and inclination in a nature while at the same time preventing that nature's operation—unless it were as a punishment for some specific reason. He has never indicated any such punishment; on the contrary, He shows the opposite.

There will be no shortage of objects, for the whole world will still be available, and God above all. It is therefore unreasonable to think that God would preserve an active, vital, intellective, volitive nature—its form, power, force, and inclination—in a noble substance and then leave it unused for hundreds or thousands of years, keeping it in vain.

It is more reasonable to suppose that some action is the constant state of such spirits; otherwise the cessation of their activity would imply the loss of their very form. All that can be reasonably said is that separated souls, and souls in spiritual bodies in the future, will have actions of a different mode—very different from those we now perceive in the flesh.

They will remain fundamentally of the same kind. They will be formally or eminently characterized by what we now call vitality, intellection, and volition. They will not be lower or less excellent; if anything, they may be far more so. What the precise difference will be, only Christ knows—and in due time I shall know.

To speak of a dead life, an inactive activity, or a sleeping soul suits a sleeping man, not a waking one.

It is true that disease or injury now hinders the soul's intellectual perceptions in the body; in infancy and sleep these perceptions are imperfect. This shows that acts commonly called intellection and volition include elements of sensation, and that sensitive operations are modified by the organs of the senses.

Pure intellection and volition without any sensation are rarely observed in us, though the soul may have such acts intrinsically and in its depths. The soul is now so united to the body that it acts in the role of our form. The acts we observe are thereby specified or at least modified by the agents and by the parts of the recipients and subagents combined.

1. Just as the sun would perform the same action ex parte sui if it sent forth its beams into a vacuum—though there were no recipient to be illuminated or warmed—it would lose nothing by the absence of objects. Likewise, the soul, even without a body to act upon, would still possess its profound immanent acts of self-living, self-perceiving, and

self-loving, together with all its external acts on other objects, which do not necessarily require sensory organs to be approximated.

2. Its sensitive faculty is either identical with itself or not separated from it; particular modes of sensation may vary with their uses. Therefore, the soul may still act on or with the senses. If one mode of sensation is hindered, another can serve.

3. We do not yet know how much the physical body helps or hinders the soul's operations; we shall know in the future. Sondius, in De Origine Animæ — though a heterodox writer — has argued much to show that the body is a hindrance, not a help, to the soul's intuition. While ratiocination may be a compound act, pure intuition can be performed by the soul alone.

4. We should not judge what powers the soul has from cases in which its acts are hindered, but from instances in which its acts are fully performed. Nor should we infer what God made souls for from their state in the womb, in infancy, or during disease; we should judge from our ordinary, mature state of life.

Therefore, we have little reason to think that the God who created them for life, intellection, and volition here will not continue the same powers for the same or even nobler purposes in the future, with or without organs, as He pleases. If in this flesh our spirits were not inactive and useless, we have no reason to suppose they will be so for eternity.

This greatest and most difficult objection forces us to admit — along with Contarenus, arguing against Pomponatius on the immortality of the soul — that, although we may know the immortality of souls by natural reason (and see that they do not lose their powers or activity), we cannot, without supernatural revelation, know what kind of actions they will perform when separated or in another world.

Here they act according to objective ends and according to the receptivity of the senses and the imagination; they are received according to the mode of the recipients. In the womb, we do not perceive that they act intellectually at all.

However, we know that:

1. If the soul did not differ in its formal power from the souls of animals, it would not differ in its actions either, and it could never be raised to something not already inherent in its nature.

2. We observe that even very young children possess quick and strong knowledge of objects within their reach. Their ignorance is not due to a lack of intellectual power but to a lack of objects or images; time, experience, and interaction with the world must supply these for imagination and memory. Likewise, a soul in the womb or in a state of apoplexy lacks objects of intellection to act upon. It is like the sun in a room without windows to let in its light.

3. If its deep vitality, self-perception, and self-love arise from a kind of sensation and intuition rather than from discursive reasoning, then some recent philosophers err by too harshly disparaging sense and the sensitive soul, as if sensation were merely a fleeting accident of mixed atoms. Sensation—though varied by organs and by use, and therefore mutable—is an act of a noble, spiritual form and virtue. Just as some classify animals as a lower rank of rational beings and humans as a higher species because of superior reason for greater ends, it is fitting that humans be the highest order of sensitive beings. We possess an intellect to organize, govern, relate, and improve sensations, even if we had no higher faculties. If intellection and volition are only higher forms of internal sensation than imagination, they still raise humanity above animals. I am increasingly convinced that intellectual souls are inherently sensitive and more, and that their sensation never ceases.

4. I hold it unlikely that the God of nature would allow a soul with an intellective power to exist in a state where it cannot use that power. Let others speculate whether the soul will have a vehicle in which to act — whether aerial, fiery, ethereal, or truly an intellectual kind of fire, as material as solar fire, with inadequate conceptual objects as a fiery substance and the formal essence of life, sense, and intellection. For my part, it is enough to believe that God will not leave its noblest powers idle. How they will be exercised is known to Him, and God's word reveals more than nature does. Moreover, life, intuition, and love (or volition) are acts so natural to the soul — like motion, light, and heat are to fire — that I cannot see how their separation would hinder them. Indeed, I suspect that embodiment may rather obscure objects and so hinder the latter two, whatever is said about abstract knowledge and memory.

The greatest challenge to natural knowledge is whether souls will keep their individuality, merge into one common soul, or return to God so as no longer to be distinct individuals, like extinguished candles blending with illuminated air or sunlight. I have treated this at length elsewhere, but for present purposes I need only this:

1. As I said above, either souls are indivisible substances or they are not. If they are not indivisible, how can they be truly united? If many can become one by the conjunction of substances, then by God's power that one could be made many again by division. Either all (or many) souls are now one, individuated only by matter — like many gulfs in the sea or many candles lit by the sun — or they are not. If they are not one now in separate bodies, what reason have we to think they will be one in the future more than they are now?

Augustine (in De Anim.) was asked whether souls are one and not many, which he completely denied. He was also asked whether they are many and not one, which he seemed unable to accept. He considered whether they could be both one and many at the same time, which he thought might seem ridiculous, though he appeared to lean toward this view.

As God is the Lord of nature, so nature—even that of the devils—depends on Him more than the leaves of fruit depend on the tree. We are all His offspring, and in Him we live, move, and have our being (Acts 17). Nevertheless, we are certain of the following:

1. We are not God.

2. We are many individuals, not all one soul or one man.

Even if our union were as close as leaves and fruit on the same tree, those leaves and fruits would remain numerous and individual parts of the tree. If this were shown to be true of our present or future state, it would not change our hopes or fears. For now, although we all live, move, and have our being in God (and, as some believe, are parts of a common soul), it is plain that some are better and happier than others: some are wise and good, others foolish and evil; some are in pain and misery, others at ease and in pleasure. As I have said, it comforts no miserable person to be told that, at bottom, all souls are one; it would not be comforting in the future either, nor can people reasonably hope for or fear such a union that would make their conditions the same.

We see in nature (as I have already noted) that if you graft many kinds of scions—some sweet, some bitter, some crabapple—onto the same stock, they form one tree but still produce diverse fruits. If souls are not unified or indivisible substances, there is no reason for this fear. If they are indivisible, they will remain what they are, even if united to a common soul. A drop of water in the sea is still a separable part and yet itself; a crab on the grafted stock or tree keeps its identity. Goodness or badness does not cease because of union with others.

We are sure that all creatures exist in God by close dependence, and yet the good remain good and the bad remain bad. God is good and has no evil; when a man suffers or is miserable, God does not suffer in the same way—just as the whole person does not suffer when only a tooth aches—because He would not harm Himself by being passive. Therefore, to suppose that our individuality could cease by union with a creature—so that the good would become less good or the bad less bad or miserable—is a baseless folly.

It is very likely that there will be a closer union of holy souls with God, with Christ, and with one another than we can now imagine. This is not to be feared; rather, it is the highest of our hopes.

God Himself, though equally present everywhere in His essence, acts very differently toward His creatures. With the wicked He works as the first cause of nature, just as His sun shines upon them. With some He works through common grace; to others He gives faith in preparation for the indwelling of His Spirit. In believers He dwells by love, and they dwell in Him. If we may use a comparison: just as Satan influences some only by suggestions but affects others so strongly that we call it possession, so God's Spirit works in holy souls with such power and constancy that it is called possession.

On the human nature of Christ, the divine nature of the Second Person exercises such a further, extraordinary operation that it is rightly called a personal union. This union does not arise from a more essential presence—His essence is everywhere—but from a unique operation and relationship. In the same way, holy souls, being under a fuller operation of God, may be said to have a closer union with Him than they now experience.

As I observed earlier, all things naturally incline toward union and communion with their like. Every clod and stone tends toward the earth; water seeks water, air seeks air, and fire seeks fire. Birds and beasts gather with their own kind, and the noblest natures are the most strongly drawn in this way. For this reason, I have natural grounds to believe that holy souls will also share this inclination.

I find that excessive self-regard — an inordinate focus on oneself and one's private interests — together with a failure to love others according to each creature's goodness, and especially a failure to love God, the infinite Good whom we should love above ourselves, is the essence of human depravity.

All injustice and harm done to others, the neglect of good works in the world, and our daily fears, anxieties, and griefs spring from this overweening self-love. Therefore I have reason to hope that in our better state we will love others perfectly as ourselves, and that selfish affection will be transformed into a common, divine love — one that issues from a preference for the common good and the divine interest.

I am keenly aware of the power and plague of selfishness and how it now corrupts, tempts, and disturbs me. When I feel fears that individuation might cease and that my soul might merge into one common soul (as the Stoics held that all souls do at death), I suspect these fears arise from the influence of that corrupting selfishness. Reason finds no cause to fear such a fate, even if it were true.

I find that the nature of love is to desire the closest union possible, and the strongest love desires it most intensely. Fervent lovers think they can scarcely be too united; since love is our perfection, so is union.

I find that when Christians first experienced the full outpouring of the Spirit they displayed the most fervent love, the closest union, and the least desire for personal possession or distance.

I find that Christ's prayer for the welfare of His disciples is a prayer for their unity (John 17:22-23). In that prayer He places much of their perfection.

I also find that man is by nature sociable; all men know by experience that joining together in societies is necessary for their safety, strength, and pleasure.

My soul longs to be nearer to God; darkness and distance are my misery. Near communion would satisfy every desire of my soul, so why should I fear a union that is too close?

It seems utterly improbable that my soul could be more closely united to any creature than to God, even though my soul is of the same kind as other souls and infinitely less than God. God is as near to me as I am to myself; I depend on Him as an effect depends on its total, constant cause. This dependence is not like a fruit's dependence on a tree, the way a fruit draws earth, water, air, and light from the tree. Rather, it is like a creature's dependence on its Creator, whose existence the creature receives entirely and continually from God.

Thus Antonine, Seneca, and the other Stoics taught that the whole world was God or one great animal, composed of divine spirit and matter as man is composed of soul and body. They sometimes called the supposed soul of the world God and at other times called the whole world God. Their meaning was that the universe is one spirit and body united, and that we are all parts of God, parts of the body of God, or at least accidental parts of it.

Even the Roman Catholic mystical theologians, in their claims to the highest perfection, express similar ideas. For example, Benedict Anglus, in his *Regula Perfectionis* (approved by many scholars), emphasized that much of his elevated life rested on the sincere conviction that there is nothing but God — just as rays are to the sun and heat to fire. He urges us to find rest in all things as good, since they are nothing but the will of God, which is Himself. From this perspective even our sins and imperfections are resolved back into God, being treated either as God's or as non-existent.

These writers have as strong a claim to a present union with God as they do to a union after death. Their reasoning runs as follows:

1. Since God is infinite, there cannot be any being additional to Him. If one supposed God and some smallest distinct being both existed, that would imply something greater than God alone, which contradicts the notion that infinity admits no addition.

2. Because being and goodness are interchangeable, and only God is truly good.

Despite all this, if we are distinct beings from God now, we will not be elevated into a deified state, nor will creatures or distinct beings be transformed into a being infinitely above us. If we are not parts of God now, we will not be then.

However, if they could prove that we are part of God now, we could quickly counter their claims:

1. This would imply that God has material, divisible parts (as the Stoics believed).

2. It would mean that we are not indistinguishable parts of one another; rather, some would be tormented while others would be happy.

3. It would not lessen the misery of the tormented or the joy of the blessed to say that they are all parts of God. Although the nature of our union with Him and our dependence on Him is beyond our comprehension, it is undeniable that we remain distinct from one

another, each experiencing our own joy or misery. Therefore, there is no union with God that holy souls should fear; on the contrary, the highest union is to be eagerly desired.

If our union with God does not eliminate our individuality or reduce us to a principle to be feared, the same can be said of a union with any common soul or with many souls. If we were unified in that way, we would still be partible, possessing a distinct, though undivided, substance that has its own characteristics. All plants are parts of the earth, truly united to it—rooted in it, living and nourished by it—yet a vine remains a vine, an apple remains an apple, a rose remains a rose, and a nettle remains a nettle. Few people would choose to be horses or toads if it were proven they were animated by a common soul.

God allows us to see that although the world is one, He delights in a wonderful diversity and multiplicity of individuals. Consider how varied and numerous they are in the sea, on land, and in the air. Are there none in the other world? How could the stars there be so numerous if they were all of the same element? Even if Saturn or other planets, or many stars, send their radiant rays into the same air that the sun's beams seem to fill and illuminate, the sun's rays and those of other stars are not the same, however close they come in the same medium.

If there were no more contraction by egoity or ownership among men—if "mine" and "thine" meant nothing, and if distance were no greater than that between the drops of water in the sea or particles of light in illuminated air—and if I had my share in such perfect unity and communion with all others, knowing that all were as happy as I, so that there were no divisions of conflicting interests or minds, but all were one, surely my comforts would be greatly increased compared to how they are now. Are not a hundred candles set together and united as splendid a flame as if they were all set apart? So would one soul, one love, one joy be.

Objection: But it is only the fuel that individuates lights. When the same sun, through a burning glass, lights a thousand candles, they are individuated only by the matter that contains them, remaining united parts of the same sunbeams. When they are extinguished, they become nothing or return to being one again.

Answer: Before they were extinguished, the lights were both one and many. Only fools believe that extinction annihilates them or any part of them; they remain as much substance and as much solar fire, though diffused, and are as much one as before, though not as many. They become parts of one. Nature has made the sunbeams evenly diffused through the air and across the earth, like blood moving equally through the body; our candles and fires resemble that same blood contracted into a bile or inflammation. Such concentrated fire is felt more strongly than the evenly diffused blood, but it is akin to the pain of a disease. When our fires go out, they are like a healed, scattered inflammation, and the same substance is more naturally and equally diffused. If the individuation of souls were only by corporeal matter, and the union at their departure were as great, their perfection and happiness would not be diminished and might even be increased; for there would be no loss of substance, power, activity, or perfection.

This refutes the foolish opinion that separated souls sleep in a state of potentiality because they lack an organized body to operate in. No doubt, if all holy souls were one, this world—whether in heaven or on earth—has a common body sufficient for such a soul to act in. Even the Stoics who believed departed souls become one maintained that this one soul operates more nobly than ours, freed from the confines of our narrow bodies, and that when our souls cease animating this body they engage in the nobler and sweeter task of animating the whole world. Those who thought various orbs had their own souls, of which particular beings participated, made similar claims about separated souls animating the bodies of their globes and orbs. Although these people are preoccupied with vain imaginations, the matter reveals a significant truth: the utmost fear of the unbeliever is that departed souls lose their individuality or activity and are absorbed into a common soul or remain in a sleepy potentiality for want of a body. They contradict themselves, as it is a well-known truth that:

1. If all holy souls were one, no one would lose by that union; rather, it would be a greater gain than we can hope for. A part of one is as substantial, noble, and active as if it were a separate person (and annihilation or loss of specific powers is not rationally to be feared).

2. That one soul is now either self-subsisting without a body or it animates a suitable body (as some ancients believed of the stars). If that one soul can act without a body, so can ours, whether as parts of it or not. If that one soul animates a suitable body, then ours, if they were united parts of it, would share in that activity; thus they refute themselves.

Objection: But this would equalize the good and the bad, or at least those who were good to varying degrees. Where then would be the reward and punishment?

Answer: It would not equalize them at all, any more than distinct personalities would.

1. The souls of all holy persons may be united in such a way that the souls of the wicked have no part in that union. Whether the souls of the wicked are united in one sinful, miserable soul, or rather in one sinful society, or are even more separated and disunited—contrary to one another and in conflict, as part of their sin and misery—is irrelevant to this case.

2. However, natural and moral unions must be distinguished. God is the root of nature even for the worst. While it is true in one sense that there is nothing in God but God, it is also true that for in Him we live

and move and have our being. Yet the wicked's existence in God does not give them any sanctifying or beatific communion with Him, as experience shows us in this life. Holy souls possess that communion because they have been made capable of receiving it. Different plants — briars and cedars, the stinking and the sweet — are implanted parts (or accidents) of the same world or earth.

3. The godly themselves may have as different a share of happiness in one common soul as they now have of holiness, and thus receive different rewards — just as roses and rosemary and other herbs differ in the same garden, and various fruits differ in the same orchard or on the same tree. If souls are unified and thus partible substances, they do not gain or lose substance or holiness by that union; each retains its proper measure. Just as a tun of water cast into the sea remains the same, so does a spoonful cast into it.

Objection: But spirits are not like bodies, extensive and quantitative, and therefore not partible or divisible; thus your supposition is vain.

Answer:

1. My supposition is merely the objectors'. If they acknowledge that spirits are substances — which cannot reasonably be denied (even those who explain their operations by motion alone still presuppose a pure proper substance as the subject or thing moved) — then when they speak of many souls becoming one, it must be through conjunction and an increase of the substance of that one. When they claim that they were always one, they must also admit that they now differ in number, as individuated in the body. Who would argue that millions are no more than one of those millions? Number is a form of quantity, and all souls in the world are more than just Cain's or Abel's. One does not feel what another feels; one does not know what another knows.

2. While souls may not have corporeal extension like passive, gross, bodily matter, they are more noble and therefore have a more refined sort of extension, quantity, or degrees by which all humanity perceives the spiritual substance of the universe. Indeed, all angels or all souls on earth are considered more substantial than a single man's soul alone.

3. If the contrary is assumed—that all souls are no more than one, leaving no room for uniting or partition—then there is no basis for the objection that all souls might become one and lose individuation, unless by "losing individuation" they mean annihilation.

The God who delights in both union and the wonderful multiplicity of creatures will not make all stars into just one. Although fire tends to unite or aggregate, He has provided further evidence that individuation exists in the other world as well as in this one: countless angels and devils, not a single being. Apparitions, witches, and many other phenomena support this claim, which I will elaborate on later. Considering all things, there is no reason to fear that souls will lose their individuation or activity (even if their manner of action changes), any more than their being or formal power; therefore it is naturally certain that they are immortal.

If holy souls are indeed immortal, I need not prove that they will also be eternally happy; their holiness implies this. Few would imagine that it would go poorly for those who are good, or that the most just and holy God would not treat well those whom He makes holy.

The belief that holy souls will be happy in the future seems to be common and inherent in human conscience. It is widely acknowledged by the majority who use their reason freely. Most, if not all, of the heathen nations today believe this, as do the Muslims; only the most barbaric cannibals and some Brazilians do not, since their understanding has seen the least development. Their ignorance is more a matter of inconsiderate unawareness than outright denial. Although a few philosophers have denied this belief, they represent a small and disregarded faction. Many others expressed doubt, but that doubt was often a confessed lack of certitude rather than a conviction that the belief is false. Both common people and the learned have generally believed it, while those who questioned it were often philosophers who had not settled in natural understanding nor reached full intellectual evidence through discourse, and so found themselves puzzled.

Even among those who have turned away from Christianity, many still recognize the soul's immortality and the happiness and reward of holy souls as common knowledge rooted in human nature. Julian was so convinced of this that he urged his priests and subjects to live strictly and holily, so Christians would not surpass them in righteousness. Among us, Lord Herbert de Veritate and many others who seem not to accept our supernatural Christian revelations fully acknowledge this truth. Philosophers who most opposed Christianity—Porphyry, Maximus, Tyrius, and others—also recognized it.

We find this understanding so deeply rooted in human nature that few who plunge into bestiality (or Sadduceeism) escape the fears of future misery. Conscience troubles them greatly, even when they do their utmost to deny it. Why should this awareness exist in humans and not in animals if humans had no greater reason for hopes and fears than they? Are a few Sadducees truly wiser in their coarse or forced beliefs than the whole world taught by nature itself?

If the God of nature has made it every person's certain duty to seek happiness in the life to come, then such happiness must exist for those who genuinely seek it. The antecedent is certain, as I have shown elsewhere. Therefore it follows that there is happiness for those who seek it.

Regarding the antecedent: the world contains three kinds of people in their beliefs about future retribution:

1. Those who regard it as a certain truth, such as Christians, Muslims, and most heathens.

2. Those who consider it uncertain but most probable or likely to be true.

3. Those who view it as uncertain but lean toward thinking it untrue.

No one can be certain that something is false if it is in fact true. I have never met anyone who would claim to be certain of its falsehood. Therefore I need not spend time on other hypothetical opinions; if anyone were to assert such certainty, it would be easy to show they are mistaken about themselves.

It is the duty of all these people — especially the first two groups — to make it their chief concern to seek their happiness in the life to come. This is easily shown. Natural reason requires every person to pursue what is best for them with the greatest diligence. And natural reason makes the possibility or probability of future, everlasting happiness more worthy of pursuit than anything attainable in this present life (which does not presuppose it). Therefore, they should seek it.

The major premise is beyond doubt. Goodness and happiness are inherent objects of the human will; therefore what is best, when known to be so, must be most desired.

The minor premise should also be beyond doubt for those who do not act against their reason. For:

1. In this life, nothing is certain to last even for an hour.

2. All things will quickly come to an end; even the longest life is short.

3. It is certain that past time and past pleasures are properly nothing, and therefore no better for us than if they had never existed.

4. While we possess them, present goods are poor and unsatisfying. The pleasures of the flesh are no sweeter to a person than to an animal, and the troubles that accompany them are much greater for us. Animals lack the cares, fears, and sorrows about the future that humans have. They do not fear death beforehand, nor fear any misery after death. They are not compelled to labor, suffer, or endure trials to obtain future happiness or to avoid future misery. Given all this, anyone who claims that this vain, vexatious life is better than the possibility or probability of everlasting glory does not speak with reason.

Now, concerning the major premise of the first argument: it is evident from God's perfection and from the nature of His works. God would not make it man's natural duty to spend his chief care and labor through life on something that does not exist, or to seek what man was never meant to attain. If that were so:

1. All duty would arise from deceit and falsehood, and God would govern the world by lies. That is impossible for One who, in power, wisdom, and love, rules by truth and justice. He has imprinted His image on His laws and on His servants, and those laws condemn lying; the better a person is, the more they detest falsehood. Liars are loathed by all mankind.

2. The better a person is, and the more faithfully they fulfill their duty, the more deluded, mistaken, and miserable they would be. They would spend their lives and labor pursuing what they could never obtain, wasting time and effort. They would deny themselves the temporal pleasures that the wicked enjoy, and suffer persecution and injury from the wicked—all for nothing and based on an error. The more wicked or unbelieving a person is, the wiser and happier they would be, since by denying the life to come they would be right to refuse all duty and labor

in seeking it or avoiding future punishment. They would indulge in their utmost pleasures here and possess all that humanity was made for. But all this is utterly inconsistent with God's perfection and with His other works. He creates nothing in vain and cannot lie; far less would He make holiness itself, and all the duties of life which reason obliges men to pursue, not only vain but harmful. I have treated this argument more fully elsewhere.

Humanity differs so greatly from animals in knowledge of God and in the possibilities regarding the future that this difference demonstrates a corresponding difference in capacity and in particular hopes.

1. Regarding the antecedent: humanity knows there is a God by His works. They know this God is their absolute Lord, their ruler, and their ultimate end. They understand that we naturally owe Him all our love and obedience. Good masters do not allow their most faithful servants to suffer loss because of their fidelity, nor do they set them to work in vain. They know that the soul of man is immortal, or at least that it is far more probable that it is; therefore a man's condition must be good or ill for eternity, and this should be of the utmost concern.

2. Why would God grant humanity all this knowledge if they were made for no greater enjoyment than animals? Every wise craftsman orders his work to its designed end; will not God do the same? Thus the consequence is also drawn from divine perfection. If God were not perfect, He would not be God. The denial of God, therefore, follows from the denial of humanity's future hopes.

Indeed, although animals possess only an analogical form of reasoning, those who argue that the difference between humans and animals lies more in the objects, tendencies, and works of our reasoning than in reasoning itself seem to be correct. They describe humans as animal religiosum rather than animal rationale. Even in their low concerns, a fox, a dog, a donkey, or a goose show behaviours we find hard to ascribe to anything below some kind of reasoning or perception of significance. Yet they do not think of God, His governance, or His laws. They do not consider obeying, trusting, or loving Him. They do not contemplate hopes or fears about another life, nor the joyful prospect of it. These pursuits are proper to humanity and mark the chief difference from animals. Shall we then unman ourselves?

The justice of God, as governor of the world, requires different rewards in the future, as I have shown at length elsewhere.

1. God is not only the mover of all that moves but also the moral ruler of mankind, governing by laws, judgments, and executions. Otherwise there would be no proper law of nature — few deny this so grossly as to reject it; mankind would have no proper duty, only motion as they are moved. How, then, could a government by law be established under God among men? There would be no sin or fault; if there were no law and duty but only necessitated motion, everyone would be moved as the mover desires, and there could be no sin. Consequently there would be no moral good, only forced or necessary motion. This is absurd. Experience shows God does morally govern the world, and His right to do so is unquestionable.

If God were not the ruler of the world by law and judgment, the world would lack universal laws, for there is no human universal ruler. Consequently kings and other supreme powers would be entirely lawless and ungoverned, having no one above them to provide laws, and so they would be incapable of sin or fault. Yet neither the interests of their subjects nor their own consciences will allow men fully to believe this.

If God is a ruler, He must be just; otherwise He would not be perfect, nor as good as He requires earthly princes and judges to be. An unjust ruler or judge is abominable to all mankind. Righteousness is the great attribute of the universal King.

But how could He be a righteous ruler if He compelled all people to obey Him through deceit?

1. If He forced them to seek and expect a happiness or reward that He would never provide?

2. If He turned man's duty into his misery?

3. If He required him to labor in vain?

4. If He allowed the wicked to persecute His servants to the death, making duty costly without any recompense afterward?

5. If He permitted the most wicked on earth to go unpunished, allowing them to escape judgment just as well as the righteous, and to live in greater pleasure here?

The objections based on the intrinsic goodness of duty I have addressed elsewhere.

But God has not left us to the light of mere nature, which is too dim for blind humans like us. The gospel revelation is the clear foundation of our faith and hope. Christ has brought life and immortality to light through the gospel. One from heaven, greater than an angel, was sent to reveal what is there and how to secure our hopes. He has risen, conquered death, and entered as our captain and forerunner into everlasting habitations. He has all authority in heaven and on earth, and all judgment has been committed to Him, so that He might give eternal life to His elect. He has frequently and expressly promised them that they shall live because He lives and shall not perish but have everlasting life. (Matt. 28:18; John 5:22, 17:2, 12:26, 3:16; Rom. 8:35–38.) How fully He has proven and sealed the truth of His word and office to us I have set out in my Reasons of the Christian Religion,

Unreasonableness of Infidelity, and Life of Faith, and since then in my Household Catechising, so I will not repeat it here.

Just as all His word is filled with promises of our future glory at the resurrection, we also have assurance that at death the departing soul enters a state of joy and blessedness. "For this reason the gospel was preached also to those who are dead, that they might be judged according to men in the flesh, but live according to God in the spirit." (1 Pet. 4:6.) For He expressly promised the penitent, crucified thief, "Assuredly, I say to you, today you will be with Me in Paradise." (Luke 23:43.) He gave us the narrative or parable of the sensualist and Lazarus (Luke 16) to instruct us, not to deceive us.

He tells the Sadducees that God is not the God of the dead but of the living. (Matt. 22:32.) Enoch and Elijah were taken up to heaven, and Moses, who died, appeared with Elijah on the mount. (Matt. 17.) He tells us that those who kill the body cannot destroy the soul. (Luke 12:4.) Indeed, if the soul were not immortal, the resurrection would be impossible. It might be a new creation of another soul, but not a resurrection of the same person if the same were annihilated. It is certain that the Jews believed in the immortality of the soul, as evidenced by their belief in the resurrection and future life of the same person.

Christ commended His spirit into His Father's hands, and His soul was in paradise while His body lay in the grave, to show us what shall become of ours. (Luke 23:46.)

And He has promised that where He is, there His servants shall be also. (John 12:26.) The life begun in us is eternal life, and he who believes in Him shall not die but shall live by Him, as He lives by the Father, for He dwells in God, and God in him, and in Christ, and Christ in him. (John 17:3; 6:54; 3:16; 36; 6:47; 50; 56; 57; 1 John 4:12, 13; Luke 17:21; Rom. 14:17.) Accordingly, Stephen, who saw heaven opened, prayed the Lord Jesus to receive his Spirit. (Acts 7:55, 59.) We have come to Mount Zion, to an innumerable company of angels, and to the spirits of the just made perfect. (Heb. 12:22, 23.) Paul expresses his desire to depart and be with Christ, which is far better. To be absent from the body is to be present with the Lord. (2 Cor. 5:8.) The dead who die in the Lord are blessed, from now on, for they may rest from their labors, and their works follow them.

If the spirits who were disobedient are in prison, and if the cities of Sodom and Gomorrah suffer the vengeance of eternal fire, then the just have eternal life. (1 Pet. 3:19; Jude 7.) If the Jews had not believed in the immortality of the soul, Saul would not have sought the witch to call up Samuel. I will pass over many others. We have many great and precious promises on which a departed soul may rely.

Christ expressly teaches that when we fail—that is, must leave this world—we shall be received into everlasting habitations. (Luke 16:9.)

It is no small encouragement to hope in Him who has made all these promises when we see how He hears prayers in this life and proves Himself the true and faithful Savior of His servants. In distress we are prone to cry out for mercy and deliverance, and when human help fails we promise God that if He saves us now we will acknowledge it as His work. Yet when we are delivered we often return not only to security but even to ingratitude, thinking our deliverance came merely through common providence rather than as an answer to prayer.

Therefore God, in mercy, renews both our distresses and our deliverances, so that what once or twice did not convince us may be reinforced by many and great deliverances. This is my own experience. How often have I cried to Him when human means were of no avail, and how often has He suddenly and mercifully delivered me! I have seen sudden removals of long afflictions beyond my own and others' expectations, when many sincere Christians have sought God on my behalf by fasting and prayer. These experiences have repeatedly convinced me of special providence and that God truly hears prayer. I have seen wonders done for others by such prayers, even more than for myself, and wonders for the church and public societies. Though I and others are too much like those Israelites who cried to God in their troubles and were often delivered, yet quickly forgot His mercies—forgetting their convictions, purposes, and promises when they should have praised the Lord and declared His works with thanksgiving to others.

What were all these answers and mercies but the fruits of Christ's power, fidelity, and love—the fulfillments of His promises and the earnest of the greater blessings of immortality to which those promises give me a title?

I know that no promise of hearing prayer puts our wills in absolute control over God, as if every desire must be fulfilled simply because we pray fervently or confidently. However, if we ask anything through Christ according to His will expressed in His promise, He will hear us. If a sinful love of this present life—comfort, wealth, or honor—leads me to pray against death or against all sickness, want, reproach, or other trials, as if I must live here in prosperity forever if I ask for it, that desire and expectation are presumption, not faith. What if God does not relieve me of my last or daily pains? What if He does not prolong my life, regardless of who prays for it or how earnestly? Shall I then forget how often He has heard prayers for me and wonderfully helped both me and others? My faith has often been strengthened by such experiences; shall I now forget them or question them without cause?

It is a secondary support for my belief in immortality with Christ to find so much evidence that angels have friendly communion with us here, and therefore we shall have communion with them hereafter. (Psalm 34:7; 91:11, 12; Luke 15:10; 1 Cor. 11:10; Heb. 1:14; 12:22, 23; Matt. 18:10; 25:31; 13:39, 49; Acts 5:19; 8:26; 12:7, 23.) They have charge over us and encamp around us; they bear us up; they rejoice at our repentance; they are the attentive witnesses of our behavior; they are ministering spirits for our good; they are our angels beholding the face of our heavenly Father. They will come with Christ in glorious attendance on the great and joyful day, and, as His executioners, they will separate the just from the unjust.

It is not only the testimony of Scripture that assures us of their communion with us, but also some degree of experience. Not only in ancient times did they appear to the faithful as messengers from God; in more recent times there have also been testimonies of their ministry for us. For more on this, see Zanchy de Angelis and Mr. J. Ambrose on our communion with angels.

God grants many mercies to us through their ministry. Those who are now so friendly to us, fit for our communion and help, and who form one society with us, encourage us to hope that we are made for the same region, work, and company with these our blessed, loving friends. They once endured a life of trial as we do now, though not on earth. (Jude 6; 2 Pet. 2:4.) Those who have overcome and are established rejoice in our victory and confirmation.

It is not an uninhabited world that lies above us, nor one beyond our capacity and hope. We have come to an innumerable company of angels and to the spirits of the perfected just—distinct individuals who enjoy a happy union and fellowship together.

And even Satan himself, though unwillingly, has in many ways confirmed my belief in our immortality and future hopes.

I have had many convincing proofs of witches, the contracts they have made with devils, and the power they have received from them. Besides the volumes of Remigius and Bodin, and the Malleus

Maleficarum, Danæus, and others, we had many dozens detected and many executed in one year in Suffolk and Essex, about 1644.

I presently own a flint-stone—one of about 160—which was expelled through the urinary passage of a bewitched child in Evesham who was still alive. Some of these stones weigh nearly an ounce. The connection was fully proven; the witch was executed, and the child was freed upon the witch's imprisonment. I will pass over many other such cases.

I have had convincing testimony of apparitions besides that famous one—the devil of Mascon—and the apparition in the shape of Lieutenant Colonel Bowen in Wales, mentioned elsewhere. There are also many testimonies of haunted houses, though many or most such reports are mere deceits.

From both of these, I gather:

1. That there are individual inhabitants of the invisible world, and that spirits have distinct numerical differences, whatever unity exists among them. Therefore, we have reason to believe the same about separated souls.

2. That our souls are destined for future happiness or misery, which is implied in the aforementioned contracts and endeavors of devils for our ruin.

3. That faith and holiness are the way to life, while unbelief and sin lead to misery, which is also implied in these observations.

I have both read and partially witnessed convincing evidence that there is such a phenomenon as diabolical possession. Whether all or most madmen are under such power, as some believe, I cannot determine, but it is evident that some are. The bodily movements I have seen seemed beyond natural human power. The ability to reveal secrets and absent things, to speak languages never learned, and the expulsion of nails, glass, hairs, and other such effects — things which many learned, sober, and impartial physicians claim to have witnessed — serve as credible testimonies.

I have felt, heard, and learned from others about temptations that plainly appear to be the work of malicious spirits, enemies of mankind. The advantage Satan takes of a corrupted imagination — once it has entertained an image that he can manipulate — is very remarkable. I knew a worthy, learned, and pious person who, from youth to old age, was so tempted with perverse pleasure to torment himself, even his own flesh, that for many years he could not refrain from it during various fits of partial melancholy, though his conscience also tormented him.

Many, by an immodest look or touch, have given Satan such influence over their imaginations that no reason, conscience, or resolution could overcome it for a long time. Few men, I believe, who observe themselves have not at some point experienced inward temptations that indicate their author to be an invincible enemy. All of this shows us:

1. That there are individual spirits.

2. That there are indeed devils who seek man's misery.

3. That through sin, we must expect a future happiness or misery for us all.

The great and sure indications of our immortal happiness come from the renewing operations of the Spirit of holiness upon the soul. All true believers perceive, to some degree, that such a renewing work exists.

That it is the earnest of heaven is proved as follows.

If it is a change of the greatest benefit to man.

If heaven is the very sum and end of it.

If it overcomes all fleshly, worldly opposition.

If it can be accomplished by none but God.

If it was promised by Jesus Christ to all true believers.

If it is universally worked in them all, either solely or predominantly above all others.

If it was promised to them as a pledge and earnest of glory, then it can be no less than such a pledge and earnest; but all the former statements are true.

The change is of immense importance to man because it renovates his mind, will, and life. It repairs depraved faculties and causes a person to live as he was meant to, rather than in a way little different from the brutes.

By allowing many to live in blindness, wickedness, and confusion, and to torment themselves and others by temptations, injuries, wars, and cruelty, God makes the saving power of grace more visible. Those who led unholy lives in youth more easily recognize the difference when they are renewed. For those pious from childhood, the change is harder to discern unless they observe others.

If man has any worth, it is for the use of his faculties; and if he is not fit for the knowledge, love, and service of his Creator, what is he good for? Certainly most ungodly people are not inclined to such works until the Spirit of Christ effectively changes them.

Men are slaves to sin until Christ makes them free (John 8:32, 33, 36; Rom. 6:18; Acts 26:18; Rom. 8:2). Where the Lord is the Spirit, and where the Spirit of the Lord is, there is liberty (2 Cor. 3:17). If the divine nature and the image of God, and the love of God poured into the heart, are not our excellence, health, and beauty, then what is?

That which is born of the flesh is flesh, and that which is born of the Spirit is spirit (John 3:6). Without Christ and His Spirit we can do nothing. Our dead notions and reason, even when they understand the truth, lack the power to overcome temptations, to restore the soul to its intended end, or to fill us with love and the joyful hope of future blessedness. It would be better to have no souls than to have souls void of the Spirit of God.

That heaven is the sum and end of all the Spirit's operations is evident to all who are truly conscious of them in themselves, and to others through all of God's precepts, which the Spirit causes us to obey, and the doctrine that it leads us to believe, and by the description of all the graces that God works in us. What is our knowledge and faith but our understanding and belief in heaven, as consisting in the glory and love of God manifested there, purchased by Christ, and given by His covenant? What is our hope but the hope of glory? (See Heb. 11:1, and throughout; 1 Pet. 1:3, 21; Heb. 6:11, 18, 19, and 3:6; Tit. 2:13, and 3:7; Col. 1:5, 23, 27.) Through the Spirit, we wait for all this hope. (Gal. 5:5.) What is our love but a desire for communion with the blessed God, initially here and perfectly hereafter? The sum of Christ's gospel was, "Take up the cross, forsake all here, and follow me, and you shall have a reward in heaven." (Luke 14:26, 33, and 18:22, 23.) The consolation of His gospel is, "Rejoice, and be exceedingly glad, for great is your reward in heaven." (Matt. 5:11, 12.) Thus, the same is the sum of His Spirit's operations, for what He teaches and commands, that He works. He works by that word, and the impression must be like the signet, regardless of which arm set it on. He does not send His Spirit to make men craftier than others for this world, but to make them wiser for salvation and to make them more heavenly and holy. For the children of this world are wiser in their generation than the children of light. Heavenliness is the Spirit's special work.

In working this, the Spirit conquers the inward aversion and resistance of a fleshly, worldly mind and will, and the habits of a carnal life. It also meets the outward temptations of Satan and all the allurements of the world.

Christ first overcame the world and now teaches and enables us to overcome it—its flatteries as well as its frowns. Our faith is our victory. Whether this victory is easy or whether it brings honor to the Spirit of Christ, let the wickedness of the ungodly world, our own weaknesses, and our falls when the Spirit departs be our teachers.

That none but God can perform this work on the human soul is shown by both the knowledge of causes and by experience. The most learned, wise, and holy teachers cannot do it, as they confess and as experience proves. The wisest and most loving parents cannot; therefore they must pray to Him who can. The greatest princes cannot; evil angels neither can nor will.

What good angels may do in the heart we do not fully know; but we know they act only as obedient ministers of God. And while we have some power over ourselves, we cannot quicken, illuminate, or sanctify ourselves. We have nothing but what we have received; conscience and experience testify to this.

Christ promised this Spirit in a special measure to all true believers, that it would be in them as His advocate, agent, seal, and mark. This is evident in the gospel and in the former prophets (Isa. 44:3-4; Ezek. 36:26; 37:14; Joel 2:28-29; Ezek. 11:19; 18:31; Eph. 1:13; John 3:5; 4:23-24; 6:63; 7:39; John 1:33; 14:16, 26; Acts 1:5, 8; John 15:26; 16:7-9, etc.).

Indeed, the Spirit here and heaven hereafter are the chief promises of Christ.

This Spirit is not given to hypocrites who abuse Christ and do not truly believe, nor to mere pretenders or nominal Christians, but to all who sincerely believe the gospel. This is evident to believers themselves in a certainty—if they are in a condition to know themselves—and to others in part by the effects.

Believers have different ends, affections, and lives than the rest of mankind. Though their heavenly nature and purpose may be less noticed in the world—because their chief difference is inward, in the heart and in secret actions, and because their imperfections mar them—the hostile world is an incompetent judge. Yet it is discernible to others that they live upon the hopes of a better life, and that their heavenly interest governs all opposing earthly interests.

They live under divine authority; God's will is the highest and most prevailing aim for them. To obey and please Him, as far as they know His will, is the chief business of their lives, even though ignorance and the opposing flesh make their holiness and obedience imperfect. The general noise and opposition of the world against them show that people recognize a notable difference, which error, conflicting interests, and carnal inclinations make offensive to those whom their heavenly aims condemn.

However, whether others recognize it, deny it, or detest it, the true believer is conscious of it in himself. Even when he groans to be better, to believe, trust, and love God more, and to share more of the heavenly life and comforts, those very desires show a different appetite and mindset than that of worldlings. Even when his frailties and weaknesses make him doubt his own sincerity, he would not change his governor, rule, or hopes for all the world can offer him.

He has the witness within that there is a sanctifying Spirit in believers, calling their minds to God and to glory, and warring victoriously against the flesh (1 John 5:9–11; Gal. 5:17; Rom. 7; Phil. 3:7–15). Thus the will to do good is present with them; they love and delight in conformity to their rule. It is never so well or so pleasant for them as when they can trust and love God most. Even in their worst and weakest condition they long to be perfect.

This Spirit and its renewing work are greatly different from the temper and desires of worldly men. It is given by Christ to all true believers.

It is true that some who do not know an incarnate Savior possess many laudable qualities. Whether this constitutes real saving holiness, and whether Abraham was mistaken in thinking that even the Sodomites might have had fifty righteous persons among them, I will not inquire. However, this much is certain:

1. That the world had a Savior about four thousand years before Christ's incarnation — even the God of pardoning mercy, who promised and undertook what was later fulfilled and will continue to the end.

2. That the Spirit of this Savior sanctified God's elect from the beginning and gave them the same holy and heavenly dispositions (to some degree) before Christ's incarnation as are given since. Indeed, it is called the Spirit of Christ, which was given before. (1 Pet. 1:11, 3.)

3. That this Spirit was given to more than just the Jews.

4. That Christ has not placed those parts of the world that have not heard of His incarnation in a worse condition than He found them. Just as the Jews' covenant of peculiar privileges did not repeal the universal law of grace that God made with fallen mankind in Adam and Noah, so the covenant of grace in its second edition, made with Christ's

peculiar people, does not repeal the earlier law of grace for those who have not heard of the second.

5. That all the wisdom and goodness found in anyone outside the visible Christian church is the work of the Spirit of the Redeemer. It is like the light that shines before sunrise, after sunset, and on cloudy days: it comes from the same sun that others see, even though they do not see the sun itself.

6. That the more similar any individuals outside the church are to sanctified believers, the better they are; and the more unlike them, the worse they are. Given these six points, it appears that it is the same Spirit of Christ that now gives all men whatever real goodness is found anywhere. Yet it is notorious that no part of the world, taken as a whole, is comparable in heavenly virtue to true and serious Christians.

Furthermore, Christ (Eph. 1:14; 2 Cor. 1:22 and 5:5; Rom. 8:23; 2 Tim. 2:19; Eph. 1:13 and 4:30; 1 John 5:9-10; Heb. 10:15), who promised the greatest measures of the Spirit and has accordingly given them, expressly promised this Spirit as a means and pledge, as firstfruits and earnest of heavenly glory. Therefore it is a certain proof that such glory awaits us.

He who can and does give us a spiritual change — a renovation that is heavenly in nature and tendency, that sets our hopes and hearts on heaven, and that directs our lives toward seeking future blessedness — and who told us beforehand that He would give this preparatory grace as the earnest of that felicity, may be trusted to fulfill His word in our actual glorification.

And now, O weak and fearful soul, why should you draw back as if the matter were still in doubt? Is not your foundation firm? Is not the way of life, even through the valley of death, made safe by Him who conquered death?

Are you not delivered from the bondage of fear, when the executioner who had the power of death has been rendered powerless by Christ? Is not all this evidence true and sure? Do you not have the witness within yourself? Have you not long ago found the motions, the effectual operations, and the renewing changes of this Spirit in you? Is He not still the agent and witness of Christ, residing and operating within you?

Whence else come your groanings after God, your desires to be nearer His glory, to know Him better, and to love Him more? Whence came all the pleasure you have found in His sacred truth, in His ways, and in His service?

Who else overcame your folly, pride, and vain desires so far as they have been overcome? Who made it your choice to sit at Jesus' feet and hear His word as the better part, and to despise the honors and preferments of the world, accounting them all as rubbish? Who breathed into you all those petitions you have lifted up to God?

Do not overvalue corrupted nature; it does not produce such fruits as these. If you doubt that, remember what you were in the hour of temptation, even in the face of small and weak temptations. How little has sometimes drawn you to sin when God left you to yourself.

Do not forget the days of youthful vanity. Do not overlook the case of the miserable world, even your sinful neighbors, who, in the midst of light, still live in darkness and do not heed God's loudest calls. Look around at thousands who, in the same land and under the same teaching, and even after the greatest judgments and deliverances, rush on to all excess of riot — past feeling, greedily vicious and unclean.

Is it not the work of Christ's Spirit that has made you different? You have nothing to boast of and much to be humbled by; but you also have much to be thankful for. Your holy desires are, alas, too weak; but they are holy. Your love has been too cold; but it is holiness and the most holy God that you have loved. Your hopes in God have been too low; but it is God's love and glory you have hoped for. Your prayers have been too dull and interrupted; but it is holiness and heaven that you have most prayed for. Your labors and endeavors have been too slothful; but they have been for God, for glory, and for the good of mankind.

Though your motion was too weak and slow, it was directed toward God; therefore it was from God. O bless the Lord, who has not only given you a word that bears God's image and is sealed by incontestable miracles as the basis for your belief, but who has also fulfilled His promises so often and notably to you — in answered prayers, in great and convincing deliverances of yourself and many others, and by wonders that have often strengthened your faith.

Bless that God of light and love, who, besides the public attestation of His word long ago given to the church, has given you the internal seal: the nearer indwelling attestation, the effects of power, light, and love imprinted on your nature, mind, and will — the witness within yourself — that the word of God is not a human dream or a lifeless thing. By regeneration He has been preparing you for the light of glory, just as by generation He prepared you to see this light and to converse with men. And will you still doubt and fear against all this evidence, experience, and foretaste?

I find it worthwhile to strengthen my soul in the firm belief of its own immortal nature, in the reality of a future life of joy or misery for mankind, and in the undeniable truth of the Christian faith. The existence of God and His perfection are so evident to me that I feel little temptation to doubt them, just as I would not doubt the existence of the earth or the sun. To me, the atheist appears no better than a madman.

The truth of Christianity is known only through supernatural revelation. Yet this revelation is so externally attested to the world and internally attested to holy souls that it makes faith the ruling, victorious, and comforting principle by which we must live, rather than living by sight.

The immortality of the soul and its future reward can be argued from natural revelation, but that argument is far less clear than the argument for God's existence. Add evangelical, supernatural revelation, and the matter becomes much clearer and more certain.

I observe that among the unbelievers of this age, most who deny Christianity also question or deny the retribution of a future life. Those who are convinced of the latter find that Christianity fits excellently with it, greatly aiding the work of faith. Thus I believe there is hardly any truth more essential to be thoroughly digested into full assurance than the soul's immortality and the hope of future happiness.

When I consider the great disparity between people's hearts and lives and the beliefs we all profess, I cannot help fearing that not only the ungodly but also many who genuinely hope for glory hold a far weaker belief — both in habit and action — in the soul's immortality and the truth of the gospel than they suppose.

Can I be certain — or fully persuaded in habit and action — of the future rewards and punishments of souls, and that we will all soon be judged according to how we have lived here, yet still not despise all the vanities of this world? Should I not set my heart, with determination and diligence, on the preparations required by a holy, heavenly, fruitful life, as one whose soul is consumed with hopes and fears about matters of such unspeakable importance?

Who could afford to linger, as most do, at the threshold of eternity if they truly believed their immortal soul would soon be there? Even if a person had no certainty of their own particular claim to salvation, the certainty that joy or misery is imminent would surely awaken them to try, cry out, search, beg, strive, watch, and spare no care, cost, or labor to secure their standing in so weighty a matter. It is impossible they would not act swiftly, with a fully resolved soul and with earnest zeal and diligence.

What man who has once seen the things we hear about—heaven and hell—would not afterwards treat these matters with more fervor than the most resolved believer you know? Reason would lead to such a conclusion; I confess that a wicked heart is very insensible.

I admit there is much weakness in the belief of unseen things, even where sincerity exists. Still, there should be some correlation between our belief and its effects. Where there is little regard, fear, hope, sorrow, joy, or resolved diligence about the world to come, I must conclude that, at least in action, there is little belief in it. Such people are largely unaware of how much they secretly doubt its truth.

I know most people complain mainly about the uncertainty of their claim to salvation, and little about uncertainty concerning heaven and hell. Yet if they were more certain of the latter and truly persuaded in their hearts, it would lead them to serious, resolute faithfulness in religion. That steadiness of faith would help them more easily ascertain their sincerity than lengthy examinations and numerous debated marks could do without such assurance.

I acknowledge that God's great wisdom has deemed it unfit for us, while in the body, to have the clear, sensible, and vivid apprehensions of heaven and hell that sight would provide. That would mean having too much of heaven or hell on earth; the taste would follow the perception, and such a full sense would be akin to possession. We are not prepared for that while in this world.

Therefore revelation must be darker than sight, allowing for a lower perception. Otherwise this world and the next would be confused, and faith and reason would be rendered ineffective—not duly tested, exercised, and prepared for reward. Yet faith is faith, and knowledge is knowledge. He who truly believes in such great, transcendent things, even without seeing them, will have corresponding affections and endeavors.

I also confess the human soul, while in the flesh, is not equipped to bear the profound sense of heaven and hell that sight would induce. The soul operates with the body and according to its capacity. It cannot endure such a deep sense without distraction; it risks overwhelming the senses and leading to a breakdown.

Yet a genuine belief in future things must bring an overriding seriousness to the soul that truly possesses it. One who is careful and serious about this world, yet looks toward a better one with only slight, unwilling, half-hearted regard, must be seen as believing only as he lives. His doubts or unbelief about the reality of heaven and hell are greater than his belief.

O then, what should my soul pray for more than a clearer and stronger faith? "Lord, I believe; help my unbelief!" I have groaned to You countless times under the burden of this remnant of darkness and unbelief. I have often reflected on the evidences of Christian truth and on the great necessity of a lively, powerful, active faith. I have begged for it; I have cried to You day and night, "Increase our faith." I have written and spoken to others in ways that might be most useful to myself, to elevate my understanding of faith and make it more like the perceptions of sense. Yet, Lord, how dark is this world! What a dungeon is this flesh! How little clearer is my sight, and how little quicker are my perceptions of unseen things compared to long ago!

Am I at the highest point a man on earth can reach, even when I feel so dark and low? Is there no further growth in these perceptions to be expected? Does the soul cease to grow in vigorous perception when the body ceases to grow in sensation? Must I settle for such a low measure while I am drawing closer to the things I believe and am almost where belief must transition into sight and love?

Or must I accept the passive silence and inactivity some friars suggest is closer to perfection, and, under the pretense of annihilation and receptivity, leave my sluggish heart alone—claiming that in this neglect I wait for Your operations? O, let not a soul that is driven from this world, weary of vanity, and thinking of little else but immortality—who seeks and cries both night and day for the heavenly light and longs for a foretaste of glory and more of the firstfruits of the promised joys—let not such a soul long, cry, or strive in vain!

Do not punish my past grieving of Your Spirit by abandoning a soul that cries for Your grace, so near its great and inconceivable change. Let me not languish in vain desires at the door of hope, nor pass with doubtful thoughts and fears from this vale of misery. This should be the season of triumphant faith, hope, and joy, especially as I am entering the world of joy! O, You who have left us so many comforting words of promise that our joy may be full, send, O send the promised Helper—without whose presence and heavenly beams, after all thoughts and strivings, it will still be night and winter for the soul.

But have I not expected more particular and sensitive conceptions of heaven and the state of blessed souls than I should, and then remained less satisfied because I anticipated such distinct perceptions for my comfort—perceptions God does not ordinarily grant to souls in the flesh? I fear this has been too true. A distrust of God, and a desire to know much (both good and evil) for ourselves as necessary for our peace and satisfaction, is a sin that has deeply corrupted human nature and is more common than usually observed.

I find that this distrust of God and my Redeemer has significantly influenced my desire for clearer, more sensible knowledge. I know I should implicitly, absolutely, and quietly trust my soul into my Redeemer's hands (of which I will speak more shortly). Distrustful care is our great sin and misery, not only regarding the body but regarding the soul as well. Yet we must desire that our knowledge and belief be as distinct and particular as God's revelations are.

We can love no further than we know. The more we know of God and of glory, the more we shall love, desire, and trust Him. It is a known, not a merely unknown, God and happiness that the soul joyfully desires.

If I must not be ambitious for too distinct and sensitive perceptions of unseen things here, I will yet earnestly desire and beg for the most fervent and sensible love for them that I am capable of. I will, in part, accept the unavoidable ignorance and the low degree of knowledge that God confines us to in the flesh—so long as He grants me such comforting foretastes in love and joy that this general, imperfect knowledge may coexist with them. Thus my soul may not pass with distrust and terror, but with suitable, triumphant hopes for everlasting pleasures.

O Father of lights, who gives to all liberally and without reproach: do not confine this sinful soul in darkness! Do not leave me to grope in unsatisfied doubts at the door of the celestial light.

If my knowledge must remain general, let it be clear and powerful. Do not deny me now the lively exercise of faith, hope, and love—those stirrings of the new creature, the dawnings of the everlasting light, and the guarantee of the promised inheritance.

Often we find ourselves agreeing with Cicero, who, after reading works like Plato's, remarked that while we held the book in our hands we felt assured of our immortality; yet when we set it aside our doubts returned. Our arguments may seem clear and convincing, but when we do not reflect on them with a composed mind we are often caught off guard by fear, worrying that we may be mistaken and that our hopes are in vain.

This, together with the common fear of death that even good people frequently exhibit, leads skeptics to conclude that we force ourselves into a hope we wish to be true. They argue, contrary to human nature, that we were not created for a better world.

However, this fallacy arises from people's failure to distinguish:

1. Sensitive fears from rational uncertainty or doubts.

2. The mind that is in the darkness of unbelief from that which possesses the light of faith.

I find within myself too much fear when I contemplate eternity. That fear interrupts and weakens my desires and joy. Yet I recognize it is largely an irrational, sensitive fear. It is produced by the darkness of the human mind, the magnitude of the change to come, the dreadful majesty of God, and humanity's natural aversion to death. These things may coexist with a reason that is otherwise fully satisfied.

If I were bound with the strongest chains or stood on the surest battlements atop a castle or steeple, I could not look down without fear—a fear that would nearly overwhelm me—yet I would be rationally sure I was secure and could not fall. The same applies to our outlook on the life to come: fear is often a necessary passion.

When a person is certain of a safe foundation, that very certainty can be violently robbed of comfort by fear. Indeed, fear is a passion that can irrationally corrupt our reason itself, leading us to doubt because we fear, even when we do not know why. A fearful person struggles to trust his own perceptions of safety. Like anxious, melancholy people who magnify every small symptom into a mortal threat, the fearful are quick to suspect deception and slow to accept words of hope.

Satan, aware of the power of these emotions and having easier access to our sensitive faculties than to our intellectual ones, seeks to infiltrate this backdoor. He tries to frighten vulnerable souls into doubt and unbelief.

He is particularly successful with timid individuals when it comes to the comforting acts of faith.

Yet God's mercy is remarkably evident in preserving many honest and tender souls from the destructive aspects of unbelief. Their fears often keep them from being reckless with sin. Meanwhile, many bold and shameless sinners become infidels or atheists by forfeiting the assistance of grace.

Irrational fears have such power to raise doubts that the two are seldom separated. Many people scarcely recognize the difference between doubts and fears. They often claim they not only fear but also doubt, when they can hardly say why, as if the trouble were not an intellectual act but an irrational passion.

If, therefore, my soul sees undeniable evidence of immortality; if it can, by irrefutable arguments, prove the future blessedness expected; and if it is convinced that God's promises are true, sufficiently sealed, and attested by Him to warrant the most confident belief—then it is not our aversion to dying, nor the sensible fears of a soul that gazes into eternity, that invalidate the reasons for hope or prove the unsoundness of faith.

However, these fears do demonstrate the weakness of faith. If they were to prevail against the choices, obedience, resolutions, and endeavors of faith, they would undermine the truth of faith or prove its nullity. Faith is trust, and trust is a securing, calming thing. "Why are you fearful, O you of little faith?" was a just rebuke from Christ to His disciples when sensible dangers raised their fears.

The established will has a political or imperfect, though not a despotic and absolute, power over our passions. Therefore our fears reveal our unbelief, and a stronger faith is the best means of conquering even irrational fears. "Why are you cast down, O my soul? And why are you disquieted within me? Hope in God;" (Psalm 42) is a necessary admonition to a timid heart.

Although many claim that faith lacks evidence and insist it is merely an assent of the mind commanded by the will, without knowledge of the truth of the testimony, Scripture often treats this same assent as both knowing and believing. Just as a bare command will not inspire love unless we perceive something admirable in the object, a mere command of the law or of the will cannot alone produce belief unless we recognize truth in the testimony believed. That would be an act without its object.

Truth is perceived only to the extent that it is somehow evident, for evidence is nothing but the objective perceptibility of truth — or, as Scripture metaphors it, light. Thus we must say that faith does not rest on sensible evidence of the invisible things believed. Rather, faith is the willing perception of the evidence of truth in the word of the one asserting it, and a trust in that word. We must have evidence that Scripture is God's word and that His word is true before we can believe it by any mere command of the will.

Therefore I neither despise evidence as unnecessary nor rely on it alone as the sufficient total cause of my belief. If God's grace does not open my eyes, come down in power upon my will, and instill a sweet acquaintance with the unseen things — together with a taste of their goodness to delight my soul—no reasons, however undeniable, will suffice to establish and comfort me.

Reason must first engage with notions, words, and signs; it must understand terms, propositions, and arguments, which are merely means to the knowledge of things. Many learned people rest on this alone. But it is God's illumination that must give us an effective acquaintance with the spiritual and invisible things these notions signify, of which our intellectual knowledge is merely the means.

To sum up, the certainty of our hopes of heaven is evident from three sources:

1. From nature.

2. From grace.

3. From other works of gracious providence.

From the nature of man:

1. Made capable of it.

2. Obliged, even by the law of nature, to seek it above all else.

3. Naturally desiring perfection:

    (i). Habitual.

    (ii). Active.

    (iii). Objective.

From the nature of God:

1. As good and communicative.

2. As holy and righteous.

3. As wise, making none of His works in vain.

From grace:

1. Purchasing it.

2. Declaring it through a messenger from heaven, both by word and by Christ's own resurrection (and others').

3. Promising it.

4. Sealing that promise through miracles.

5. And by the work of sanctification until the end of the world.

By subordinate providence:

1. God's actual governance of the world through the hopes and fears of another life.

2. The many helps He gives us for a heavenly life and for attaining it — which are not in vain.

3. Especially the ministry of angels, their love for us, and communion with us.

4. Additionally, even devils themselves convince us:

    (a) Through the nature of their temptations.

(b) Through apparitions and haunted houses.

(c) Through witches.

(d) Through possessions. These, although merely a satanic operation on the body, are so extraordinary that they differ from the more usual operations; just as God's Spirit's operations on the saints, which are called His dwelling in them or possessing them, differ from His lesser operations on others.

Having proven that faith and hope have a certain future happiness to expect, the text directs me next to consider why it is described as "being with Christ":

1. What is included in our "being with Christ."

2. That we shall be with Him.

3. Why we shall be with Him.

To be with Christ includes:

1. Presence.

2. Union.

3. Communion, or participation of felicity with Him.

Question: Is it Christ's godhead, His human soul, or His human body that we shall be present with and united to, or all? Answer: It is all, but in various ways.

We shall be present with the divine nature of Christ.

But are we not always so? And are not all creatures so?

Yes. His essence encompasses all places and beings, but not as it is operative and manifested by His glory. Christ directs our hearts and tongues to pray, "Our Father in heaven," yet He knew that all places are in and with God. It is because God operates and shines forth most gloriously to holy souls in heaven. Just as a man's soul is said to be in the head because it understands and reasons there—not in the foot or hand, though it is also present there—so when we speak to someone we look them in the face; similarly, we look up to heaven when we pray to God. God, who is and operates as the root of nature in all the works of creation (for in Him we live and move and have our being), and through grace in all that is gracious, is eminently present and active in heaven through the works and splendor of His glory. Therefore, by this glory we must mean some created glory, for His essence has no inequality.

We shall be present with the human nature of Christ, both soul and body. However, our limited understanding must not too boldly presume to resolve the difficulties that should be overcome for a distinct understanding of this. We should not expect anything more than a dark and general knowledge of them, such as:

What is the formal difference between Christ's glorified body and His flesh on earth?

Where Christ's glorified body is, and how far it extends.

How the soul and the glorified body differ, since the latter is called a spiritual body, is beyond our present understanding.

What can we conceive of a spiritual body except that it is pure, incorruptible, invisible to mortal eyes, and fitted to the soul's most perfect state? How closely it resembles a spirit (and thus the soul), and how far they agree or differ in substance, extent, divisibility, or activity, we know very little.

Nor do we know where and how far Christ's body is present. The sun is commonly regarded as a body, and, according to the most probable philosophy, its moving, illuminating, and heating rays are a real emanation of its substance. Thus it is essentially as extensive as those rays: it fills the air and touches the surface of the earth. How much further it extends we cannot tell. The differences between Christ's glorified body and the sun, in terms of purity, splendor, extent, or excellence of nature, remain largely unknown to us.

Therefore, let no one argue, "How can a multitude of glorified bodies all be present with the one body of Christ when each must occupy its own space?" Just as the body of solar rays and the encompassing air coexist so that no one can discern the difference in the places they occupy, and a multitude of bodies can be present with them both, so may all our bodies be with Christ's body without any real confusion.

Besides being present with Christ, there will be a union that we cannot now comprehend. A political or relational union is beyond doubt—like the union subjects have with their king in one kingdom—but we know little of how much more there may be. We observe a remarkable corporeal continuity among the material works of God. The more spiritual, pure, and noble a nature is, the greater its inclination toward union. Every plant on earth is united with the soil in which it lives; plants are real parts of it. What natural connection our bodies shall have with Christ's, and what influence will flow from it, is beyond our knowledge. Although the similitudes Christ uses in John 15 and John 6, and the teachings in Ephesians 5 and 1 Corinthians 12, seem to reach far, being only similitudes we cannot fully know their extent.

Similarly, we may speak of our union with Christ's human soul. Souls, being more inclined to union than bodies, suggest that, just as plants are united parts of the earth yet retain their own individuating form and matter, invisible souls may also have some kind of union or connection while keeping their individual substances and forms. We cannot assert that our bodies will have a closer union with Christ's body than our souls will have with His soul. The nature, manner, and measure of this union remain unknown to us.

It is far from us to suppose that Christ's glorified, spiritual body is composed of the same forms, parts, and dimensions as His earthly body. It will not have hands, feet, brain, heart, stomach, liver, or intestines as it did on earth. Nor will it be a compound of earth, water, and air as it was here, nor confined to the same extent. If it were so, then only His disciples and a few Jews would be present with Him, while the rest of the world would be absent and without His company. But it is such that not only Paul but all true believers from creation to the end shall be with Christ and shall see His glory. Although differences of fitness or degrees of holiness will produce differences of glory, no one can prove any inequality based on local distance from Christ. Even if such distance exists, it is beyond our comprehension; yet none in heaven are so distant from Him that they do not share in the joy of His presence.

When we argue against those who hold to transubstantiation and the ubiquity of Christ's body, we conclude that the senses judge whether real bread and wine are present; but they cannot judge whether Christ's spiritual body is present any more than they can determine the presence of an angel. We conclude that Christ's body is not infinite or immense like His Godhead. As for its dimensions, limits, or extent, and where it is absent, we must refrain from deciding. We cannot ascertain how far the sun extends its secondary substance or emanating rays, nor can we fully understand the locality of Christ's soul or of any spirit in relation to a spiritual body.

The fear is vain and carnal of those who worry that their union with Christ or with one another will be too close—that they will lose their individuality like rivers flowing into the sea, or like extinguished candles whose fire becomes merely a sunbeam or part of the common element of fire in the air, or like the vegetative spirits that retreat from the leaves into the branches and trunk of a tree in autumn. I have already shown that our individuality, our numerical existence, does not cease; and no union should be feared that does not destroy the being, formal powers, or actions of the soul. This fear springs from the root disease of selfishness and from a lack of holy love toward God, our Savior, and one another. Selfishness makes people prefer their own wills and pleasures above God's, and their own happiness above that of others. It makes them more ready to endure God's injuries and the sufferings of countless others than to forgo their own. The One who implanted a strong desire for the body's preservation into the soul, while it is its form, will diminish that desire when the time for separation comes, for then it will serve no purpose until the resurrection; otherwise it would be a torment to the soul.

As we shall have union, so also communion with the divine and human natures of Christ. Both will be the objects of our soul's noblest and most constant acts, and both will be the source or communicative cause of our receptions.

Our various faculties have different objects suited to their natures. The objects of sense are sensible things; the objects of imagination are images; the objects of the intellect are things that can be understood; and the objects of the will are things that are desirable. The eye, a nobler sense than the others, has light as its object, which is not an object for the other senses. Therefore, as our glorified souls and our spiritual, glorified bodies will differ, so will Christ's glorified soul and body be their respective objects; to behold the glory of both will be part of our glory.

Still, it should not be inferred that the separated soul, before the resurrection, will not have Christ's glorified body as its object; the objects of the body are also objects of the soul. More precisely, the objects of sense are also objects of intellect and will, though not all objects of intellect and will are sensible. The separated soul can know Christ's glorified body, even though our present bodies cannot see a soul. We cannot, however, determine how much our spiritual bodies will surpass these passive bodies now composed of so much earth and water.

Although our souls are now like a candle in a lantern, requiring external objects admitted through the senses before they can apprehend them, this does not mean a separated soul cannot know such objects.

1. The soul now knows things abstractly, through species, because its act of reasoning is a composite of soul and body. In the future it will know such things intuitively, as it can already do now when the lantern is removed.

2. Despite the claims of many recent thinkers who style themselves ingenious, we have little reason to believe that the sensitive faculty is not an essential, inseparable power of the same soul that is intellectual. Sensation does not cease for separated souls, although particular modes of sensation may cease with their organs and uses. To feel intellectually, to understand, and to will in a feeling way are actions we have reason to think will belong to separated souls. If this is so, why should they not have communion with Christ's body and soul as their objects in their separated state?

3. Moreover, we are uncertain whether the separated soul has any vehicle or body at all. We should not assume as true or false what we do not know.

Some maintain that the sensitive soul is material and, like a body related to the intellect, is never separated. I do not agree with those who assert two distinct substances, yet I cannot with certainty pronounce them mistaken. Others hold that the soul is material, of a purer substance than visible things, and that the common notion of its substantiality amounts to nothing more than a pure, so-called spiritual materiality. This view was held not only by Tertullian but also by almost all the early Greek doctors who wrote on the subject, and by many Latin doctors, as I have shown elsewhere and as Faustus recounts in the treatise answered by Mammertus.

Some suppose the vegetative soul to be an ignited body, akin to what we call the solar or other fire, though of a higher, purer kind. They argue that sensation and intellection are the formal faculties that distinguish it from mere inferior fire. Few of the early doctors denied some sort of materiality in the soul; consequently, they held it to be extensive and divisible by divine power, though not naturally so, for it is most strongly inclined to unity. If any of these uncertain opinions proved true, the objections now under consideration would have no place.

Let us not forget the notion of some that, just as the spirit that departs from falling leaves in autumn yet continues to animate the tree, so too a man's soul, when departed, may continue to animate some more noble, universal body to which it is united. These are bold speculations by men who would do better to leave unknown matters alone. Still, they may be mentioned to counter the more perilous boldness that denies the soul's action—an action that is certain, though alleged objections rest on uncertain grounds.

I may confidently conclude, despite such objections, that Christ's divine and human natures, both soul and body, will be the objects of happiness and love for the separated soul before the resurrection. To be with Christ means to have such communion with Him, not merely to be present where He is.

The primary aspect of this communion will be our receptivity—specifically, Christ's communications to the soul. The infinite, incomprehensible Deity is the root and first cause of all communication—natural, gracious, and glorious—relating to being, motion, life, rule, reason, holiness, and happiness. All creation depends on God even more than fruit depends on the tree, plants on the earth, or members on the body; yet they are not parts of the Deity nor deified, because this communication is creative.

God employs secondary causes in His communication to lower natures. It is highly probable that the human soul of Christ primarily, and His body secondarily, will be the chief secondary causes by which grace and glory are communicated to men both in the body and in the separated state. Just as the sun is primarily an efficient, communicative secondary cause of sight to the eye and is also the object of our sight, so Christ is to the soul. The glory of God will illuminate the heavenly city, and the Lamb will be its light.

Although He will deliver the kingdom to God the Father and put an end to all rule and authority, and though the last enemy to be destroyed is death, yet He will not cease to be our Mediator, the head of the church, or the conveying cause of everlasting life, light, and love to all His members. Just as we live because He lives, even as the branches in the vine, and the Spirit that quickens, enlightens, and sanctifies us is first the Spirit of Christ before it is ours—communicated from God by Him to us—so it will be in the state of glory. Our union and communion with Him will be perfected, not destroyed or diminished. Unless I were so arrogant as to think myself the most excellent of all God's creatures and therefore nearest to Him, how could I suppose that I am under no secondary cause, but receive grace or glory from God alone?

I am far from such arrogance as to imagine I will be so near to God that I will be above the need for Christ's communications or above the need for other subordinate causes. Just as I am now lower than angels and in need of their help, subject to the governance of my superiors, and, as a poor weak member, of little worth compared to the whole body—the church of Christ—from which I receive continual help, so I expect there will be differences in glory. I do not know how it will be in that state, but I am convinced God will still use secondary causes for our joy, and that there will not be absolute equality among us.

It is consistent with God's all-sufficiency and our happiness in Him that we will forever have use for one another. To sit down with Abraham, Isaac, and Jacob in the kingdom, to be carried to Abraham's bosom, to sit at Christ's right and left in His kingdom, to have authority over ten cities, and to join with the heavenly host in the joyful love and praise of God and the Lamb—these are not false or useless notions of our celestial glory.

Certainly, if I am with Christ I shall be with all who are with Christ—that is, with the whole heavenly society. Our present bodies of gross, passive matter require so much room that the earth seems barely enough for its inhabitants; those at the antipodes are almost as strange to us as if they were in another world, and people from another kingdom, province, county, or even another parish are often strangers, sometimes even those from another house. Our capacity for communion here is therefore narrow.

Yet many scriptural expressions give us good reason to believe our heavenly union and communion will be closer and more extensive. All the glorified will know one another, or at least be far less distant and strange than we are now. Consider how far the sunbeams extend, how they penetrate our densest glass, and how they confound those who claim all bodies are impenetrable. Observe how little they hinder the presence of other creatures and how intimately they mix with all, seeming to possess the whole region of the air while the air itself appears to fill it. On that account I cannot believe that glorified spirits, nor even spiritual bodies, will be such strangers to one another as we are here on earth.

I must say it is a pleasant thought to me, and it greatly aids my willingness to die, to think that I shall go to all the holy ones—Christ and the angels, as well as departed, blessed souls. For:

1. God has convinced me that they are better than I individually, and therefore more amiable than myself.

2. Many are better than one, and the whole is greater than a poor, sinful part; the New Jerusalem is the glory of creation.

3. God has given me a love for all His holy ones, as such.

4. I have a love for the work of love and praise, which they continually and perfectly perform to God.

5. I have a love for the celestial Jerusalem as it is complete, and for God's glory shining in them.

6. My old acquaintances—many holy persons who have gone to Christ—make my thoughts of heaven more familiar. O, how many of them could I name!

7. It is no small encouragement for one about to enter an unseen world to think that he does not tread an untrodden path, nor enter a solitary state; he follows all who from creation to this day have passed through death to endless life.

Is it not an encouraging thought to consider that I will go no other way, and to no other place or state, than all the believers and saints who have gone before me from the beginning until now? More on this later.

4. Departing to Be with Christ

But I must be loosed, or depart, before I can be with Christ. Here I must consider: (1) from what I must depart, and (2) how, or in what manner, I must depart. I must not refuse to know the worst.

First, I know that I must depart from this body itself and from the life that consists in animating it. These eyes will see no more; this hand will move no more; these feet will walk no more; this tongue will speak no more. As much as I have loved—and over-loved—this body, I must leave it to the grave. There it must lie and rot in darkness, a neglected and loathed thing.

This is the fruit of sin, though nature would not have it so; I mean the nature of this compound man. But what if it is so?

1. It is but my shell or tabernacle—the clothing of my soul, not the soul itself.

2. It is merely an elementary composition that is dissolved: earth returns to earth, water to water, air to air, and fire to fire, each to that union toward which the elemental nature inclines.

It is but an instrument laid aside when all its work is done, a servant dismissed when his service is at an end. What should I do with a horse when I need to ride no more, or with a pen when I must write no more? It is simply the laying aside of the passive receiver of my soul's operations when the soul has no more to do with it — just as I cast aside my lute or other instrument when more pressing matters than music occupy my time.

Or, at most, it is like flowers dying in the fall and plants in winter, when the retiring spirits have completed their work and are unwilling to dwell in such a cold and unsuitable habitation as the season makes their former matter to be. Its retirement is not annihilation but a transition to a more fitting place.

It is merely a separation from a troublesome companion, like putting off a shoe that pinched me. I have endured many sad and painful hours in this frail and faltering flesh — many weary nights and days. What cares, what fears, what griefs, and what groans has this body cost me! How many hours of my precious time have been spent maintaining it, pleasing it, or repairing it! A considerable part of my life has been spent in necessary sleep and rest; how much in eating, drinking, dressing, taking medicine; and how much in laboring or using means to procure these and other necessities! Many times I have thought that life costs me so dearly — even a painful, weary life — that were it not for the work and higher purposes of life, I would have little reason to love it or to be reluctant to leave it. Had God not instilled in our nature a necessary, unavoidable, sensitive love for the body and for life — just as He does in a mother and in every creature for their young — how unclean, impotent, and troublesome would it be for the propagation and continuation of man on earth? Had God left it to mere reason, without this necessary pre-engagement of our natures, it would have been more doubtful and difficult whether this life should be loved and desired; many would wish daily that they had never been born — a wish I have struggled to suppress, even when I knew it to be sinful, and even when the work and pleasure of my life have been sufficient to overcome its evils as few have experienced.

Yes, to depart from such a body is merely to be removed from a foul, unclean, and sordid habitation. I know that the bodies of men and animals are the curious, wonderful work of God and are not to be despised or dishonored, but admired and well used. Yet it is a wonder to our reason that so noble a spirit should be housed so meanly, and we may call it "our lowly body," as the apostle does (Philippians 3:21). It is made up of the airy, watery, and earthly parts of our daily food, acted upon by the fiery part as the instrument of the soul. The greater part of that same food, presented with great cost, pomp, and pleasure on our tables and then in our mouths today, is tomorrow a fetid, loathsome excrement—cast out to avoid the sight and smell that annoy us—though yesterday it was the sumptuous fruit of our abundance, the glory of great housekeeping, and the pleasure of our eyes and taste. Is not the rest that turns into blood and flesh of the same general kind as that which turns into loathsome filth? The difference is that it is more suitable for the soul by the fiery spirits, yet longer to operate on and keep from corruption; our blood and flesh are as stinking and loathsome a substance as our filthiest excrements, except that they are kept longer from putrefaction. Why then should it grieve me more that one part of my food, which turns into flesh, should not stink in the grave than that all the rest should daily stink in the draught? Yes, while it is within me, were it not covered from my sight, what a loathsome mass would my intestines appear! If I could see what is in the guts, the mesentery, the ventricles of the brain—what filth, what bilious or mucous matter, and perhaps crawling worms there are in the most proud or comely person—I should think that the cover of a cleaner skin and the borrowed ornaments of apparel make little difference between such a body and a carcass (which may also be covered with an adorned coffin and monument to deceive those who see only the outside). The change from corruptible flesh, filled with such fetid excrements, to corrupted flesh is not as great as some foolishly imagine.

Moreover, to depart from such a body is merely to be loosed from the bondage of corruption and from a clog and prison for the soul. I do not say that God placed a pre-existent soul in this prison as punishment for former faults; I must say no more than I can prove or know. However, that body, which was once a suitable servant to innocent man's soul, has become a prison for him now. I have no reason to assert what alteration sin made upon the nature of the body, whether it is more terrene and gross than it would have been otherwise; it was made from earth or dust at first, and to dust it shall return. No doubt it has its part in that dispositive deprivation which is the fruit of sin. We find that the soul, as sensitive, is so imprisoned or shut up in flesh that sometimes it requires more than one door to be opened before the object and the faculty can meet. In the eye, indeed, the soul seems to have a window to look out at and to be almost visible to others; yet there are many interposing layers, and a suffusion or winking can make the clearest sight as useless for the time as if it were none. If sense is thus shut off from its object, it is no wonder if reason also faces difficulties from corporeal impediments; and if the soul yoked with such a body can move no faster than its heavy pace.

Furthermore, to depart from such a body is merely to be separated from an accidental enemy—one of our greatest and most harmful foes—though we say that it is not by any fault of our Creator's work but by the effects of sin that it is so. What could Satan or any other enemy of our souls have done against us without our flesh? What is it but the interests of this body that stand in competition with the interests of our souls and of God? What else do the profane sell their heavenly inheritance for, as Esau sold his birthright? No one loves evil as evil, but as it seems to be a real or apparent good; and what good is it but that which seems good for the body? What else is the bait of ambition, covetousness, and sensuality but the interests and pleasures of this flesh? What occupies our thoughts and care, which we should direct toward spiritual and heavenly matters, but this body and its life? What pleasures steal away men's hearts from the heavenly pleasures of faith, hope, and love, but the pleasures of this flesh? This draws us into sin and hinders us from our duties. This body has its interests that must be attended to, and its inordinate appetites that must be satisfied; otherwise, what complaints and disquiet must we expect? Were it not for bodily interests and temptations, how much more innocently and holily might I live! I would have nothing to care for but to please God and to find pleasure in Him, were it not for the concerns of this bodily life. What employment should my will and love have but to delight in God and love Him and His interests, were it not for the love of the body and its concerns? Through this, the mind is darkened and thoughts are diverted; our wills are perverted and corrupted; by loving corporeal things, we develop a strangeness and aversion to spiritual things. Through this, heart and time are alienated from God; our guilt is increased; our heavenly desires and hopes are destroyed; life becomes unholy and uncomfortable, and death becomes terrifying. God and our souls are separated, and eternal life is set aside and in danger of being utterly lost. I know that it is the sinful soul that is the chief cause and agent in all this; but what is it but bodily interest that serves as its temptation, bait, and end? What but the body, and its life and pleasure, is the chief, objective, alluring cause of all this sin and misery? And shall I regard such a body as better than heaven, or be reluctant to be loosed from such a troublesome yoke-fellow, or to be separated from such a burdensome and dangerous companion?

Objection: But I know this habitation; the next I do not know. I have long been acquainted with this body and this world, but the next I am unacquainted with.

Answer: If you know it, you know everything I have mentioned before; you know it to be a burden and a trap. I know from long experience that this flesh has been a painful dwelling for my soul, and this world is like a tumultuous ocean or the uncertain, stormy region of the air. It is well-deserved bondage, pain, and enmity for anyone who loves them simply because they are familiar with them and who is reluctant to leave them because they have had them so long, and who is afraid of being well because they have been sick for so long.

And do you not know the next and better dwelling? If you believe God's promise, you know that such a state exists. You know, in general, that it is better than this world, and that we shall be in holiness and glorious happiness with Christ. Is this not knowledge?

And what we do not know, Christ, who prepares and promises it, does know. Is that nothing to us if we truly entrust our souls to Him? He who can discern no more good in heaven than on earth remains so earthly and unbelieving that it is no wonder he is afraid and unwilling to depart.

In departing from this body and life, I must leave behind all its familiar pleasures. I will no longer taste the sweetness of food, drink, or rest. I will no longer enjoy sports or any other present delights. Houses, lands, goods, and wealth must all be left behind. The place where I live will no longer know me.

All my possessions will mean no more to me, nor all that I labored for or delighted in, than if they had never existed at all.

And what if it must be so? Consider, O my soul! Your old pleasures are already past; you lose none of them by death, for they have been lost already—unless immortal grace has sanctified them and made their benefits everlasting.

All the sweet drinks, morsels, sports, and laughter; all the pleasant thoughts of your worldly possessions or hopes that you ever had until this hour are gone, dead, and past. All that death does to such things is to prevent you from having them on earth any longer.

Is this not the case for every brute animal, which has no comfort from the prospect of another life to compensate for its loss? Just as our dominion diminishes their pleasure while they live—by keeping them under fear and labor—so, at our will, their lives must end.

To satisfy a gentleman's appetite for half an hour or less, birds, beasts, and fish must lose their lives and all the pleasure life might have given them for many years. Many of these (birds and fish at least) must die to become but one feast for a rich man, if not one ordinary meal.

And is not their sensual pleasure of the same nature as ours? Food is as sweet to them, comfort as welcome, and desire as strong in season. The pleasure that death deprives our flesh of is a pleasure common to man and brute. Why then should it seem hard for us to lose, in the course of nature, what our wills deprive them of at our pleasure?

If we are believers, we can say that we are merely exchanging these delights of life for the greater delights of life with Christ—a comfort our fellow creatures do not possess.

Indeed, the pleasures of life are often embittered by so much pain that for many people the sorrows outweigh the joys. The vanity and vexation are so great and grievous that pleasure seldom compensates.

Nature prefers life—even under tolerable suffering—rather than death. But that inclination arises less from sensible pleasure than from a deep, God-given natural bent, which free will cannot easily overcome. As I said before, the human body is such that, if we could see through the skin (as one might look through a glass hive to watch bees) and observe all the parts and motions, the filth and excrements within, the soul would hardly be willing to dwell in such a mass of unclean matter.

Were it not for this necessitating inclination, a cow would not lick an unclean calf, nor would mothers bear the burdens of children who bring so much uncleanness, crying, and helplessness. I now say of the pleasure of living that the sorrows are for many so much greater than the sensible delight that life would not be so commonly chosen and endured were it not for natural inclination — or the fear of the misery of the separated soul.

Yet even this did not prevent some, counted the best and wisest of the heathen, from viewing it as valor and wisdom to end their lives in times of extremity. They made this the great answer to those who grumble at God for making life miserable: "If the misery is greater than the good of life, why do you not end it? You may do that whenever you wish."

Our food and drink are pleasant to the healthy, but they cost the poor so much toil, labor, care, and trouble to procure even a meager diet that I think if they could live without eating and drinking, they would gladly exchange the pleasure for relief from the care and toil of obtaining it. And when sickness comes, even the most pleasant food becomes loathsome.

Do we not willingly interrupt and set aside these pleasures every night when we go to sleep? A man may have pleasant dreams, but few go to sleep for the pleasure of dreaming. Either no dreams, or vain or troublesome dreams, are far more common.

To say that rest and ease are my pleasure is merely to say that my daily labor and cares outweigh my waking pleasures so much that I am glad to put them aside. What is ease but deliverance from weariness and pain? In deep, dreamless sleep there is little positive sense of the pleasure of rest itself.

It is more from nature's necessitated inclination toward self-care and repair than from the positive pleasure of rest that we desire sleep. If we can thus be content every night to die, as it were, to all our waking pleasures, why should we be unwilling to die to them all at once?

If it is the inordinate pleasures forbidden by God that you are reluctant to leave, those must be forsaken before you die; otherwise it would have been better for you never to have been born. Every wise and godly person casts them off with detestation.

You must be hostile to holiness for that reason, as well as to death. The same cause that makes people unwilling to live a holy life also makes them unwilling to die — simply because they are reluctant to leave the pleasures of sin. When the wicked are converted, they must give up gluttony and drunkenness. They must no longer live in pride, vanity, worldliness, and sensuality. Therefore they draw back from a holy life as if it were death itself.

Thus they are more reluctant to die because, for eternity, they must forgo the pleasures of riches, pomp, honors, sports, and lusts. But what does this mean for those who have mortified the flesh, with its affections and lusts?

Yes, these forbidden pleasures are the great impediments to both our holiness and our truest pleasures. One reason God forbids them is that they hinder us from better things. If for our own good we must forsake them when we turn to God, then they should not be a reason against our willingness to die. Rather, being freed from their danger should make us more willing.

But the great, satisfying answer to this objection is that death will lead us to far greater pleasures, with which these earthly ones cannot be compared. More on this will be discussed in due time.

When I die, I must depart not only from sensual delights but also from the more noble pleasures of study, knowledge, and conversation with many wise and godly men. I must leave behind the pleasure of reading, hearing, and participating in public and private exercises of religion.

I will leave my library and will no longer turn over those pleasant books. I will no longer be among the living, nor see the faces of my faithful friends, nor be seen by men. Houses, cities, fields, countries, gardens, and walks will mean nothing to me.

I will no longer hear of the affairs of the world—of men, wars, or other news—nor see what becomes of that beloved concern for wisdom, piety, and peace which I desire may prosper.

Answer. Though these delights are far above those of sensual sinners, yet, alas, how low and little are they! How small is our knowledge compared to our ignorance! How little does the knowledge of learned doctors differ from the thoughts of a silly child?

From our childhood we take knowledge in by drops. As trifles form the matter of childish understanding, so words, notions, and artificial forms make up much of the learning of the world. Many learned men know little more of truly great and excellent things than rustics who are looked down upon for their ignorance.

God and the life to come are little better known by many scholars—if not much less—than by many of the unlearned. What is it but child's play that many logicians, rhetoricians, grammarians, and even metaphysicians and other philosophers are engaged in with their eager studies and disputes? Of how little use is it to know what is contained in the hundreds of volumes that fill our libraries? Or to know the most glorious speculations in physics and mathematics that give some the title of virtuosi and ingeniosi in these times, when they have little more wit or virtue to live for God, to overcome temptations from the flesh and the world, and to secure their everlasting hopes?

What pleasure or peace does it give to a dying man to know almost any of these trifles?

Indeed, it would be better if much of our reading and learning did us no harm, rather than cause harm. I fear that for some, books are merely a more honorable form of temptation than cards and dice. Many precious hours may be lost in them that should be spent on higher matters.

Many make such knowledge merely an unholy, natural, and even carnal pleasure—just as worldly people do with thoughts of their lands and honors. These pursuits may be more dangerous precisely because they are less suspected. The one saving feature is that the pleasure is fenced off from the slothful by the thorny labor of hard and long studies, so that laziness often saves more from it than grace and holy wisdom do.

Yet the imagination and natural intellect can, with as little sanctity, find pleasure in reading, knowing, disputing, and writing, just as others spend their time playing chess or other clever pastimes.

For my part, I know that the knowledge of natural things is valuable and can be sanctified, much more so than mere theological theory when it is rightly employed. When sanctified, it is of real use. I have little knowledge that I do not find useful in some way for my highest ends.

If wishing or money could procure more, I would gladly spend for it. Yet if many scores or hundreds of books that I have read had been unread, and I had that time now to devote to higher things, I would consider myself much richer than I am.

I must earnestly pray that the Lord forgive me the hours I have spent reading things less profitable, for the sake of pleasing a mind that desired to know all—hours I should have spent increasing holiness in myself and others. Yet I must thankfully acknowledge that from my youth He taught me to begin with matters of greatest weight, to refer most of my other studies to them, and to spend my days under motives of necessity and profit to myself and those with whom I had to do.

I now think better of the course of Paul, who determined to know nothing among you except Jesus Christ and Him crucified — that is, to converse with them so as to use and glory in that as if he knew nothing else. And so of the rest of the apostles and the primitive ages.

Though I still love and honor Augustine (and am not of Dr. Colet's mind, who, as Erasmus says, most slighted Augustine), I now censure less even that Carthage council which forbade the reading of the heathens' books of learning and arts than I once did. I would have men savor most that learning in their health which they will or should savor most in sickness and near death.

And, alas, how costly is this knowledge! What is merely theoretical and notional is just a fleeting delight of the mind, little different from a pleasant dream. But how many hours, how much strain on weary eyes, and how many stretching thoughts of an impatient brain must it cost us to attain any excellence?

Solomon wisely warned: "Of making many books there is no end, and much study is a weariness of the flesh; for in much wisdom is much grief, and he who increases knowledge increases sorrow." How many hundreds of studious days and weeks, and how many hard and taxing thoughts, have my very small store of knowledge cost me? How much infirmity and pain to my body, an increase of painful diseases, and loss of comfort and health! How much pleasure of other kinds, and how much acceptance with others, have I lost by it — pleasures I could have had through a more sociable and agreeable way of life!

And when all is said and done, if I happen to know more than others about my position and duties, I am usually obliged to differ from them. If I hide that difference and keep my knowledge to myself, I sin against conscience and against nature. The love of humanity and the love of truth compel me to share knowledge responsibly.

If I were indifferent to truth and learning—so indifferent that I could easily refrain from sharing them—I would show that I valued them little, despite the high cost at which I acquired them (even though they are, in truth, the free gifts of God). Just as nature is inclined to propagate the species through generation, so the intellect is inclined to communicate knowledge. Yet that same intellectual impulse can produce pride, ignorance, and hasty disputes among teachers, just as the generative faculty can lead to fornication and adultery.

But when I obey nature and conscience by sharing the knowledge that distinguishes me, dissenters often feel insulted, however peaceably I present it. Just as the wicked take the piety of the godly as an accusation of their own impiety, many teachers feel accused of ignorance when the light of truth condemns their errors.

Even if I do not address a particular person, they take opinions so personally that any critique of those opinions feels like a personal attack.

And then, alas! what envy, what whispered disparagements, what backbiting—if not malicious slanders and undermining—do we encounter from the carnal clergy! And oh, that it were only them. Even among the zealous and suffering band of faithful preachers, there is too much iniquity; too many preach Christ out of strife and envy.

It is a tragedy that error so often finds refuge in the selfishness and pride of pious men, and that friends of truth are tempted, in their ignorance, to reject and misuse much that is good. The reality is plain and sorrowful.

Especially when we face a clergy that is proud and has large worldly interests at stake, or when they sit in councils and synods with a secured majority, they too readily assume that their grandeur, numbers, or reputation prove them orthodox and right. They will hastily label and defame anyone who contradicts them or claims superior knowledge as erroneous, heretical, schismatic, singular, factious, or proud.

The cases of Nazianzen, Martin, and Chrysostom sadly prove this, as do the actions of too many general and provincial councils. Thus our diligent studies and cherished truths may make us appear as owls or reproached persons among those reverend brethren who find ignorance easier and far more comfortable, since it allows them to think and speak as the most esteemed do rather than to endure reproach and obloquy at great personal cost.

The people in various regions will echo what they hear from their teachers, becoming militant followers of overly militant leaders. At home, in shops, in the streets, and even in church, the talk will be that such a person is erroneous and dangerous because he is not as ignorant and mistaken as they are — especially if they follow a teacher who is greatly provoked by refutation and entangled in controversy.

If the contradicted man happens to be a suffering confessor or someone highly esteemed for extraordinary piety, imagine the cruel judgments he must expect when he seeks to correct their errors with tenderness.

Oh! What sad instances of this exist:

1. The case of the confessors in Cyprian's days, who, as many of his epistles show, became the great disturbers of that church.

2. The Egyptian monks at Alexandria, in the days of Theophilus, who became Anthropomorphites and raised abominable tumults, bringing woeful scandal and odious bloodshed.

3. And oh, that this age had not even greater instances to prove the matter than any of these!

And now, should a man be reluctant to die for fear of leaving behind such troublesome, costly learning and knowledge as the wisest men can attain here?

But the chief answer is yet to come. No true knowledge is lost; it is perfected and transformed into a much nobler, sweeter, and greater knowledge. Men may debate whether acquired habits of intellect and memory die with us, since they depend on the body; yet, by whatever means it happens, it is undeniable that we shall have far clearer knowledge than we can attain here.

The cessation of our present way of knowing will be merely the end of our ignorance and imperfection—just as waking ends the confused knowledge of a dream, and maturity ends the trifling understanding of childhood. As the Holy Spirit says, "Love never fails. But whether there are prophecies, they will fail; whether there are tongues, they will cease; whether there is knowledge, it will vanish away. For we know in part and we prophesy in part. But when that which is perfect has come, then that which is in part will be done away. When I was a child, I spoke as a child, I understood as a child, I thought as a child; but when I became a man, I put away childish things. For now we see in a mirror, dimly, but then face to face. Now I know in part, but then I shall know just as I also am known." (1 Cor. 13:8–12.)

Our knowledge and God's cannot be compared in the same way. Just as holy spirits know us now and forever, so we shall both know and be known by immediate intuition.

If a physician must describe the parts of a man and the hidden diseases of his patient, he must search hard and devote much thought to it. Long reading and patient conversation are needed before he can claim knowledge. And after all that, he still relies heavily on conjecture; his knowledge remains mixed with uncertainties and mistakes. But when he opens the corpse, he sees everything. His knowledge then is more complete, truer, and certain; moreover, it is quickly attained with a single glance.

A countryman knows the town, fields, rivers, plants, and animals where he lives with ease and clarity, while someone who learns these things only from maps and books knows them in a general, often mistaken way. Alas! When our present knowledge has cost a man forty, fifty, or sixty years of study, how lean, poor, doubtful, and unsatisfactory it often is.

But when God reveals Himself and all things, when heaven is known by its own light like the sun, the knowledge will be clear, sure, and satisfying: "Blessed are the pure in heart, for they shall see God." (Matt. 5:8) "Pursue peace with all people, and holiness, without which no one will see the Lord:" (Heb. 12:14) This sight will rightly be called wisdom, while our present glimpse is only philosophy—a desire and love of wisdom. We should not fear death because of losing our present means of knowledge. Rather, death should make us long for the world of glorious light, so that we may escape darkness and know with an easy look what now we know only with troublesome doubts or not at all. Shall we fear the darkness of heaven, or dread ignorance when we will see the Lord of glory?

And as for the loss of sermons, books, and other means, it is no real loss to cease using the means once we have attained the end. Can we not put away our winter clothes in summer and sit by the warm fire without gloves? Can we not leave our horse or coach at home when our journey is done? Can we lie in bed without boots and spurs? Is it burdensome to stop taking medicine when we are well?

Even here, the man who needs little from creatures and is content with less is happier than the man who has much and needs much. All creature comforts and aids bring their own inconveniences; applying and using many remedies is tedious. As God needs nothing and is self-sufficient—perfectly and essentially happy—those who need least from without are most like God and possess the greatest fullness of inward goodness. What need have we to preach, hear, read, or pray to bring us to heaven when we are already there?

And as for our friends and our interactions with them—whether relatives or wise, religious, and faithful individuals—anyone who does not believe there are far more and far better friends in heaven than on earth does not truly believe in heaven. Our friends here are wise, but also foolish; faithful, but partly unfaithful; holy, but, alas, too sinful. They bear God's image, but it is marred and dishonored by their faults.

They serve God and His church greatly, yet they do much against Him and too much for Satan, even when they intend to honor God. They promote the gospel, but they also hinder it. Their weaknesses—ignorance, errors, selfishness, pride, passion, division, contention, scandals, and negligence—often cause so much harm that it is hard to tell whether their good outweighs their damage to the church or their neighbors. Our friends are our helpers and comforters, but how often are they also our hinderers, troubles, and sources of grief? In heaven, however, friends are wholly wise, holy, faithful, and harmonious; nothing in them or done by them displeases God or man.

Among our faithful friends here we find a mixture: useless and burdensome people, unfaithful hypocrites, self-conceited factious wranglers, malicious envious underminers, and implacable enemies. How many such persons are there for every one worthy, faithful friend? How many troublesome individuals exist for each who will genuinely comfort you?

In heaven there are none but the wise and holy—no hypocrites, no burdensome neighbors, no treacherous, oppressive, or persecuting enemies. Is not the pure good there far better than a little good mixed with such a troublesome array of vile evils?

Christ loved His disciples, His kin, and all mankind, and took pleasure in doing good to all, as did His apostles. But how poor a return did He or they receive from anyone except God? Christ's own brothers did not believe in Him but argued with Him, almost like those who said to Him on the cross, "If You are the Son of God, come down from the cross." Peter himself was once a Satan to Him (Matt. 16), and later, with cursing and swearing, denied Him; and all His disciples forsook Him and fled. What, then, could be expected from others?

No friends are perfectly compatible. The roughness and inequalities closest to us are the most troublesome. The variety and contradiction of perceptions, interests, education, temperaments, occasions, and temptations are so great that, while we are scandalized by the world's discord and confusion, we should also marvel at the providence that preserves as much order and harmony as exists. We are like people in crowded streets going different ways and jostling one another, or like boys playing football, each striving to overthrow the other for the ball. It is a wonder of divine power and wisdom that the world is not in constant conflict.

Even when I harm no one, if I merely cross another's will it is taken as a grievous injury. With as many wills as there are people, who can please them all? Who has enough money to satisfy every poor person or every greedy desire? Who can live among discontented people without feeling the sting of their displeasure? What day passes without my being burdened by impossible expectations placed on me? How many demand unrighteous things!

I displease many by refusing to please God and my conscience. I am accused most harshly for not sinning. The world will not accept anything that contradicts its opinions and carnal interests, however much it conforms to God's commands. I must confess that, though I suffer from all sides, few men receive more insincere praise from their persecutors than I do. They praise me in general or for other matters, while highlighting my refusal to conform to their opinions and wills, and thus consider me more harmful.

The greatest crimes charged against me have been for those things I regarded as my greatest duties — acts of obedience to conscience and to God that cost me most. Had I conformed to their wishes and accepted a bishopric with its honors and riches, how good a man I would have been called by the diocesan faction! And what praise I would have had from the papists, had I turned papist; all the backbiting and bitter censures from the antinomians, Anabaptists, and separatists would have become praise if I had aligned with them. Otherwise, there is no escaping their accusations. Is this tumultuous, militant, indeed malignant world a place I should be reluctant to leave?

Alas, our darkness, weakness, and passions make it hard even for a household or a small circle of faithful friends to live steadily in love without frequent unpleasant conflicts. What, then, can be expected from strangers and enemies? Thousands will judge my words and actions without knowing my reasons. Each person's view is shaped by reports and how matters are conveyed to them; with differing perspectives and false accounts (and human imperfection makes them false), what can be expected but harmful and unjust judgments?

Although nothing on earth is more precious than the holy Word, worship, and ordinances of God, I still see reasons that point higher and tell me it is far better to be with Christ.

Should I love the name of heaven more than heaven itself? The holy Scriptures are precious because they contain the promise of glory; yet possession of that glory is far better than the promise. If a light and guide through this wilderness is good, surely the end must be better.

It pleases God that earthly means, even the sacred Scriptures, bear marks of our imperfection: imperfect men wrote them, and imperfect human language conveys them. Their method and phrasing, though true and blameless, fall short of heavenly perfection. If this were not so, so many commentators would not find it hard to explain countless difficulties and reconcile seeming contradictions. Nor would unbelievers find such temptation and so much to criticize.

Peter himself warned that in Paul's epistles there are some things hard to understand, which the untaught and unstable twist to their own destruction. Heaven will not be the source of so many errors, controversies, and quarrels for perfect spirits as the Scriptures are for us imperfect men on earth. Indeed, heaven is more desirable because I shall understand the Scriptures there far better than I ever can here. All the hard passages now misunderstood will be made plain, and seeming contradictions will be reconciled. God, Christ, the New Jerusalem, glory, and the happiness of souls — now known darkly and enigmatically — will be known intuitively, just as the face that a mirror only formerly showed us is then beheld directly.

Leaving my Bible to go to the God and heaven revealed will be no greater loss than laying aside crutches or spectacles when they are no longer needed, or abandoning an image for the presence of the friend it once represented.

I need not fear losing all other books, sermons, or verbal instruction. Much reading has often wearied my flesh, and the pleasure of my mind is greatly diminished by the imperfections of the means. Many books must be skimmed only to discover they are hardly worth reading. Others must be read to satisfy expectations or to refute those who misuse authors against the truth. Many good books add little to what we have already read elsewhere; many contain glaring errors that, if we fail to detect them, become snares for the unwary. If we do detect them and point them out — even gently and truthfully — we are thought injurious to the reputations of learned, godly authors and accused of overvaluing our own opinions.

The lamentable state of mankind, due to the imperfections of human language, is that words meant to communicate ideas so poorly fit that purpose that they often produce misunderstanding and contention. Hardly any word has a single meaning, and most require many more words to convey the speaker's true intent. Each word is a signum that has three relations:

1. To the matter being spoken of.

2. To the mind of the speaker, signifying his conceptions of that matter.

3. To the mind of the hearer or reader, which is to be informed by it.

It is difficult to find and use words truly suited to all these purposes, and to keep a store of such words without mixing in others. Few, if any, have attained it. If words are not suited to the matter, they are false to their proper use. The scarcity of suitable words, the abundance of unsuitable ones, the authority of scientific masters imposing arbitrary terms, and the customs of the populace dictating meanings have all made words inadequate and uncertain. Thus, after long, arduous study, students are often little closer to true knowledge and are frequently misled to false conceptions by inapt language. The saying that a great book can be a great evil is often true, especially when it contains many uncertain words that provoke great contention.

When the mind of the speaker or writer is poorly informed by such notions—when his conceptions are sometimes false, sometimes confused and undigested—what wonder if his words fail to convey his meaning? Even the clearest minds find it hard to have words ready to communicate their concepts with truth and clarity. To form true sentiments into apt, significant words is an art requiring a skilled teacher, a serious learner, and long practice. Too many overestimate their skill in prayer, conversation, or preaching, and too readily condemn those unaccustomed to it.

Even if we fit our words well to the matter and to our minds, it is still hard to fit them to the reader or hearer. Without that fit, they are lost to him; since his understanding is our goal, they are therefore lost to us. What is most appropriate to the subject is seldom suited to the capacity of the receiver.

"Recipitur ad modum recipientis, et pro capiu lectoris, etc." Some readers or hearers—indeed, most—are so used to unsuitable words and notions imposed by the masters of language that they cannot understand us if we change their terms and offer more fitting ones. They least understand those things they think they understand best. All must learn the art of words before they can understand and use them readily. The duller a person is, and the less understanding they have, the more words are needed to make them comprehend; yet their memory can retain fewer. This difficulty affects not only catechizing but all writings and teachings. A short catechism or concise style is not understood by the ignorant, while a lengthy one they cannot remember.

He who adapts his writing or speaking to suit one discerning reader or listener with deep thought and precise style must necessarily put many others at a disadvantage, because they cannot follow it. Such a person must be content with a few approving minds and leave the applause of the crowd to more popular speakers — unless he can adjust his words to suit both groups.

Anyone who resolves not to be deceived by ambiguous words and makes it their first task — whenever they read or argue — to distinguish carefully between words, meanings, and things, and to examine every disputed term until the speaker's intent is clear, will soon see how lamentable the state of the church and of mankind is. They will recognize the shadowy knowledge that deceives the world and the useless fantasies in which most people, even some learned men, spend their days. Much of what some men laboriously study and consider the honor of their minds or their lives, and much of what multitudes rest their piety and hopes of salvation upon, is merely a play of words and vain notions. It is rightly called vanity and vexation, like the rest of the empty show in which most men walk.

I will not here open my sad and bitter reflections about the heathen, infidel, and Mahometan world, nor about the common corruptions of rulers and teachers, cities and countries, senates and councils. I will not cry out, as Seneca did, "Omnes mali sumus," or "Stultorum plena sunt omnia," nor rehearse at length the furious spirit, ignorance, unrighteous calumnies, and schisms of the clergy, as Gregory Nazianzen and others have done. I will not lament at great length the seemingly hopeless condition of the earth on account of the boldness, blindness, and fury of men. Rather, I will use such sorrowful thoughts to loosen my attachment to this world and to make me willing to be with Christ.

If the writings and words of others are so full of imperfection, why should I suppose my own are blameless? I must always be thankful for the holy instruction and writings of others, despite human frailty and the contentious misuse of words. I must also be grateful that God has made any use of my own work for the good of souls and the building up of His church. Yet how many faults are mixed in with those comforts?

We are not the teachers of a well-ordered school, where learners are arranged in classes so each receives teaching suited to their capacity. Instead, we must open the door to all who will crowd in and publish our writings to every kind of reader. Since there are as many degrees of capacity as there are people, and therefore a wide variety and contradiction of understandings, it is easy to predict the varied reception our work will get. We cast out our doctrine almost like a ball tossed among boys in the street: few understand it, and yet everyone criticizes it.

Few come as learners or teachable disciples; most come to sit as judges over their teacher's words. Yet they lack the skill, patience, or diligence needed for fair judgment. As our words meet or clash with each hearer's prior beliefs, they are judged to be wise or foolish, sound or unsound, true or false, fitting or unfit.

Hardly any sermon I preach passes without one person praising it and wanting it printed, while another accuses it of some grave fault. Some value the clarity and accuracy of doctrine; others say it is too lofty and that the preacher "shoots over the congregation's heads," preferring only the fervent application of what they already know. Most listeners dislike most what they most need. If they err, they call the doctrine erroneous that would cure them. If they are guilty of a common sin, they take the application of the truth as a personal affront. Many enjoy plain and zealous reproof of sin—so long as it is the sins of others, not their own.

The poor love to hear about the wickedness of oppression, unmercifulness, pride, gluttony, and idleness—the sins of the rich. People enjoy hearing their rulers' faults and say, "Oh, this man is no flatterer; he dares to tell the greatest of their sins." But if they hear about their own faults, they take offense. Rulers like sermons on submission and obedience, but how few love to hear about injustice, oppression, pride, and sensuality, or to read Luke 16 or 12 or James 5, or to hear the necessity of holiness, justice, temperance, death, judgment, and the life to come! Every sectarian and dogmatist delights when their own opinion is praised and their party exalted as the chief saints. Yet anything that praises those they oppose and regard as adversaries to the truth is distasteful to them; it seems to endorse iniquity and strengthen the enemies of Christ. All the uncharitableness they expect from us against others is returned toward them and their kind.

Today, as I write these words, my pockets are full of letters. On one side I am importunately urged to conform to the oaths, declarations, covenants, and practices now imposed, or else to stop preaching (which would please them). On the other side I am vehemently censured as guilty of grievous sin for expressing the degree of conformity I have shown, and I am blamed for the sufferings of all who think otherwise for participating in the sacrament and the common prayers of the church. Others, taking the middle ground, urge me to testify against unjust separation and persecution while trying to save a self-destructive people from the tearing fury of those two extremes. How should I answer these conflicting expectations, or escape the censure of such claimants?

It has pleased God, who for over thirty years has tried me by human applause, to exercise me lately in this city — where multitudes of people with contrary minds are, like passengers in crowded streets, constantly jostling and offending one another — with daily backbitings and criticisms. So many have made me the subject of their conversation that I may say, as Paul did (1 Cor. 4:9, 10, etc.), "for we have been made a spectacle to the world, both to angels and to men. We are fools for Christ's sake, but you are wise in Christ!" etc.

If I did not live in retirement away from the noise, occupied with illness and the expectation of my change, how vexing it would be to hear religious people—who have a God, a Christ, and a heaven to talk about—spend so much time and breath on someone so inconsequential, who has so little to do with them or they with him. While some overvalue me, others still quarrel and make me the subject of their idle, sinful talk.

For several years the persecutors have sought to silence me (if they have not succeeded), and the separatists have shown such strange jealousy and quarrelsomeness that they seem bent on promoting my defamation. Much of their effort goes to searching for anything that might serve as grounds for accusation in every sermon I preach and every book I write. Though the fury of persecutors makes them incapable of the sober consideration needed for true judgment, most of the more religious critics are satisfied once I have spoken with them. It all ends in a "putarem" or a "non putarem." For want of accuracy and patience, they judge rashly before they understand; when they do understand, they sometimes confess their error. Yet many continue on, unmoved by repeated proofs of their mistakes.

Even in books that remain before their eyes—and in passing words and sermons—they heedlessly omit, insert, alter, and misreport plain statements. They confidently claim things were said that were never said, and sometimes the opposite was said. When people judge the worth or harm of our words by what they suppose we ought or ought not to say, how can we satisfy those who are out of earshot and whom we cannot personally explain ourselves to? Most have a narrow view and judge our words by the company they keep. When I show them that my positions on many questions (which offend them) are correct, they call it an ill-timed and hurtful truth. When I urge them to look more widely and explain my reasons, they say, "Had these been all set down, men would have been satisfied."

On what hard terms must we instruct those whose narrow understanding cannot grasp obvious reasons for what we say until they are told? To explain the reasons for everything they can quarrel with would make every book swell with commentaries to a size they could neither buy nor read. They do not come to learn our reasons, nor do we have the leisure to explain them to every person. Thus suspicious individuals, whose understanding lacks the humble awareness of their ignorance and whose consciences lack the tenderness that should restrain rash judgment, continue to attack necessary truths of which they know not the use or reason. What living man has the leisure and opportunity to inform every ignorant person in city and country of the reasons for all he says, writes, or does? Or who, unless he writes a book instead of a sentence, can write so that every unprepared reader will understand him? What hope has that tutor or schoolmaster of preserving his reputation if every student who does not grasp his words and reasons judges him erroneous and accuses him of unsound or harmful doctrine?

But God, in great mercy to me, has appointed this as my lot—not causing, but permitting the sins of the contentious—so that before death I might be better weaned from all below. Had my temptations from excessive applause gone unchecked, they might have been dangerously strong. Even now, while church-dividers at both extremes daily slander me, the continued respect of the sober and peaceable is so great that it tempts a weak person like me to delay my desire to leave the world.

For a long time riches and worldly honor have appeared to me as they are: they do not make the world particularly lovely or desirable. The love and concord of religious people, however, have a more amiable face. There is so much holiness in these that I was reluctant to call them vanity and vexation. Yet, because flesh and blood would turn them to selfish ends and value them as a carnal interest, I must call them so and count them among the things that are loss and rubbish (Phil. 3:7, 8).

Selfishness can prey even upon things that are good and holy. If good men, good books, and good sermons make the world seem overly attractive to us, it will be God's mercy to lessen that temptation. If my soul, set on the heavenly Jerusalem, is hindered—like Paul was on his journey to Jerusalem (Acts 20 and 21)—by the affection of ancient friends and hearers, I must say, "What do you mean by weeping and breaking my heart? I am ready to leave the dearest friends on earth, and life, and all the pleasures of life, for the presence of far better friends with Christ and the sweeter pleasures of a better life."

The little amiableness found in things below is in godly men like life in the heart: it dies last. When that is all gone—when we are dead to the love of the godly themselves, and to learning, books, and mediate ordinances insofar as they serve a selfish interest and tempt our hearts from heavenly aims—the world is truly crucified to us, and we to it.

I rejoice to walk in the footsteps of my Lord, who had some weeping around His cross and was forsaken by all His disciples; in the hour of temptation they all fled. My desertion is far less than His, and far less than I am fit to bear.

If God justifies, who is he who can condemn? If He is for me, who can be against me? O may I not be put to that dreadful case of crying out, "My God, My God, why have You forsaken Me?" May nothing separate me from His love!

If I were forsaken by the sober and peaceable, as I am in part by some quarrelsome dividers, how tolerable a trial that would be! Man is as dust in the balance, adding little and signifying nothing when God is on the other end. Yet I still suspect that I place too much value on man, for this situation has occupied too much of my attention.

Of all things, surely a departing soul has the least cause to fear losing awareness of the affairs of the world—of peace or war, of church or kingdom.

If the sun can send forth material beams and operate at such a distance—that is, by motion, light, and heat—why should I think that blessed spirits are such local, confined, and impotent substances that they cannot be aware of earthly matters? If I had bodily eyes, I could see more from the top of a tower or hill than anyone below can. Shall I know less of earth from heaven than I do now? It seems unlikely that my capacity will be so limited. And even if it were, it seems unlikely that Christ and all the angels would be so strange to me as to give me no awareness of things that concern my God and Redeemer (to whom I am united), the holy society of which I am a part, and myself as a member of Christ and that society.

I do not think the communion of celestial inhabitants is as narrow and slow as that of walking clods of earth or souls confined to such dark lanterns as this body. Stars can shine to one another, and we on earth can see them from afar in their heaven. Surely, if they have a seeing faculty, each can see many of us—even the kingdoms of the world.

Spirits are most active and possess powerful, quick communication. They need not send letters or write books to one another, nor lift up a voice to make each other hear. There is no unkindness, division, or unsociable selfishness among them that would cause them to conceal their notices or joys.

As activity, so unity is greatest where there is most perfection: they will be many, yet still be one. Their knowledge will be one knowledge, their love one love, and their joy one joy. Not by the absolute unity that belongs to God Himself—who is one and only one—but in a way suitable to created imperfection, which participates in the perfection of the Creator. As an effect shares in the virtue of its cause, so the creature has some part in His unity.

(O foolish soul! If I fear this union with God, Christ, and all the holy spirits lest I lose my present separate individuality, I forget how closely related perfection and union are.) In short, I have no cause to think that my celestial advancement will diminish desirable knowledge of earthly matters; rather, I believe it will be inconceivably increased.

If indeed I shall know less of things below, it will be because the knowledge of them is part of vanity and vexation, which has no place in heaven. The knowledge of good and evil in lower matters—introduced to us through sin—is unworthy of our fond attachment or of fearing its loss.

Surely the sad tidings we receive weekly in our newsbooks—the lamentable reports of heathen and infidel kingdoms, the overwhelming prevalence of barbarism, idolatry, ignorance, and infidelity; the rage and success of cruel tyrants; the bloody wars of proud, restless, worldly men; the misery of oppressed, desolate countries; the scattered churches; and the persecuted, innocent Christians—are not such pleasing things that we should dread to hear of them no more.

To know or hear of the poor in famine, the rich in folly, the church in disarray, the kingdom discontented, the godly scandalized by the effects of their errors, imperfections, and divisions; of the wicked growing worse; of the falseness, miscarriages, or sufferings of friends; of the fury or success of enemies—are these reports I cannot spare?

What are the daily tidings I hear but of bloody wars, ruined countries, persecuted churches, silenced, banished, or imprisoned preachers; of the best being removed by death from an unworthy world, with worse succeeding them; of renewed designs and endeavors of the church's enemies; of the relentless rage of worldly and restless clergy; of new divisions among self-conceited sectarians; and of the slander and backbiting of each party against the other?

How often do I hear the sad news of one friend's sickness or death, another's discontent, and yet another's fall—and the sufferings of many, many more? My ears are daily filled with the cries of the poor whom I cannot relieve and with the endless complaints of fearful, melancholy, despairing individuals.

I am burdened by the wranglings of ignorant and proud professors and contentious divines, who boldly criticize where they are most erroneous or dark. I endure the troublesome discontent of those I converse with. Should I fear the end of such a sad tragedy or the waking from such an unpleasant dream?

Have I not often thought of the privilege of the deaf, who do not hear these troublesome and provoking things, and of the blind, who do not see the vanities and temptations of this world? One benefit of solitude or of a private life and habitation is freedom from many of these displeasing objects. A great part of the benefit of sleep is that I can lay aside these troubling thoughts along with my clothes.

But others tell me that the church cannot yet spare me; there is still this and that necessary work to be done; there is this and that need, and so on.

But who must choose His servants and determine their work—us or God? Whose work am I doing? Is it my own or His? If it is His, is it not He who must tell me what to do, when to do it, and how long to serve? Will not His will and choice be best? If I do not believe this, how can I call Him my God? Does God or I know better what He still intends to do, and who is fittest to do it? The church's service and its benefits must be measured out by our Master and Benefactor, not by ourselves.

What am I compared to those more excellent persons whom, in all ages, He has taken out of the world? Would men's thoughts about the church's needs keep them back? The poor heathen, infidel, and Mahometan nations have no preachers of the Gospel. If their need does not prove that God will send them such, no country's need will prove that God will continue them.

Many useful servants of Christ have died in their youth. John Janeway preached only one sermon. Joseph Allen and many other excellent men died in the midst of vigorous, successful labors. Both were far more fit for God's work and more likely to win souls and glorify God than I am or ever was—though their greater light was partly kindled from my lesser.

Yet both of these, under painful, consuming languishings of the flesh, died as they had long lived — in the lively, triumphant praises of their Redeemer and in joyful desires and hopes of glory. Shall I, at seventy-six years of age, after such a life of unspeakable mercies and almost fifty-three years of comfortable help in the service of my Lord, now be afraid of my reward, shrink at the sentence of death, and still desire to stay here under the pretense of further service? We do not know what is best for the church as God does. The church and the world are not ours but His; not our desires, but His will must measure out its mercies. We are not as merciful as He is. Whether we live or die, we are the Lord's.

It is not inappropriate for us to desire many things that God will not give, nor is it fitting for Him to grant the particulars of such desires. Nothing has ever weighed so heavily on my heart as the sin and misery of mankind, and to think how much the world lies in folly and wickedness! For what can I pray so earnestly as for the world's recovery? It is His will that I should show a holy and universal love by praying, "Hallowed be Your name. Your kingdom come. Your will be done on earth as it is in heaven." Yet, alas, how unlike earth is to heaven, and what ignorance, sin, confusion, and cruelty reign and prosper here! Unless there is a wonderful change to be expected, even as by a general miracle, how little hope appears that these prayers should be granted!

It makes us better to desire that others may be better, but God is the free disposer of His own gifts. It seems to be His will that the permitted ignorance and confusions of this world should help us value and desire that world of light, love, and order which He calls us to prefer and hope for.

If I am in any way useful to the world, it is undeserved mercy that has made me so, for which I must be thankful. But how long I shall be so is not mine to determine, but my Lord's. My many sweet and beautiful flowers arise and appear in their beauty and sweetness, but only for one summer's time; they do not murmur that they flourish for so short a space. The beasts, birds, and fishes that I feed on live until I choose to have them die. Just as God is served and pleased by a wonderful variety of animals and vegetables, He will also be served by many successive generations. If one flower falls or dies, it suffices that others will arise from the same root, summer after summer. If my pears, apples, plums, etc., fall or serve me when they are ripe, it suffices that not they, but others the next year, will do the same. God will have other generations to succeed us.

Let us thank Him that we have had our time. If we could overcome the great (and often overlooked) crime of selfishness and love others as ourselves, and God, as God, above all the world, it would comfort us at death that others will survive us, that the world will continue, and that God will still be God and glorified in His works. Love will say, "I shall live in my successors, and I shall more than live in the life of the world, and yet most of all in the eternal life and glory of God."

And God, who made us not gods but mere creatures, as it pleased Him, knows best our limits. He will not subject us to a long life filled with temptations, lest we become too familiar with what should be foreign to us and completely estranged from our true home. It is no wonder that a world ripe for a deluge of sin allowed men to live for six, seven, eight, or even nine hundred years. If our great sensualists had any hope of such long lives, they would resemble incarnate devils, and there would be no place for the holy seed among them. If angels were present, they would, like the Sodomites, seek to abuse them with fury.

Nor will God wear us down with a long life of earthly suffering. We often perceive short cares, fears, sorrows, persecutions, sickness, and trials as lengthy. Should we begrudge the wisdom and love that shortens them? Yes, even though holy duty is excellent and sweet, the weakness of the flesh makes us susceptible to weariness and diminishes the spirit's willingness. Our wise and merciful God will not prolong our struggles or our race, lest we grow weary and faint and fall short of the prize. By our complaints, fears, and groans, one might think we consider this life too long; yet when we should yield to God's call, we hesitate as if we desired it to last forever.

Willingly submit, then, O my soul. It is not you, but this flesh, that must be dissolved — this troublesome, vile, and corruptible flesh. It is merely the other half of your sustenance, which your presence kept uncorrupted for longer while it pursues the excremental part. You do not die when man (the composite being) dies by your departure. And as you do not live for yourself, you do not die for yourself. Whether we live or die, we are the Lord's. He who set up the candle knows how long He has use for its light. Work the works of Him who sent you while it is day, and let God choose your time, willingly submitting to His disposal. The gospel does not die when I die. The church does not die. The praises of God do not die. The world does not die, and perhaps it will improve, and those prayers that seemed lost will be answered. Yes, some of the seeds I have sown may yield benefits for the dark, restless world after I am gone. And is not this much of the end of life? Is not that life good which achieves its purpose? If my purpose was to do good and glorify God, and good is done, and God is glorified when I am dead, even if I were annihilated, is not my purpose fulfilled? Do not pretend to be God, whose interest (that is, the pleasing of His will) is the end of all things, and whose will is the measure of all created good. Do not pretend to be the whole world: God has not lost His work; the world does not dissolve when I dissolve. Oh, how strong and unreasonable a disease is this inordinate selfishness! Is not God's will infinitely better than mine and more fitting to fulfill? Choose to fulfill His will, and you will always have your choice.

Lord, now You are letting Your servant depart in peace, even in Your peace which surpasses all understanding, that guards the heart and mind in Christ Jesus, which Christ, the Prince of Peace, gives and nothing in the world can take away. Oh, grant me that peace which befits a soul so near the harbor — the world of endless peace and love — where perfect union (as much as I am capable) will free me from all the sins and troubles caused by the convulsions, divisions, and confusions of this divided, selfish world. Call this soul home with the encouraging voice of love, that it may joyfully hear and say, "It is my Father's voice." Invite it to You through the heavenly messenger. Attract it with tokens and foretaste of love. The messengers that invited me to the feast of grace compelled me to come in without constraint. Your effectual call made me willing; is not glory better than preparing grace? Shall I not come more willingly to the celestial feast? What was Your grace for but to make me willing for glory and the way to it? Why did You send down Your beams of love but to make me love You and call me up to the everlasting center? Was not the feast of grace a sacrament of the feast of glory? Did I not partake in it in remembrance of my Lord until He comes? Did not He who told me, "Come, for all things are now ready," also say, "I go to prepare a place for you"? It is His will that we shall be with Him and see His glory. Those who are given to Him and drawn to Him by the Father on earth do come to

Christ. Give now, and draw my departing soul to my glorified Head; and as I have glorified You on earth, to the extent that Your grace has prevailed in me, pardon the sins by which I have offended You, and glorify me in the beholding and participation of the glory of my Redeemer. Come, Lord Jesus — come quickly, with fuller life, light, and love — into this too dead, dark, and disaffected soul, that it may come with joyful willingness to You.

Willingly depart, O lingering soul! It is from a Sodom, even though there are righteous Lots within it, who are not without their woeful blemishes. Have you not often groaned over the general blindness and wickedness of the world, and are you reluctant to leave it for something better? How often would you have rejoiced to see even the dawning of a day of universal peace and reformation? And would you not see it where it shines forth in its fullest glory? Would a light at midnight have pleased you so much? Have you prayed and labored for it so hard? And would you not see the sun? Will the things of heaven please you only on earth, where they come in the least and weakest influences, and are confined to gross, earthly, obscure, and unkind recipients? Away, away — the vindictive flames are ready to consume this sinful world! Sinners who blindly rage in sin must soon rage in the consequences of sin and God's justice. The pangs of lust prepare for these pangs! They are treasuring up wrath against this day. Look not behind you. Away from this unhappy world! Press on toward the mark (Phil. 3). Looking for and hastening the coming of the day of God. As this world has treated you, it would treat you still, and it will treat others. If you have fared well in it, it is no thanks to it, but to God. If you have experienced manifold deliverances and marvelous preservations, and have been fed with angel's food, do not love this wilderness for it, but love God and His angel, who has been your guide, protector, and deliverer.

And has this troublesome flesh been such a comfortable companion to you that you are so reluctant to leave it? Have your pains, weariness, languishings, labors, cares, and fears about this body been pleasing to you? And are you hesitant for them to end? Did you not find a need for patience to endure them, and of greater patience than mere nature provided? Can you now hope for better when nature fails, and that an aged, worn, and more diseased body should be a more pleasant dwelling for you than it was before? If from your youth it has been both a tempting and troublesome thing to you, surely, though it may be less tempting, it will not be less troubling when it is returning to dust and, above ground, smells of the grave. Had sensible things been ever so pleasant in your youth, and had you indulged yourself in health with that sort of delight, in old age you must say by nature, "I have no pleasure in them." Does God, in great mercy, make pain and weakness the harbingers of death, and will you not understand their purpose? Does He mercifully take away the pleasure of all fleshly things and worldly vanities beforehand, so that there may be nothing to relieve a departing soul (as the shell breaks when the bird is hatched, and the womb relaxes when the infant must be born), and yet shall we linger when nothing holds us back, still reluctant to depart? Would you dwell with your beloved body in the grave, where it will rot and stink in loathsome darkness? If not, why should it now, in its painful languor, seem to you a more pleasant dwelling than the glorious presence of your Lord? In the grave it will be at rest, not tormented as it is now, nor wishing at night, "Oh, that it were morning!" nor saying in the morning, "When will it be night?" And is this a dwelling fit for your delight? Patience in it, while God will so try you, is your duty, but is such patience a better and sweeter life than rest and joy?

But, alas! how deaf is flesh to reason. Faith possesses the reason that can easily shame all contrary reasoning, but the senses are unreasonable, especially this inordinate, tenacious love of present life. I have enough reason to be willing to depart, even much more willing than I am. Oh, that I could be as willing as I know I should be! If I could love God as much as I know I should love Him, then I would desire to depart and be with Christ as much as I know I should desire it. But God, in nature, has placed upon me some necessity of aversion (though the inordinateness comes from sin), else Christ would not have feared and deprecated the cup. Death must be a penalty, even where it is a gain, and therefore it must meet with some unwillingness: because we willingly sinned, we must unwillingly suffer. The gain is not the pain or dissolution itself, but the happy consequences of it. All the faith and reason in the world will not make death a non-penalty, and therefore will not remove all unwillingness. No man has ever reasoned or believed himself into a love of pain and death as such, but seeing that the gain is unspeakably greater than the pain and loss, faith and holy reason may make our willingness greater than our unwillingness, and our hope and joy greater than our fear and sorrow. It is the deep and effectual awareness of goodness, which is God's way, in nature and grace, to change and draw the will of man. Come then, my soul, and think, believingly, about what is best for you. Will you not love and desire most that which is certainly the best?

5. Why Being with Christ Is Far Better

To say and hear that it is far better to be with Christ is not enough to make us willing. Words and notions are instruments that God uses to work on souls, but the convincing, satisfying, powerful light and the inclining love are other things. The soul now operates as the form of man on and with the corporeal spirits and organs, and it perceives its own perceptions, but it is a stranger to the mode of its future action when separated from the body and can have no formal conception of such conceptions as it has never experienced. Therefore, its thoughts of its future state must be analogical and general and partly strange. However, general notices, when certain, can be very powerful and satisfy us sufficiently for our consent and to a measure of joy suitable to this earthly state. Such notices we have from the nature of the soul, the nature of God, the course of Providence and the governance of mankind, the internal and external conflicts we perceive about men's souls, the testimony and promises of the word of God, the testimony of conscience, along with the witness of the sanctifying Spirit of Christ, and in it the earnest and foretaste of glory and the beginnings of eternal life here, all of which I have considered before.

The Socinians, who interpret this as referring only to the state of resurrection, against clear evidence, violate the text: for Paul expressly speaks of his gain by death, which will be his abode with Christ upon his departure from this life. In 2 Corinthians 5:7-8 he calls this to be absent from the body and to be present with the Lord; and Christ, to the penitent thief, refers to being with Him in Paradise. In Luke 16, in the parable of the steward, Christ indicates that wise preparers, when they depart, are received into everlasting habitations; as He further tells us that Lazarus was in Abraham's bosom.

Goodness is primary in two senses: as the absolute essence and will of God, or as something secondary and measurable. The first is God's perfect essence and will. The second can be understood in two ways:

1. Greater goodness: the welfare or perfection of the universe.

2. Lesser goodness: what pertains to the various parts of the universe, either:

a. In a nobler sense, when they contribute to the perfection of the whole;

b. In a lesser sense, when they are perfect or happy in themselves;

c. In the lowest sense, when they are good for creatures lower than themselves.

Accordingly, it is far better to be with Christ:

1. Properly and simply: because it fulfills God's will.

2. Analogically: because it contributes to the perfection of the universe and of the church.

3. Because it will be for our own good or happiness.

4. Because it may be beneficial to our lesser fellow creatures; although this last point is somewhat doubtful and does not seem tied to the meaning of this passage.

Let us consider these points in order.

It is a repugnant consequence of idolatrous selfishness to see no goodness beyond our own pleasure. We then reduce God's goodness to being merely useful, benevolent, and generous toward creatures, treating the creature as the ultimate end and God as only a means. In doing so we honor His name while denying Him in truth, elevating the creature to the place of God.

What is simply best is what God wills. So remaining here is best while I am meant to stay, and departing is best when the time for my departure comes. What is best is what exists, for it is God's work; the world at any moment cannot be better than it is, nor can anything that is of God be better than He wills it to be. When God changes things, then it will be best that they are changed. Even if the only good in my departure were this simple good — the fulfillment of God's will — reason tells me I should be fully satisfied. Yet there is also a subordinate kind of good.

My change will contribute to the perfection of the universe, including the material good that relates to its fitness for the purpose for which God created and sustains it. Just as every part, position, and movement of a clock or watch serves the ends of its maker, so everything in creation serves a divine purpose.

Although God has not revealed to me specifically why everything is as it is, I trust that it is all done with perfect wisdom and is suited to its proper use and end. For example, if a hen or other bird knows how to build her nest, lay her eggs discreetly, when and how to sit on them until they hatch, how to feed and protect her young, and when to leave them to become self-sufficient, then surely God, who made these creatures, knows what is best.

If a bee knows when, where, and how to gather honey and wax, how to build its honeycombs, and how to store its provisions, and if it displays all the marvels of its intricate behavior, can I believe that God lacks knowledge of what is best or that He is deficient in skill, will, or power?

And should the stone resent being hewn, the brick being burned, the trees being cut down, sawn, and framed, the lead and iron being melted, and so on, when all this is for the purpose of forming a useful building and fitting every part to perfect the whole?

Shall the waters resent that they must flow away, the plants that they must die or partly die every winter, the fruits and flowers that they must fall, the moon that it must have its changing motions, or the sun that it must rise and set so often, when all of this is simply the action and order that creates the harmony and perfection the Creator designed and which pleases His will?

Lawful self-love is further satisfied here: the goodness spoken of in the text is that analogical, subordinate good — my own happiness and what leads to it. It is most reasonable to love God best and then to love what is most like Him (when known). Why should not the latter be the easiest and sweetest? Experience shows how easy it is to love ourselves. So if I firmly believe that it is best for me, I will desire to depart and be with Christ. Have I not reason to believe that?

I will consider the reasons for this in the following order:

1. The general reason from the efficient causes and the means.

2. The final reasons.

3. The constitutive reasons from the state of my intellect, and its action and enjoyment there.

4. The constitutive reasons from the state of my will.

5. The constitutive reasons from my practice there, leaving out those which the resurrection will provide me, because I am only speaking of my present departure to Christ.

What is best for me is what Love itself — my heavenly Father — designs and chooses for my good. I hope I will never dare to think or say that He is mistaken, or that He lacks skill or love, or that I could have chosen better for myself than He does if He had left all to my choice. Many times the wise and good will of God has crossed my foolish, rebellious will here on earth; afterward I have always perceived that it was best — usually for myself, but always for a higher good than mine.

He is not an enemy or a tyrant who made me, preserved me, and now calls me hence. He has not treated me as an enemy: the more I have tested Him, the better I have found Him. Had I better obeyed His ruling will, how happy I would have been! And is not His disposing and rewarding will equally good?

Human work is flawed and corrupted by evil; God's work is perfect and uncorrupted. If I would not die until my dearest friend desired it, how much less should I wish to delay until I myself preferred it (when not constrained by misery)? I should then rejoice and think my life secure. O foolish, sinful soul! If I do not recognize that it is far better to be under God's choice than under my own or anyone else's, then how blind I am. Should I not prefer that He choose the time rather than I?

Be of good cheer, then, O my soul! It is your Father's voice that calls you: the same voice that called you into the world and bade you live; that called you out of a state of sin and death and bade you live to Him;

that so often brought you back from spiritual death, forgave your sins, renewed your strength, and restored you to the comforts of His house and service; that so graciously led you through this howling wilderness and brought you almost to the sight of the promised land. Will you not willingly go when infinite, fatherly love calls you hence? Are you not yearning for His presence? Are you afraid to go to Him who is the only cure for your fears?

Was it not to this glory that He finally elected you? Where do you read that He elected you to the riches and honors of this world or to the pleasures of the flesh? No; He elected us in Christ to the heavenly inheritance (Eph. 1:3, 4, etc.). Indeed, He elected you also to bear the cross and to endure manifold sufferings here. But is that what you prefer over the crown? Those sufferings were merely a means to the kingdom, to conform you to Christ so that you might reign with Him after suffering with Him. If God chooses you for blessedness, do not refuse it or act like one who rejects a gift.

Surely that state is my best which my Savior purchased and promised me as best. As He did not buy me with silver and gold, so neither did He intend that I be rich or exalted in this world. If that had been His chief design, His incarnation, merits, sacrifice, and intercession would have been of small account. Who has more of these things than those who have least of Christ?

But He purchased us to an incorruptible crown; to an inheritance incorruptible and undefiled, that does not fade away, reserved in heaven for us, who are kept by the power of God through faith unto salvation. Is it heaven that cost such a dear price for me, the end of such a wonderful design of grace, and shall I now be unwilling to receive the gift?

That is surely best for me — the very thing for which God's Holy Spirit has been preparing me, the thing He gives to believers, and the end of all His holy operations on my soul. Yet the Spirit is not persuading me to love this world more each day; rather He urges me to turn from such love and to set my heart on the things above. Should I love this life, fleshly interests, vanity, and vexation, or should I love the invisible perfection that this blessed Spirit has worked so earnestly to form in my heart?

Would I now undo all or frustrate all His work? Has grace been preparing me for glory so long, and shall I be unwilling to take possession of it? If I am not willing, then I am not yet sufficiently prepared.

If heaven is not better for me than earth, then God's Word and ordinances have been all in vain. Surely my best is the gift of the better covenant, secured to me by so many sealed promises and pointed out by so many sacred precepts, doctrines, and examples. I have been called to hear, read, meditate, pray, and watch for this end for so long.

Was it the interest of the flesh on earth, or a longer life of worldly prosperity, that the gospel covenant secured to me? Was it what the sacraments and the Spirit sealed to me, what the Bible was written to direct me to, what ministers preached to me, what books were written for, what I prayed for, and what I served God for? Or was it not His grace on earth and glory in heaven?

Is it not far better to attain the end of all these means than to lose them all and lose my hopes? Why have I used them if I would not attain their end?

That is my best state toward which all the course of God's fatherly providences tends. All His gentler mercies and all His sharper corrections are designed to make me a partaker of His holiness and to lead me to glory by the same path my Savior and all His saints have walked. All things work together for my good by preparing me for what is truly best.

Both calms and storms aim to bring me into that harbor. If I take them merely for themselves and for this present life, I mistake their purpose, misunderstand them, and ungratefully despise them — thus losing their end, life, and sweetness. Every word and work of God, every day's mercy, change, and experience looks toward heaven and intends eternity.

God leads me no other way. If I do not follow Him, I forsake my hope by forsaking Him. If I follow Him, shall I be unwilling to come home and reach the end of this journey?

Surely my best is that which God has required me principally to value, love, and seek, and to make the business of my whole life, referring all else to it. I am fully certain this is my duty, as has been demonstrated elsewhere.

Is my business in the world only for the things of this world? How vain a creature, then, is man; and how little difference between waking and sleeping! If one believes there is no life but this to seek or hope for, no wonder he lives in uncomfortable despair. He will seek only to palliate his misery with brutish pleasures and will not hesitate at any wickedness to which his fleshly lusts incline him — especially tyrants and multitudes who have nothing but God to fear.

It is my certain duty to seek heaven with all the fervor of my soul and the diligence of my life. Is it not best to find it?

That must surely be best for me, for which all other things must be forsaken: it is folly to give up the better for the worse. Scripture, reason, and conscience tell me that when the world stands in competition or opposition with heaven, it should be forsaken — even for the least hopes of heaven. A possible everlasting glory ought to be preferred over a certainly perishing vanity.

I am sure this life will soon be nothing to me; therefore it is next to nothing now. If I must forsake all for my everlasting hopes, why then be unwilling to enter into the possession of them?

Our best state is likely our most mature state. Nature moves things toward their perfection: apples, pears, grapes, and every fruit are best when ripe. Though then they hasten to decay, that is due to the incapacity of their bodily matter to retain the vegetative spirit, which is not annihilated at separation.

Created things are not made for their own happiness but for man's use. Their ripeness is the state in which man uses them before they corrupt, and their corruption serves for his nourishment; the spirits and best parts of his food become his very substance. Would God cause saints to grow to ripeness only to perish and drop into useless rot? That is not credible.

Though our bodies may become like our filthiest excrements, our souls return to God who gave them. Though He does not need them, He uses them in their separated state for such heavenly purposes as their maturity and ripeness have prepared them for. Seeing then that love has ripened me for itself, shall I not willingly drop into its hand?

Our best is likely what the wisest and holiest in all ages have preferred above all else and most desired—the thing almost all mankind acknowledges to be best in the end. It is unlikely that all the best people should be most deceived and led into fruitless labors and sufferings by such a deceit, and that God should rule nearly all mankind through such illusions. Were that so, the common insights of human nature and the final judgments of conscience would be in vain.

It is beyond doubt that those who believe in no life but this are usually worse in temper and practice. None are so holy, just, sober, charitable to others, and useful to mankind as those who firmly believe and hope for immortality. Shall I fear that state which all the wise and holy in every age have preferred and desired?

It is also likely that my best state is what my greatest enemies most oppose. Think how much Satan works to keep men from heaven, and how much worldly honor, pleasure, and wealth he offers to accomplish that end. I need not elaborate; I have said much about it in the Treatise of Infidelity.

Shall I then adopt so much of Satan's mind toward myself? He would not have me come to heaven; shall I therefore be unwilling? All these considerations point to the same conclusion: it is best to be with Christ.

6. The Final Reasons

Is it not far better to dwell with God in glory than with sinful men in such a world as this? Although God is everywhere, His glory—the presence we must behold for our happiness—and the perfecting communications of His love are found in the glorious world, not on earth.

Just as the eye is made to see light and then to see other things by that light, so the human mind is made to see God and to love Him, and to see other things in, by, and for Him. The One who is our beginning is also our end; our end is the primary motive of all moral action, for it is for this end that all means are used. The end attained is the rest of souls.

How often has my soul groaned under the sense of distance, darkness, and estrangement from God! How often has it looked up and longed for Him, saying, "As the deer pants for the water brooks, So my soul pants for You, O God. My soul thirsts for God, for the living God; When shall I come and appear before God?" (Psalm 42:1). Would I not have my prayers heard and my desires granted? What else is the sum of lawful prayers but God Himself? If I desire anything more than God, what sinfulness lies in those desires, and how sad their implication!

How often have I said, "Whom have I in heaven but You? And there is none on earth that I desire besides You. But it is good for me to draw near to God; I have put my trust in the Lord God, That I may declare all Your works." (Psalm 73:25, 28). Woe to me if I were to dissemble! If not, why should my soul draw back? Is it because death stands in the way? Do not my fellow creatures die for my daily food? Is not my passage secured by the love of my Father and the resurrection and intercession of my Lord? Can I see the light of heavenly glory in this dark shell and womb of flesh?

All creatures display more or less excellence and glory according to how much God operates and shines through them. By that operation He communicates more of Himself to them. Although He is immense and indivisible, His operations and communications are not equal.

That which is nearest to Him receives the most of those operations, without the intervention of any second, created cause. Thus creatures stand in order toward Him according to their nobler natures and the fewer intervening causes they involve.

I do not presume to think I am or will be the best and noblest of God's creatures, such that I would be under the influence of no second or created causes. I will say more about that later. To be as near as my nature was ordained to approach is simply to attain the end and perfection of my nature.

Just as I must not expect to be the nearest to Him as He is the first efficient cause, I must also not expect to be nearest to Him as He is the first directing or governing cause. Since I am now under the governance of His officers on earth, I expect to be under subordinate governors in heaven as well.

My glorified Savior will be my Lord and ruler, and I do not know who else will be under Him. If angels differ in perfection and, as commonly believed, in power and order among themselves, I must not conclude that no created angel or spirit will have any governance over me. Yet whatever administrators there are, the divine governance will be so pure and divine that the blessed effects of God's rule will be sweetly powerful within it.

If the law was given by angels, if the angel of God appeared in the burning bush, and if an angel conducted the people through the wilderness, and yet these things are attributed to God, how much more near and glorious will divine governance be—regardless of who the administrators are?

Since I must expect to be under some created efficient and directing causes there, I must also expect subordinate ends; without them there would be no proportion and harmony of causes. Whatever nobler creatures are above me and exercise causal influence upon me, I must ultimately exist for their purposes.

When I look up and consider the multitude of glorious beings above me, I dare not presume I will be the nearest to God or that I am made solely for Him. I find that I am made, ruled, and sanctified for the public or common good of many beyond myself. I am certain I must ultimately exist for my glorified Redeemer; as for what other spiritual beings or intelligences are above me, I know little.

God has arranged all His creatures so that they are means and ends to one another, though not equally or in the same respects. Whatever nearer ends there may be, He who is the first efficient and directing cause will be the ultimate, final cause. In this respect I shall be as near to Him as is appropriate to the rank and order of my nature, and I shall be useful to the ends that correspond to my perfection.

If it is an honor for a servant to have an honorable master and to be appointed to honorable work, and if it is some distinction for a horse over a swine, or for a worm or a fly to serve more closely the use of man — yes, even for a prince — will it not also be my advancement to be ultimately for God and subordinately for the highest created natures, in services fitting my spiritual and heavenly state?

I am far from thinking I will be above service and have nothing to do. Activity will be my perfection and my rest. All such activity will be regular, in harmony and order of causes, and used for its proper purpose.

Although I do not yet fully know what service I will perform, I know it will be good and suitable to the blessed state I will be in. It is enough that God and my Redeemer know it, and that I shall know it in due time when I come to practice it. I will say more about this later.

The inordinate love of this body and present composition seduces souls into thinking all their use and work is for the body's maintenance and prosperity. When the soul has served that end and is separated from the flesh, it is not left idle or without work or pleasure. It is a mistake to imagine the world contains nothing but this little mass of matter for a soul to labor upon; as if the soul itself, all creatures, and God were unfit objects for a soul.

Nor is it true that what operates in our composite state by means of its organs has no other way of operating without them. As a musician is not dead when his instrument is broken — he has other powers — so the living principle of the soul continues. The fiery part of a candle is not annihilated when the flame goes out, and a sunbeam does not cease to be light when it is outside our horizon.

Though I will not always have a body to operate in and upon, I will always have God, a Savior, and a world of fellow creatures. When I do not shine in this lantern or see by these spectacles, I shall still see things intuitively, as face to face. That which is essentially life will live; that which is essentially active, intellective, and volitive will remain so while it is itself and not annihilated or changed into another thing. Such a nature cannot lack an object until all things are annihilated.

Reason assures me that if my will were now what it ought to be — fully obedient to my understanding — then fulfilling God's will would also fulfill my will. My will would perfectly comply with His, and to please Him perfectly would be my perfect pleasure.

It is only the unreasonable attachment to this body and sinful selfishness that make anyone think otherwise now. I am sure my soul shall live, for it is life itself. I am sure I shall live to God, fulfill His blessed will, and please Him; this is far better than happiness considered by itself. Yet, insofar as I take pleasure in doing so, it will also be my happiness.

I now begin to think that the soul's deep love for this body (so long as it is not excessive) is given by God, in part to signify the great love Christ has for His mystical, political body and for every member of it, even the least.

He will gather His elect, and those who come to Him will not be cast out; those given to Him shall not be lost. As truly as His flesh is food and His blood is drink, He nourishes them for eternal life. His Spirit within them makes the sacrament, the Word, and Christ as believed in become spirit and life for us — just as our soul and natural spirits convert our food into flesh, blood, and spirit — something that never happens in a dead body or any lifeless vessel.

As we take delight in the comfort and prosperity of our body, and enjoy the nourishing food that sustains it and other things that serve it, Christ likewise delights in the welfare of His church and all the faithful. He is pleased when they are fed with good, nourishing food and when they prosper.

Christ loves the church not only as a man loves his wife but as we love our own bodies; for no one ever hated his own flesh (Ephesians 5:27, etc.). In this I must acknowledge my Savior's superiority, for He surpasses me in powerful, faithful love. He will save me from pain and death far better than I can save my body, and He will hold me to Himself far more inseparably.

If it pleases my soul to dwell in this house of clay and to act upon something as humble as flesh, how much more will it please my glorified Lord to dwell with His glorified body—the triumphant church—and to cherish and bless every member!

It would be a kind of death for Christ to be separated from His body and to see it perish. Whether Augustine and other fathers were right in thinking that, just as our bodies shed hair and lose much flesh through sickness and decay, so Christ's militant body also loses hypocrites and perhaps some nominally living members, I cannot say for certain. But it is certain that confirmed members, and most certainly glorified members, shall not be lost. Heaven is not a place where Christ or we should suffer such loss.

Will Christ love me more than I love my body? Will He be more unwilling to lose me than I am to lose a member of my own body or to die? Will He not take infinitely greater delight in animating and empowering me forever than my soul takes in animating and empowering this body?

Oh, then, let me long to be with Him! And although I am naturally reluctant to be absent from the body, let me, by His Spirit, be even more unwilling to be absent from the Lord. Though I would not wish to be unclothed were it not for sin's effects, let me not groan to be clothed with my heavenly dwelling. Let me desire to become the delight of my Redeemer and to be perfectly loved by love itself.

Even this blessed receptivity of my soul—receiving the love and delight of my glorified Head—will surely be happiness to me. Insensible creatures are merely beautified by the sun's light and heat; sentient beings enjoy pleasure from it as well.

Shall my soul be senseless? Will it be a clod or a stone? Shall that which is now the form of man be then more lifeless or incapable than the form of brutes is now? Doubtless not. It will be a living, perceiving, sensible recipient of the felicitating love of God and my Redeemer. I shall be loved as a living spirit, not as a dead, senseless thing that cannot comfortably perceive love.

If I must rejoice with my fellow servants who rejoice, shall I not be glad to think that my blessed Lord will rejoice in me and in all His glorified ones? Union will make His pleasure much mine; and it will be aptly said by Him to the faithful soul, "Enter into the joy of your lord." (Matt. 25:21). His own active joy will objectively be ours, and our joy will efficiently come from Him. Can that be a bad state for me in which my Lord most rejoices? It is best for Him, and therefore best for me.

The heavenly society will joyfully welcome a holy soul. If there is now "Likewise, I say to you, there is joy in the presence of the angels of God over one sinner who repents." (Luke 15:10), who has so little holiness and so much sin, what joy will there be over a perfected, glorified soul? Surely, if our angels there behold our Father's face, they will be glad, in season, for our company.

The angels who carried Lazarus to Abraham's bosom undoubtedly rejoiced in their work and their success. Is the joy of angels and the heavenly host of no significance to me? Will not love and union make their joy my own? If love here makes my friends' and neighbors' comforts become mine, then because their joy—measured by their perfection—will greatly exceed what I now know, participating in such joy will be far better than occupying my little separated apartment.

The Final Reasons

Surely my best condition will be that in which angels and blessed spirits most delight, and I shall rejoice most in what they most rejoice in.

7. Reasons Arising from My Intellect

Though the tempter would argue — by pointing to infants in the womb, apoplectics, and others — that the understanding will be merely inactive when separated from bodily organs, I have already given sufficient reasons to counter that temptation.

I will grant that it will not have the same mode of conception as it does now through these organs. Still, 1. The soul will remain essentially a vital, intellective substance, naturally inclined to act. This inclination is like fire's inclination to shine and give heat. Since it is life itself — that vital substance — it cannot die so long as it remains what it is in essence. Nor can it fail to be intellective, as an inclined power, because that is essential to its nature. Of course, God can change or annihilate anything if He wills.

2. It will exist amid a world of objects.

3. It will continue to depend on the first Cause and receive His continual, actuating influx.

4. No one can produce the least evidence that it will cease to have sensation — whether the sensitive faculties are the same substance as the intellective (which is most probable) or in some conjunct, as others

suppose—even if the particular species and modes of sensation tied to organs cease.

5. Indeed, no one can prove that the departing soul does not carry with it the fiery spirits it immediately actuated in the body. If ever so certain that those Greek fathers were mistaken (and some were hypocritical) in believing the soul to be a sublime intellectual fire, still the argument remains unsettled.

As for the objection that some make—that the soul pre-existed before it was in the body, while others, and most, believe it received its first being at that time—if the former were true it would mean the soul had intellectual activity before incorporation, though it remembers nothing of that once united to the body. It would operate only as the form of man, and its forgetfulness would be taken as part of its penalty. Those who think of it as a ray of the anima mundi or of the world-soul must believe it intellectually animated the world or part of it; to suppose it would do so again is the harshest conjecture one can make about it.

Just as the rays of the sun that heat a burning glass and ignite a candle remain the same rays when diffused through the air—illuminating, heating, and moving it—and are not annihilated or weakened when their contracted operation ceases by breaking the glass or extinguishing the candle, so too the spirit of a tree continues to animate the tree even when it withdraws from the leaves and allows them to fall. But this is merely an unproven imagination of men, and we have no need of it except to refute their own argument.

But if the soul did not exist until its incorporation, what wonder is it that it operates only as the form when united to the body for that purpose? What wonder if its initial actions, like a spark in tinder or the first lighting of a candle, are weak and barely perceptible? What wonder if it acts only for the uses that creation appointed: first preparing its own body as the maker's instrument, then feeling, and then understanding? What wonder if it operates only insofar as it admits objects? Therefore, what wonder if, in cases of apoplexy, those operations are interrupted?

The departing soul, however, is:

1. In its maturity.

2. No longer united to this body, and thus not confined to sense and imagination in its operations or in the reception of its objects.

3. Under the aspect of merit, ordered as a governed subject to its reward—something it could not receive in the womb or during an apoplexy.

As we have previously established, I hold that:

1. The soul shall not be annihilated.

2. Nor dissolved.

3. Nor lose its essential faculties or powers.

4. Nor shall those essential powers be rendered useless by the wise and merciful Creator, although by natural reason we do not know how they shall act, on what other body, by what conjunction, or to what extent.

However, through supernatural revelation we are assured there is a reward for the righteous, that holy souls remain members of Christ and live because He lives. On the day of their departure they will be with Him in Paradise, and being absent from the body they will be present with the Lord. Christ died and rose, that He might be Lord both of the dead and of the living—those who, though dead, live with Him, and those who yet live in the body. For He said, "God is not the God of the dead, but of the living," indicating that He does not relate to them as His people like a king to subjects; He is not the Lord of the absolutely dead, but of the living.

Therefore, as Contarenus said against Pomponatius on the Immortality of the Soul: the immortality of the soul can be demonstrated by the light of nature, but the manner of its future operation must be known by faith. Blessed be the Father of spirits and our Redeemer, who has sent and established this excellent light by which we see farther than blind infidels can!

I do not deny that Scripture itself tells us little about the manner of our understanding when we are out of the body. It is not improbable that there is more imperfection in that mode of notional, organical, abstract knowledge which the soul exercises in the body than most suppose. Just as the eye has an ability to act in sleep and when we blink—an internal action of the visual spirits—yet it sees nothing outside until the eyelids are opened, so the soul in the body is like a winking eye toward all things not brought within its reach by sense and imagination.

Whether I can say, "I do not see the sight, nor the faculty, nor the substance that sees, yet I certainly perceive that I see," it may also be said, "I do not immediately understand the act of understanding, nor the faculty, nor the substance that understands, yet I certainly perceive that I understand," because the act of intellect is felt in the sensitive spirits. Or whether we must further say, with Ockam, that "the intellect understands both intuitively and abstractly," I leave to wiser men to judge. I am, however, very suspicious that the body is more a lantern to the soul than some will admit. This secondary, abstract knowledge of things—knowledge by organic images, names, and notions—seems caused by the union of the soul with the body as its form. It is that childish knowledge which the apostle says will be done away.

I cannot tell how much of man's fall consisted in such knowledge of good and evil, or in overvaluing that kind of knowing. When vain philosophy at Athens diverted people's thoughts and desires from great realities to the logical and philological games of words and notions, Socrates was wise to call them to more serious studies. Paul was wiser still in warning men to beware of such vain philosophy and to labor to know God and Jesus Christ and the things of the Spirit, rather than to overvalue this ludicrous, dreaming, worldly wisdom.

If I have none of this kind of notional, childish knowledge when I am absent from the body, then the glass and spectacles may be spared when I come to see with an open face, indeed face to face.

Our future knowledge is usually called seeing. "Blessed are the pure in heart, For they shall see God." (Matt. 5:8). "But then face to face." (1 Cor. 13:12). "We shall see Him as He is." (1 John 3:2). "Father, I desire that they also whom You gave Me may be with Me where I am, that they may behold My glory which You have given Me." (John 17:24).

An intuitive knowledge of all things, as they are in themselves, is a more excellent sort of knowledge than this knowledge by similitudes, names, and notions which our learning now consists of, and is but an art acquired through many acts and use.

If the sun were, as the heathens thought, an intellective animal, and its emitted rays were vitally visual, then when one of those rays was received by prepared seminal matter (as in insects), it would become the soul of an inferior animal. In that case the ray would operate in that insect according to the capacity of the recipient matter. The sun itself, by all its emitted rays, would see all things intellectually and with delight. When that insect died, that ray would remain what it was: an intellective, intuitive emanation.

Although the soul in the flesh does not know how it shall be united to Christ, to all other holy souls, and to God Himself, nor how near or of what sort that union will be, yet it will be united. Therefore it will participate accordingly in the universal light or understanding to which it is united. The soul now, as it is when it operates in the foot or hand, does not understand there but only operates. It understands in the head. Yet the same soul that is in the hand understands in the head. The soul does not act selfishly in the hand or resent that it does not understand there; it is content that it understands in the head and performs its due operation in the hand.

This diversity of operations seems to arise from the organs and the body's use or need. Souls dismissed from the body, however, seem to be like all eye or intuitive light. So, although it might suffice to say that our Head sees all things and we are united to Him, we may go further and assert that we ourselves shall see God and all things that are appropriate for us to see.

Since it is certain that the superior, glorious regions are full of blessed spirits who see God and one another and have far more perfect operations than we experience here below, why should I — who find an intellective nature in myself — doubt that I shall have more perfect operations when I am dismissed from here? I am assured that a soul will not lose its simple essence.

Either those superior spirits have ethereal bodies to act in (or are such themselves), or they do not. If they do, why should I doubt the same for myself and think that my substance or vehicle will not be suited to the region of my abode? If they do not, why should I think that my departed soul cannot know or see without an igneous or ethereal body or vehicle, just as all those orders of spirits do? The certainty of apparitions, possessions, and witches tells us not only that there are inhabitants of other regions ordinarily invisible to us, but also that we are on the path to the happiness or misery that belongs to our invisible state.

Having reviewed these matters (some mentioned before), I am assured that I shall have actual understanding in my separated state. The region and its objects—and, above all, the holy Scriptures—will tell me as much as it is fitting for me to know about what I shall intuitively understand.

The apostle (1 Cor. 13:10–12) distinguishes between our partial and our perfect knowledge: knowing as a child and as a man, knowing darkly and enigmatically, as in a mirror, dimly, and knowing face to face as we are known. The great question is, when does this time of perfection occur? Does he mean at death or at the resurrection?

If Dr. Hammond's and Mr. Beverly's observations in his Great Soul of Man hold—that ἀνάσασις (anastasis/resurrection) in Scripture, when "the flesh or body" is not joined with it, signifies the life which the soul enters immediately after our death—then people will be led to think there is less difference between a man's state at his first departure and at his last resurrection than most believe, perhaps even more than Calvin thought.

However, the difference between our first and last states of after-life or resurrection cannot be distinctly known now. What difference exists between Enoch, Elijah, those who rose at Christ's resurrection, and the rest of the saints—even the spirits of the perfected just—and whether the first have so much greater glory than the rest as we conceive we shall have at the resurrection above that which immediately follows death, what mortal man can tell?

I have no doubt that flesh and blood cannot inherit the kingdom of God (see Hammond in loc.), but that our natural bodies shall be made spiritual bodies. How a spiritual body differs from a spirit or soul I do not pretend to understand well; I must wait until God, through experience or fuller light, informs me.

Surely the difference is not likely to be so great that a soul in the flesh shall know in part, a soul in a spiritual body shall know perfectly, and a soul between both shall not know at all. If perfection is what we shall have in our spiritual body, it is likely that we are closer to that perfection in knowledge and happiness while we are between both than when we are in the flesh.

Surely a soul that, as Solomon says, returns to God who gave it is more likely to know God than one confined in flesh and operating only as its form, according to its capacity and state. A soul that is with Christ is more likely to know Christ and the Father in Him than one that is present with the body and absent from the Lord. What less can the promise of being with Him signify?

As for the kind of knowledge: how excellent and more satisfying will that of intuition, or the intellective sense, be compared with our present methods of abstraction, similitudes, and signs? What a tremendous amount of time, thought, and effort it costs us now to learn grammar, rhetoric, and logic — our arts of speaking, saying, and reasoning — to learn the wordy rules and axioms of metaphysics, physics, etc.

And when we have learned them all (if all can be learned), how little nearer are many to the knowledge of the signified realities? We often acquire only a set of words to play with, to occupy our time and divert us from the matter; just as carnal men use the creatures that signify God, which were made to lead them up to Him, to entangle themselves and become the greatest and most pernicious diversion from God.

So likewise do many learned men use their organical, signal knowledge. They treat it as men do cards, romances, and plays — merely to delight their fancies — yet they know less of the things worth knowing than many unlearned persons do, as I mentioned before. Had not much of the Athenian learning been a mere pastime that squandered men's precious time and nourished pride while they remained ignorant of saving realities, Christ and His apostles would not have neglected it as they did. Nor would Paul have so often warned against that vain sort of philosophy. I judge that Paul had a higher regard for the famed Athenian arts than some, Dr. Hammond among them, suppose when they confine his rebuke to mere Gnostic pretensions.

This poor, dreaming, signal, artificial knowledge is:

1. Costly.

2. Uncertain.

3. Contentious.

4. Unsatisfactory in comparison to intuitive knowledge.

It is costly in the hard labour and precious time it demands, as has already been shown. We grow old fitting ourselves with horses, boots, and spurs for a journey, and it is fortunate if we begin it at last. It is like a man who studies the newly discovered planets and the forms of Saturn's and Jupiter's satellites, yet spends his whole life acquiring the best tubes and telescopes and never uses them for their intended purpose.

Or it is like one who, instead of learning to write, spends his life acquiring the best ink, paper, and pens; or, rather, like him who learns to write and print perfectly yet does not understand the meaning of any of his words. Men take their spectacles instead of eyes.

And once this learning is acquired, how uncertain it is whether the words are free from ambiguity, or whether they truly convey the speaker's mind and the matter under consideration. As I said before, how poor and yet how redundant are our words: how various and unstable their meanings, altered by custom or by arbitrary design; sometimes by common usage and sometimes by learned men. Those very men, aware of the speaking art's inadequacies, still meddle with it and attempt to amend it.

Some speak obscurely on purpose to create in their readers an admiration for their supposed subtle and sublime thoughts. He who understands most clearly and speaks most plainly — the true mark of learning — will yet find it hard to extract the matter from dark and bewildering obscurities and to make others understand both it and him.

Hence arise the greatest part of the world's contentions, most fierce among men who pretend to wordy knowledge. Just as in trade and common dealings, the more men and business there are, the more quarrels and differences arise; so the greater the pretence of this verbal learning instead of acquaintance with realities, the more disputes and controversies are bred. The very instruments of knowledge thus become instruments of error and contention.

Alas! How many celebrated volumes are snares and troubles to the world! How much of our libraries consists of vain janglings, strifes of words, and traps for the more ingenious sort, who will not be taken by cards and dice. These books rob us of our time, destroy our love, and depress our minds, which should ascend to God. They divert us from the great and holy matters that ought to occupy our thoughts and joys, and fill the church with sects and strife, while everyone contends for the preeminence of his wit and notions and few strive for holy love, unity, and good works.

And all the while, alas, too many learned men but lick the surface of the glass and leave the wine within untasted. To know God, Christ, heaven, and holiness supplies the soul with a nourishing, strengthening pleasure, much like the appetite satisfied by food. But this game of words is only a knowledge of images, signs, and shadows, and so is itself but an image and shadow of true knowledge.

This is not the grace Augustine called "No one misuses it." Rather, it is that grace which the sanctified use rightly, while the unsanctified are puffed up by it and use it to oppose truth, to display foolish wit, and to deceive their own souls. When knowledge is sanctified, it is merely mediate—meant to lead us to knowledge of the things it signifies. The real good is the reality that satisfies and blesses; the notions may serve as a subordinate recreation, but intuition feasts on those realities.

As for the objects of this intuition, their excellence will reflect the excellence of our knowledge.

1. I shall know God better.

2. I shall know the universe better.

3. I shall know Christ better.

4. I shall better know the church, His body, along with the holy angels.

5. I shall better understand the methods and perfection of Scripture, and all of God's guiding word and will.

6. I shall better comprehend the methods and sense of disposing providence.

7. I shall better know the divine benefits, which are the fruits of love.

8. I shall better know myself.

9. I shall better know every fellow creature, which I am concerned to know.

10. And I shall better understand all that evil, sin, Satan, and misery from which I am delivered.

Aquinas and many others regarded as the chief natural proof of the soul's immortality the fact that man, by nature, desires not only to know effects and secondary causes but to rise to knowledge of the first cause. Therefore, man was made for such knowledge in the state of his perfection. Yet grace excites this desire far more strongly than nature does.

This does not mean we should be discontent to be without much knowledge that would be unsuitable, useless, troublesome, or dangerous to us. Nor should we aspire to know what is beyond our capacity, or to fathom the unsearchable things of God. Yet to fail to know God is to know nothing; it is an understanding worse than none.

I do not presume to pry into the secrets of the Almighty, nor to claim I know more of God than I truly do. But oh, that I might know more of His glorious perfections, His will, His love, and His ways — with that knowledge which is eternal life: to know the only true God and Jesus Christ whom He has sent. Blessed be that love that sent the Son of God from heaven to reveal Him to us in the gospel, as He has done.

However, all who hear the same words and believe them do not possess the same degree of light or faith. If an angel from heaven came down to earth to tell us all about God that we would want to know, and might lawfully desire and ask him, who would not turn his back on libraries, universities, and learned men to go and converse with such a messenger?

What journey would I consider too far, what cost too great, for one hour's talk with such a messenger? Yet here we are given only intimations that will exercise faith, stir desire, and test us amid the temptations of the world and the flesh. The glorious light will be the reward of the victory won by the guidance of the light of grace.

God, in great mercy, even here begins the reward. Those who are true to the first light and faithfully pursue knowledge of the Lord usually find an increase of light— not vain notions, but vivifying and comforting knowledge of God—that greatly encourages them to seek more.

It is very pleasant here to increase in holy knowledge, though it commonly brings an increase of malignant opposition and sorrows to the flesh. The pleasure the mind takes in ordinary knowledge drives people through much labor to attain it.

How many years of travel over land and sea do some undertake to see and know more of this lower world, when they often bring home little more than increased acquaintance with sin, vanity, and vexation! How many more years do thousands spend reading multitudes of tedious volumes simply to know what others knew before them? Printers and booksellers thrive on our desire for knowledge.

What soul on earth can possibly conceive how great a pleasure it will be for a glorified soul to see the Lord? I cannot now fully conceive what that intuition of God Himself will be, whether it will be a glorious concluding or abstract knowledge, or whether the glory we shall see will be merely a created appearance of God or His very essence. It suffices me that it will be as perfect a knowledge as is fitting for me to desire.

I will then desire no more than is appropriate, and what that is I shall know by experience, for it cannot be clearly known in any other way.

Reasons Arising from My Intellect

All the pleasure I shall have in heaven in knowing any of the works of God will be in my beholding God Himself — His being, His vital power and action, His wisdom, and His love and goodness in those works; for He is the life and glory of them all. "Blessed are the pure in heart, For they shall see God."

Undoubtedly, it will be a great delight to see and know God's perfect works — that is, the universe itself. I cannot claim I will have such vast capacity as to comprehend the entire world perfectly; however, I shall understand it in a manner suitable to my capacity. It is exceedingly pleasant to know even the smallest parts of God's creations. With what diligence and delight have people dissected a body, even a small part of a carcass, and tried to know and describe insignificant worms and insects, plants, and minerals! Yet no one has ever perfectly understood even the least of them. No herbalist or physician has fully grasped the nature and uses of any single herb.

With what delight and diligence are physical inquiries pursued in the world, even though we are all groping in the dark — ignorant of many things for every one thing we do know — and therefore we do not know any one thing perfectly because we are unaware of the rest. If we were to rise above our erroneous hypotheses and see the nature of every creature, both in sea and land — this little corner of God's creation and the entirety of it — oh, what a delightful spectacle it would be! How much more to see the whole creation, or even one system of the globes, and to understand their unity and relation; to behold their beautiful symmetry and to hear them, in concord and melodious harmony, praising the glory of their great, wise, and amiable Creator. This would indeed be a delectable sight. I shall experience as much of this as I am capable of, and the wonders and glories of God's works shall fill my soul with admiration and joyful praise forever. Although here we know but a fraction of God's works, I have great reason to believe it will be quite different there.

1. Because the state of perfection must far exceed our dark and immature state of imperfection. We now have desires for such knowledge. His works are great, sought out by those who take pleasure in them; and these desires, being from God, shall not be frustrated.

2. Because there will be a proportionality in the parts of our perfection; thus, as our love for God and His works is perfected there, so too will our knowledge.

3. Because we shall know God Himself as much as we are capable, and therefore we shall know His works in Him, or through a subordinate knowledge — the lesser being known in the greater.

4. Because God has made His works to be known for His glory; however little is known of them here by mortals, they will be known by those in heaven, who are equipped to enhance that knowledge for His praise.

If Christ, who is the wisdom of God, teaches me the true philosophy of how to love God and live here in a manner pleasing to Him, I shall quickly become a perfect philosopher in heaven. Experience will show me that the surest way to be truly learned and to know the wonderful works of God is to know, love, and serve the great Creator; for in Him we shall have everything, and without Him we know nothing and possess nothing at all.

Satan tempted Christ by showing Him "all the kingdoms of the world and their glory," promising to give Him all these things if He would fall down and worship him.

In heaven, I shall better know Jesus Christ and all the mysteries of our redemption through Him, which will be no small part of my happiness. For in whom are hidden all the treasures of wisdom and knowledge. To know the mystery of His eternal Godhead, in the second person, and His created nature, and the union of these, and to see God's wonderful design and work of grace in Him laid open to our clearest view — oh, what beatifying knowledge this will be! All dark texts concerning His person, His office, and His works will then be explained and fully understood. All those strange and difficult matters, which were the great exercise and honor of faith, will then be plain. Difficulties will no longer be Satan's advantage to tempt us to unbelief or doubt. The sight of my Lord's glory will be my glory. (John 17:24.) If Paul had not yet attained perfection in the knowledge of Christ and the power of His resurrection, but was pressing forward to reach that crown in the life to come, which he calls "that I may attain to the resurrection from the dead" (Phil. 3:9-12), I must not expect to attain it here; but when that which is perfect comes, this imperfect knowledge of faith will be done away, as childish knowledge is in adulthood. The glass and riddle shall be set aside when we "but then face to face. Now I know in part, but then I shall know just as I also am known" (1 Cor. 13:10-12), regarding our sight and knowledge of Christ and His triumphant body; for I dare not apply that phrase to the sight and knowledge of the divine essence, nor do I deny it.

If now, though we do not see Him, yet believing we rejoice with joy inexpressible and full of glory, what love and joy will the everlasting sight of our blessed Head excite in the souls of all the glorified!

I shall much better know the heavenly Jerusalem, the triumphant church, the blessed angels, and glorified saints; and as my love for them grows, so too will my knowledge of them, which will not be the least part of my heavenly delight. As strangely as I now look upward to that world because I cannot see it with these eyes, it shall be my well-known everlasting habitation. Oh! what a sight, what a joyful sight, will death reveal to me by drawing aside the veil — or rather, what the Lord of Life will show me by turning death to my advantage! When I am there at home, I shall no longer think with confusion, fear, or doubt about that blessed place or state. My fears, which now arise from the smallness of my faith, will end when faith is turned into vision. Just as I know the various rooms in my house, the houses in the street, and the streets in the city, so shall I then know the many mansions which Christ has said are in His Father's house. Words now give me such a poor, imperfect conception of the world and things I have never seen that sometimes I can scarcely tell whether the joy of my faith or the trouble of my dark apprehensions is greater. But when I shall see the place and persons, the glory I have heard of, that will be the delightful, satisfying, and possessing kind of knowledge. If Nehemiah and the godly Jews made such a great matter of seeing the walls of Jerusalem repaired, and others of the imperfect rebuilding of the temple, oh, what a joyful sight the heavenly Jerusalem will be to me! The most glorious sight will be at the great marriage day of the Lamb, when Christ shall come to be glorified in His saints and admired in all who now believe; but next to that will be the day of my particular deliverance, when I shall come to Christ and see the saints admiring Him in glory.

If I were of the opinion of those Greek fathers who believed that stars were angels or had intellectual souls (matters unknown to us), I would love them as my guardians and consider it even more important to advance to a fuller knowledge of them. But since I know that angels love us and, by their office, attend to and keep us, rejoicing at our good and our repentance, and, which is far more, are more holy and excellent creatures than we are, it is therefore my comfort to think that I shall know them better and live in close and perpetual acquaintance and communion with them—a more tangible and sweet communion than we can have with them here.

Devils are aerial and close to this dark and sinful world, often appearing to men more than angels. But the angels do not seek such descending appearances until love and obedience to their Lord make it pleasing to them. Thus, we have but little knowledge of those who know, love, and keep us. However, when we come home to their closest society and fellowship, knowing them will be sweet and joyful knowledge; for they are more excellent creatures than the most glorious beings below the intellective nature. They are full of light and full of love for God and man. If God had commanded me to pray to them, I would not have refused it, but would have taken it as an honor; but since He has not, I will do what He has commanded me—love them and rejoice in my relation to the innumerable company of them in the city of the living God, the heavenly Jerusalem (Heb. 12:22), and long to know and love them more, expecting soon to take part in the praises of God and of the Lamb, in the same choir where they lead.

That I shall know the spirits of the perfected just and be in communion with them will be no small addition to my joy. How sweet has one wise and holy, though weak and blemished, companion been to me here on earth! And how lovely have God's graces in such individuals appeared to me, even though they were sullied. Oh! then, what a sight it will be when we shall see the millions of souls that shine in perfect wisdom and holiness with Christ! To see a garden that has some beautiful flowers is something; but if you could see whole fields and countries shining with them, it would be a glory, though fading, to the earth. A well-built city is a more pleasant sight than a single house, and a navy is more impressive than a single ship, and an army is more glorious than one man. If this poor, low world consisted entirely of wise, just, and holy persons, oh, what an orderly, lovely world that would be! If one kingdom consisted of such individuals (princes, magistrates, pastors, and people), what a blessed kingdom it would be! The plague of wicked men's deceits, falsehoods, oppressions, and iniquities may help us appreciate this. It would be a great temptation to us to be reluctant to die and leave such a country, were it not that the more the beauty of goodness appears, the more we desire the state of perfection. It is pleasant for me to pray in hope, as Christ has commanded me, that earth may become more like heaven, which has now become so like hell. But when I shall see the society perfected in number, holiness, glory, and heavenly employment, the joyful praises of Jehovah, the glory of God, and the Lamb shining upon them, and God rejoicing over them as His delight, and myself partaking in the same, that will be the truly blessed day. And why does my soul, imprisoned in flesh, not desire it more?

I shall better understand all the word of God, its content, and its method. Although I will not have the same use for it as I do now in this life of faith, I shall see more of God's wisdom and goodness, His love, mercy, and justice, appearing in it than any man on earth could ever perceive! Just as the creatures, so too the Scriptures are perfectly known only by perfect spirits. I shall then know how to resolve all doubts, reconcile all seeming contradictions, and expound the hardest prophecies. That light will reveal to me the admirable order and design of those sacred words, where dark minds now suspect confusion. How evident and clear everything will appear to me then! Like a small print when the light comes in, which I could not read in the dim twilight. How easily shall I then refute the objections of all our present unbelievers! And how joyfully shall I praise that God and Savior who gave His church such clear light to guide them through this dark world, and such a sure promise to support them until they reach eternal life! How joyfully shall I bless Him who, by that immortal seed, regenerated me to the hopes of glory and ruled me by such a holy and just law!

In that world of light, I shall better understand God's present and past works of providence, by which He orders the affairs of this world. The wisdom and goodness of these works are little understood in small fragments; it is the union and harmony of all the parts that reveals their beauty, even when the individual pieces seem deformed or are not understood. No one can see the whole at once but God, and those who see it in the light of His celestial glory; it is a perspective of that end by which we have any true understanding of the fragments we see here. Then I shall clearly know why or for what purpose God prospered the wicked and tried the righteous with so many afflictions. I shall know why He set up the ungodly and put the humble under their feet; why He permitted so much ignorance, ungodliness, pride, lust, oppression, persecution, falsehood, deceit, and other sins in the world. I shall know why the faithful are so few and why so many kingdoms of the world remain in heathenism, Mahometanism, and infidelity. The strange permissions that now puzzle me and are the source of my astonishment will then be as clear as day. I shall know why God disposed of me as He did throughout my life, why I suffered what I did, and how many great deliverances I experienced that I did not understand here, and how they were accomplished. All our misinterpretations of God's works and permissions will then be corrected, and all our controversies about them, which Satan has exploited to his advantage (by a pretended zeal for some truths of God), will then be reconciled and brought to an end. All the works of Divine Providence, from the beginning of the world, will then appear as a most delightful and beautiful framework.

Among all these works, I shall especially know more about the nature and excellence of God's mercies and gifts of love, which we here too ungratefully undervalue and make light of. The special works of love should be the subject of our most constant, sweet, and serious thoughts, and the fuel for our ongoing love and gratitude. The lively sense of love and mercy makes for lively Christians, abounding in love for God and mercy towards others. However, the enemy of God and man works hard to obscure, diminish, and disgrace God's love and mercies to us, or to make us lose our appreciation for them, so that they may be unfruitful regarding their excellent ends and uses. Little do most Christians know how much they wrong God and themselves, and how much they lose by their diminished, poor thoughts of God's mercies. Ingratitude is a grievous misery to the sinner, while gratitude is a very pleasant endeavor. We receive many thousands of mercies now, which we greatly undervalue. But when I come to the state and work of perfect gratitude, I shall have a more complete knowledge of all the mercies I have ever received in my life, and which my neighbors, friends, God's church, and the world have ever received. For although the events are past, their usefulness is not. Remembered mercies must be the matter of our everlasting thanks; and we cannot be perfectly thankful for them without a perfect knowledge of them. The worth of Christ and all His grace, the worth of the gospel, the worth of our church privileges, and all of God's ordinances, the worth of our books and friends, and the aids to our life and health, and all conveniences will be better understood in heaven than the most holy and thankful Christian here understands them.

And it will add to my future happiness that I will then be much better acquainted with myself, both in terms of my nature and my sin and grace. I will understand the nature of the soul and its formal faculties (three in one). I will know the nature and manner of its operations, and how far its acts are simple, compound, or organic. I will discern how memory, imagination, and both internal and external senses relate to the rational soul, and whether the sensitive and rational aspects are two or one; I will understand which senses will perish and which will not.

I will know how the soul acts upon itself and what actions it performs that are not felt during sleep, in apoplexies, or in the womb. I will understand whether the vegetative nature is anything other than fire, whether it shares the same essence with the sensitive or rational soul, and whether fire is a common fundamental substance of all spirits, specified diversely by their forms (mental, sensitive, and vegetative). I will explore whether fire serves as a body or vehicle for spirits, or if it is a nature designed for the interaction of spirits and bodies, and how it operates between the two.

I will know how far souls are one yet many, how they are individuated, and whether their discrete quantity, being numerically many, proves that they possess any continuous quantity. I will consider whether they are a purer sort of bodies, as the Greek fathers, Tertullian, and others believed, and what immateriality signifies; I will examine the substantiality of spirits, how substance and matter differ, how far they are penetrable and indivisible, and whether a soul is properly a part. I will investigate whether individual souls are parts of any common soul, how individuation continues, and whether, when separated from the body, they operate through any other vehicle or independently, and how.

I will know whether they carry with them any fiery nature, as a vehicle or as a constitutive part. I will understand how God produces souls, how His production by emanation or creation aligns with generation, how forms are multiplied, and what role the parent's soul plays in the production of the child—whether through the communication of substance or merely by preparing the recipient matter. I will explore whether all souls originated from Adam's own substantiality, whether there is more substance in all souls than in that one, and whether one substance causes more by generation.

I will consider whether the same applies to the souls of animals, or whether any common soul informs many organic bodies of animals, like the sun lighting many candles that are individuated by matter, which they variously contract and upon which they operate. I will investigate whether they were individuated in preexistence or will be individuated after separation. I will know how far the semen in generation is animated, how the animated seeds of two create one, and if animated, what happens to the soul of the lost seed and to an abortive fetus. I will explore whether the body is animated as vegetative or sensitive before the entrance of the rational soul, or if the same soul, which in its faculty is rational, being one with the sensitive and vegetative, is the constitutive form of the first animated body and the creator of its own dwelling.

I will understand how far the soul is receptive, what the final cause does to it, and what each object contributes to the constitution or production of an act. I will discern what an act is and what a habit is, how a soul, when acting or habited, differs from itself when not acting or habited, and how its acts are many yet one, or at least how its faculties are. Many other such difficulties will be resolved, which philosophers currently debate in the dark, often relying on uncertain conjectures, or are known only to very few.

I shall know how God's Spirit operates on souls, how it is sent from Christ's human nature to work upon man, and whether grace is properly, or only metaphorically, called a nature (a new nature, a divine nature) in us. I shall know what free will is, and how man's will can be the first determiner of any act of its own in moral species (good or evil) without being that prima causa which none but God can be. Thus I shall know how far free acts are necessitated or are not.

I shall know what power the intellect has over the will, and the will over the intellect; and what power the senses and imagination have over either. I shall know what any active intellect does, and whether it is to our understanding as the sun is to our sight. I shall know what is meant by degrees of acts and habits in the soul, and whether there are different degrees of substantiality or of the formal virtue or faculty of several souls.

I shall better understand the difference between habits called acquired and those called infused; what common grace is and what it effects; and what nature can do of itself, or by common grace, without that which belongs properly to the justified. Finally, I shall learn how far any degrees of grace can be lost.

I shall know what measure of grace I had, and how far I was mistaken in my self-assessment. I shall see which acts were sincere, how much that was unsound was mixed in, and what was truly mine and what was my sin.

I shall know much more about my sins than I ever knew here—their number and their magnitude—so that I may know, with the greatest thankfulness and love, how much I owe to pardoning and healing grace.

Yes, I shall know more about my body, since it was the dwelling place of my soul or the organic matter with which the soul worked in unity. I shall understand how it helped or hindered me, and what those obscure diseases were that puzzled all the physicians and myself. I shall see how marvelously God sustained, preserved, and often delivered me, and what actions were to be attributed to the body and what to the soul.

And every fellow creature I care to know, I shall know far better than I do now—both things and people. The good and the bad, the sincere and the hypocrites, will be clearly discerned. Many actions that here were considered honorable, or covered and colored with wit, worldly advantage, or false pretenses, will then be found odious and unjust. Wickedness will no longer be flattered or excused.

Many good and holy works, which false men reproached as some odious crime through wickedness and worldly interest, will be justified, honored, and rewarded. All sciences will be perfected there, freed from our ambiguous terms, imperfect axioms, and faulty rules of art.

Lastly, I shall better understand from what enemies, sins, and dangers I was delivered here: what schemes and malicious endeavors of Satan and his instruments God defeated, and how many snares I escaped. I shall better comprehend the magnitude of my deliverance by Christ from the wrath to come.

Though we shall not know hell by painful experience, we shall understand it sufficiently to fill us with gratitude toward our Redeemer. Indeed, we shall know much of it far better than the damned spirits who feel it, for we shall experience, through sweet and full fruition, the joy and blessedness they have lost, while they have no such knowledge of it.

All this knowledge will be brought to my glorified soul beyond what I can now conceive in the flesh. Is it not far better to be with Christ?

8. Reasons Arising from My Will

The will is to the soul what the heart is to the body. Just as the heart is the primary seat of physical well-being, the will is the central seat of morality and happiness. My greatest evil resides there, and my greatest subjective good will also be found there. Satan has done the most damage to it, while God will accomplish the most for it. Is it not far better to be with Christ than to remain here?

There, my will will not be tied to a body of conflicting interests and inclinations, which is now the greatest snare and enemy to my soul. It continually draws my love, care, fears, and sorrows to itself, diverting them from my highest good. What a deliverance it will be to be freed from the temptations, inordinate love, cares, and fears for this corruptible flesh!

My will shall not be tempted there by a world of inferior goods, which now serve as bait and provision for the flesh—food, sleep, possessions, houses, lands, and friends, all become snares and dangers. God's mercies will not be used as instruments of temptation. I shall not be subjected to the flatteries or frowns, the promises or threats, of the tyrants of the world. Bad company will not infect or divert me. The errors of good men will not seduce me, nor will the reputation or reverence of the wise, learned, or religious draw me into any sin.

I shall have none of Satan's solicitations to pervert my will there; he will not have the same advantage over my senses and imagination as he does now. But I have spoken of this before.

My will shall be better there than here.

Negatively, because:

1. There will be nothing in it that is displeasing to God: no sinful inclination, habit, or act; nothing to resist God's Spirit; no grudges against God's words or works; and no principles of enmity or rebellion will remain.

2. There will be nothing against the good of others: no inclination to harm, nor anything contrary to my neighbor's or the common good.

3. There will be nothing in it that contradicts itself; no more internal conflict or striving. No law in my mind will contradict a law in my members. There will be no discord between sense and reason, nor between the sensitive appetite and the rational. All will be in unity and peace within.

Positively, Christ will have completed His work on my will. The process of sanctification will be perfected.

My will will be made conformable to the will of Christ through union and communion, and thus to the will of the Father. This is surely what is meant (among other things) in Christ's prayer, where He prays, "That they all may be one, as You, Father, are in Me, and I in You; that they also may be one in Us, that the world may believe that You sent Me." (John 17:21-22). The will of Christ and the Father will become my will; that is, I will love and will (both dispositionally and actually) the same things that God loves and wills (in a measure that is infinitely below Him).

And if so, how can the will of man have greater honor than to be aligned with the will of God? To be likened to a king among us mere mortals is considered an honor; to be likened to angels is even more so. That we shall be like or equal to angels is a significant aspect of the blessed's praise; but how much greater is it to be, in this way, like God? Indeed, the image of God and the divine within us here can be no less than this similarity to God's will, to the degree that we possess it.

But, alas! that degree is so very low that we can hardly discern whether our similarity or dissimilarity is greater; I mean whether our wills align more with what God wills or oppose it more. Oh, how many thousands of wishes and desires have we had that are contrary to the will of God!

But there, we will have the full impression of God's will upon our wills, just as face answers face in a mirror, or as wax responds to a seal. Just as the hand on the outside corresponds to the motion of the clock within, so in all matters pertaining to our duty and perfection we will respond to the will of God. Just as an echo answers a voice — imperfectly, yet truly, without contradiction or discord — so will our wills be like the echo of God's will.

And then I am sure that there will be nothing in my will but good, for God wills no evil.

This will virtually encompass all obedience, for all sin is voluntary, and all true goodness resides primarily in the will.

Then there can be no disquiet within me; all will be in perfect peace, for all that is like God will be pleasing to both God and me. No troubling discord will remain.

How easy and sweet then will all my obedience be, when I shall perfectly will it, without any reluctance or aversion! Everything I do will be my very pleasure.

And since my will shall be the same as the will of God, it follows that it shall never be frustrated. I shall have everything I desire and shall be and do whatever I wish to be and do. I will desire nothing but what God wills, and God's will shall certainly be accomplished. I shall have as much love and joy as I desire; I shall be as happy as I wish to be. I shall desire nothing for others that shall not be fulfilled.

Indeed, if God's will were unknown to me there, I might ignorantly go against it, as I do here; but there, before I will or desire anything, I shall know whether it aligns with God's will or not. This ensures that I shall never wish for anything that will not be accomplished. Just as it is God's perfection to have His will always done (even if all His laws are not obeyed), my perfection will consist in this likeness to God: my will shall always be fulfilled.

And then Christ's promises will be perfectly fulfilled: "Whatever you ask the Father in My name He will give you. You will ask what you desire, and it shall be done for you." (John 15:16; 16:23; 14:13, 14; 15:7). While our will aligns with the will of Christ, He does not say that everything will be given to us here. We ask for perfection, and we shall receive it, but not in this life.

Yes, my will itself will be my fulfillment, for it will not be the will of one in need; I will desire nothing, and therefore it is said that we shall thirst no more. Instead, it will be a satisfaction in what I possess, and in this my perfection will reflect God's perfection.

All creatures still receive from God and, in that sense, may be said to need, since they have nothing of themselves but everything by gift and communication from Him. However, as full possessors, they cannot be said to want. Satisfaction in what we possess is love and pleasure in a single act; indeed, pleasure and love are the same thing. To love anything is to find that thing pleasing to my mind. Even when it is desired, it is considered a pleasing thing, and thus the act of desire is merely a secondary act prompted by want, following the primary act, which is satisfaction or simple love. I desire it because I love it. Therefore, the will itself is rightly called love, for in the first act — love — will and rational appetite are all synonymous.

My will must be perpetually filled with perfect joy when enjoying love and pleasure becomes my very will. Thus, I will have within me a spring of living waters, and the Comforter will perfectly fulfill His work when my constant will itself becomes my comfort. Glory is rightly said to be the perfection of sanctifying grace, as this grace is the beginning of that love and joy which glory ultimately perfects; and perfection is the work of the Spirit.

Much of my happiness will stem from my will being confirmed and fixed in conformity to the will of God, with holy love as its nature. Currently, both understanding and will are so lamentably changeable that, beyond what God promises to uphold us, we do not know what we will think, judge, or desire from one day to the next. But when love becomes a fixed nature within us, we will remain the same, consistently adhering to amiable goodness without interruption or cessation.

It will be as easy for us (and even more so) to love God and holiness as it is for the hungry and thirsty to love food and drink, or for the proud to love praise or power, or for anyone to love their own life. We will grow no more weary of loving than the sun grows weary of shining, or the hungry grow weary of feasting, or a friend grows weary of friendly love and companionship. Indeed, the comparison is far too low, for all creatures here possess a fading vanity that wearies the satisfied or failing appetite, but such a thing does not exist in heaven.

And as much as the nature of the act, so much more from the nature of the object, my love will be my happiness. The objects (which are the matter of the act) will be these:

God Himself will be the full and everlasting object of my love. Anyone who could understand, as those in heaven do, what it means to love God and be loved by Him would say that there is no better description of perfect happiness: perfect, joyful satisfaction in God is the heaven I desire and hope for.

This is my happiness, and so much more. As I am the agent of love toward God and the object of God's love for me, it is my happiness. As God is the ultimate object of my love and the agent of His love for me (that is, of its effects), it is infinitely more exalted than merely being my happiness. Love binds the wills of God and man. As it pertains to God's part (efficiently or objectively), it is infinitely more excellent than as it pertains to my part and interest.

In God there is everything that love can desire for its full, everlasting feast.

He is infinitely good in Himself — most lovable — and the nature of the human will is to love good as good. If we could love God with a love adequate to the object, we would be God ourselves, which is impossible; only God can adequately know God or love Him.

In God's love for Himself, both the act and the object are infinite and, in a sense, one. There is no formal distinction between what we call act and object; those are our inadequate ways of conceiving the divine activity that is His very essence. In our love for God the act is finite and falls infinitely short of the object. The object, though truly infinite, is present to our mind only as a known being — a conception or idea of God in the intellect — which serves as the proper and nearest object of the will. It is like a reflection in a mirror, a shadow, the finite little shadow of an infinite Being. The same infinite good is a source of happiness to different people in varying degrees, according to how they love Him and how receptive they are to His love.

God, who is infinitely good in Himself, will be the most suitable good for me and the most fitting for the deepest embrace of my will. First, He has everything in Himself that I need or can desire. There is no room, nothing above Him, beyond Him, or outside of Him for love to cling to. Though the creature exists below Him and not without Him, it is loved apart from Him only by the deception of the mind.

He is willing to be loved by me. He does not disdain my love. He could have refused to be embraced by affections that have so often and sinfully polluted themselves by clinging to vanity and filth. Just as people of high status and cleanliness will not allow themselves to be touched by filthy hands, much less let dogs or dirty swine leap upon them after wallowing in the mire, God could have driven me away from the happiness of loving Him and denied me the opportunity for such a high calling.

Instead, He commands my love and makes it my greatest duty. He invites and entreats me, as if He were the one gaining from my happiness. He urges me to seek Him, and as He is the first, so is He the most earnest suitor. He is far more ready to receive my love than I am to give it. All the compassionate invitations I have received from Him here, through His word and mercies, assure me that He will readily receive me there. He who valued my poor, cold, imperfect love for Him on earth will not reject my perfect love in heaven. He who made it the great work of His Spirit to bring it about will not refuse it when it is made perfect by Himself.

And He is near to me, not a distant God out of my reach and thus unsuitable to my love. Blind unbelievers may dream that He is far off, but He is as near to us even now as we are to ourselves. He is not far from each one of us; for in Him we live and move and have our being. The light of the sun is not as near to my eyes as God will be to my mind forever.

When He desires to sanctify us to love Him, He brings us close to Him in Christ. Just as we easily love ourselves, being nearest to ourselves, so we will easily love God as ourselves when we see that He is as near to us as we are to ourselves, and infinitely more lovable in His essence.

Because of the disparity between the creature and the Creator, He has provided means to demonstrate His nearness that are necessary for the exercise of our love. We will see His glory and taste His love in our glorified Mediator, and in the glory of the church and the world. God will condescend to reveal Himself to us according to our capacity to behold Him. Here we see Him in His works and word; there we will see Him in the glory of all His perfect works. But this leads me to the second object of my love.

Under God, as I shall see, I will delightfully love the glorious perfection of the universe, even the image of God in all creation. As my love will be my delight, I will love best that which is best and find the most joy in it. The whole is better than any part, and there is a unique beauty and excellence in the whole world — perfect, harmonious, and well-ordered — which cannot be found in any part, not even in Christ Himself as a man, nor in His church.

The marvelous inclination that all things have toward union, even the inanimate, might persuade me, if I did not feel it certainly within myself, that it is most credible that man also has a similar inclination, one agreeable to the nature of his faculties; therefore our love and delight in all things is that uniting inclination within man.

I will have a special love for the holy society, the triumphant, universal church, consisting of Christ, angels, and saints, as they are especially lovable in the image and glory of God. God Himself loves them more than His lesser works; that is, His essence, which is love and has no degrees or change, sends forth fuller streams of goodness upon them, making them better and happier than the rest. My love will imitate

God's love, to the best of my ability. If societies on earth, more holy and wise than others though imperfectly, are very lovable, how much more will the heavenly society be? I have spoken of this before (regarding knowing them).

Consider, O my soul, how sweet it will be for you to love the Lord Jesus, your glorified Head, with perfect love! When the glory of God, shining in Him, feasts your love with full and everlasting pleasure, the highest created perfections of power, wisdom, and goodness, radiant in Him, will not allow your love to cease, intermit, or diminish in fervor. When you see in the glorified church the precious fruits of Christ's redemption, grace, and love, this will also nourish your love for Him, from whom this heavenly glory comes.

And when you feel yourself filled with perfect happiness through His love for you, will this not also contribute? Yes, the remembrance of all His former love — what He did for you and what He accomplished in you here on earth: how He called you with a holy calling, how He washed you in His blood from all your sins, how He ignited in you those desires that lead to that perfect glory, how He renewed your nature, how He instructed, guided, and preserved you from your childhood, and how many and how great sins, enemies, dangers, and sufferings He saved you from — all this will compel you to love Him eternally.

Thus, although He gives the kingdom to the Father, ceasing His mediatory, healing, and saving work of acquisition, He will remain your Mediator of fruition. God in Him will be accessible and will condescend to a suitable communion with us. (John 17:24). As Christ is your life, both radically and efficiently, as He is the giver of grace and the Spirit of love, so He will be objectively your life as He is lovely, and it will be formally your life to love Him and God in Him forever.

Consider, O my soul, how delightful it will be to love (as well as to know) those angels who fervently love the Lord! They will be lovely to you because they have loved you, and even more so because they have been lovers and benefactors to the church and to humanity. But they will be far more admirable as they are like shining stars, continually moving, shining, and burning with purest love for their Creator.

Oh, what a blessed difference there is between that amiable society of holy spirits and this dark, mad, distracted, wicked world! Here, devils tempt me from within, and devils incarnate persecute me from without. There is blasphemy against God, reviling of godliness, derision of the sacred Scriptures and sacred practices, malignant slander against the servants of God, hatred, persecution, silencing, and all manner of evil spoken falsely against them for their righteousness' sake, as once was falsely charged against Christ Himself.

This is the conversation of those I have long dwelt with in the world: atheism, infidelity, papal church tyranny, bloody wars, destruction of the righteous, oppression of the poor, adultery and fornication, perjury, ambition, violence, covetousness, deceit, ignorant foolishness, willfulness in sin, hatred of reproof, and vengeful malice. These, and similar evils, are the fruits of the soil where I have long sojourned (though, through the grace of Christ, among the faithful there have been better fruits).

Is not the company of the holy angels preferable to this world? They are those in whom God is all. They are made up of shining wisdom, holy love, and beneficent action. They are the blessed choir that melodiously sings the high praises of their Maker. With them, God dwells as in His presence-chamber, His temple, and He takes great delight in them.

Among these angels I shall neither see nor hear evil. No mixture of fools or wicked ones pollutes or troubles their society. There will be no false doctrine, no evil example, no favoring of wickedness, no accusations against goodness, and no harmful violence. Instead, holy, powerful, operative love will be all and do all, as their very nature, life, and work.

Is it not better to be a doorkeeper in that holy society than to dwell in the tents of wickedness? Is not one day with them better than a thousand here?

With the holy angels, I shall love holy souls who are made like them and joined with them in the same company. It is likely that with them I will judge—that is, rule—the world. Their infirmities will be put off with the flesh. They will be spirits composed of holy life, light, and love.

There will be none of their former ignorance, error, imprudence, selfishness, contentiousness, impatience, or any other troubling, hurtful thing. When I think of the fervent love they will have for God, for Jesus Christ, and for one another, I feel sorrow and shame that they are prone here to disaffections and divisions. How sad that they hardly agree to call each other servants of God or to worship together in the same assemblies.

The remaining causes of division—pride, error, and uncharitableness—will all be left behind. Society with imperfect saints is sweet; the imperfect image of God in them is lovable. Yet their frailties here are so vexatious that it is hard to live in peace with some. But perfect love will unite them. Oh, how delightful that communion of saints will be!

I can never forget how sweet God has made my pilgrimage by the fragrance and usefulness of His servants' graces. How sweet my close friends have been, though changeable! How sweet the fellowship of the godly has been! How sweet the holy assemblies have been, and how many hours of comfort I have experienced there! How profitable their writings, discussions, and prayers have been! What then will it be to live united in perfect love with perfect saints in heaven forever, and with them to love the God of love together?

Just as the act and the object of love will constitute my happiness, so my reception of love from God and His creatures will be sweeter to me than anything I can produce myself. It is mutual love that creates this joy. I will not be the source of my own delights. I cannot act until I am acted upon, nor can I offer anything to God that I have not first received from Him.

I shall receive abundantly and continually, overflowing toward God. Receiving and returning will be a circular, endless motion. That will embody our true, perpetual life and happiness.

All my receptions will come from God. His love is not merely an internal will or a wish that does not touch the object. It is like the heat that emanates from the sun or from fire; it is an outpouring of goodness. It is the most powerful, sweet, and communicative principle or action. All love is communicative, but none compares to God's love, for He alone is the source of all goodness.

How much does love influence human affairs? Everything pleasant in the world is either love itself or its effects. Without sensual love, there would be no generation of humans or animals; God has made it a generating principle. Hatred does not foster connection but rather conflict or avoidance.

Without natural love, mothers would never endure the pain, trouble, and care necessary for birth and upbringing. Without love, parents would not labor throughout their lives to ensure their children are well instructed and provided for after they are gone.

My food would not please me if I did not love it, and I would neglect it to my own harm. If I did not love my books and learning, I would not have spent so many years poring over them in search of knowledge. If I did not love my home and its necessities, I would neglect them and render them of little use to me.

If I did not love my friends, I would be less useful to them, and they to me. If I did not love my life, I would neglect it and would not have endured its labor and cost. A person who does not love their country, future generations, and the common good will be like a burdensome drone in the hive or like harmful vermin. What good is done in the world, if not through love?

If created love is so necessary, so active, and so communicative, how much more will the infinite love of the Creator be! His love is now the life of the world. It is the life of nature in living beings, the life of holiness in saints, and the life of glory in the blessed.

In this infinite love I and all the saints shall dwell forever. If I dwell in love, and love dwells in me, surely I shall experience its sweet and abundant communication and shall continually drink from the river of Your pleasures.

It is pleasing to nature to be loved by others, especially by the great, the wise, and the good. How much more delightful it is to have all expressions of love—in conversation and gifts—in abundance and continuity, continually unfolded for our greatest benefit! If I had a friend who did for me even a fraction of what God does, how dearly I would love him!

Consider, O my soul, what a life you shall live forever in the presence, the face, the bosom of infinite, eternal love. He now shines upon me through the sun and upon my soul through the Sun of Righteousness; but it is as if through a lantern or the crevices of my dark habitation. Then He will shine upon me and in me openly, with the fullest streams and beams of love.

God is the same God in heaven and on earth, but I shall not be the same person. Here I receive comparatively little and live in darkness. I face frequent doubts and sorrows because my capacity to receive is limited; the windows of my soul are not open to His light. Sin has raised clouds and storms against my comfort.

The entrances to my soul through the flesh and senses are narrow, and sin has made them narrower than they were by nature.

Alas, how often would love have spoken comfort to me, but I was not at home to listen. I was caught up in a world of vanities, or I was not at leisure, or I was asleep and unwilling to be awakened! How often would love have come in and dwelt with me, but I unkindly shut my doors against Him!

How often would He have been with me in secret, where He would freely embrace me, but I was preoccupied with some pleasing company or business that I was reluctant to leave! How often would He have feasted me and prepared everything, but I was too busy to come.

When His table has been spread before me, with Christ, grace, and glory offered to me, my appetite has been dulled and I have almost neglected it, failing to find it pleasant enough to draw my mind away from harmful distractions. How often would He have shined upon me, but I have shut my windows or my eyes.

He was indeed jealous and did not want a partner. He would have been everything to me if I had been entirely devoted to Him. Yet I divided my heart, my thoughts, my love, my desires, and my affections; and alas, how much of it went elsewhere, even against Him, to His enemies, even when I knew that everything lost, and worse than lost, was not His.

What wonder, then, if such a foolish and unkind sinner found little pleasure in His love; and if such great ingratitude and neglect of sovereign goodness were punished with strangeness, fears, and faintness, which I have long lamented with groans. "Recipitur ad modum recipientis."

But in heaven I shall have none of these obstructions; all past unkindness and ingratitude will be forgiven. The great Reconciler, in whom I am beloved, will have perfected His work. I shall then be wholly separated from the vanity that deceived me here. My open soul will be prepared to receive the heavenly influx.

With an open face, I shall behold the open face of glorifying love. I shall joyfully attend to His voice and delightfully savor the celestial provisions.

No disease will corrupt my appetite, and no sluggishness will again make me guilty of my old neglects. The love of the Father, by the grace of the Son and the communion of the Holy Spirit, will have triumphed over all my deadness, folly, and disaffection. My aversion and enmity toward God will be gone forever.

The perfect love that God first instills in me will be my everlasting receptivity to the fullest love of God. Benevolent love will make me good — that is, a holy lover of God. Pleased love will make me His delight, and benevolence will continue to sustain me.

Study this heavenly work of love, O my soul. These are not dead or barren studies, nor are they sad or unpleasant. Only love can relish love and understand it; the will here has its taste. Some philosophers even say that "voluntas percipit" is a fitting phrase.

What can poor, carnal worldlings know of glorious love who study it without love? What sounding brass or a clanging cymbal, what lifeless voice, are they who preach of God, Christ, and heavenly glory without love?

Gazing upon the face of love in Christ, tasting its gifts, and looking up to its glorious reign is the way to kindle the sacred fire within you. Look upward if you wish to see the light that must lead you upward. It is not for nothing that Christ taught us to begin our prayers with "Our Father in heaven,"; it is fatherly love that must win our hearts and comfort them. It is in heaven where this is gloriously manifested.

As I said before: just as the soul is in all parts of the body but does not understand in the hand as it does in the head, and does not rejoice in the foot as it does in the heart, so God, who is everywhere, does not glorify His love everywhere as He does in heaven.

Therefore the mind and eye are naturally drawn to look up to God, just as we look a person in the face when we speak to them, rather than at their feet, even though their soul is present there too.

My sinful heart has needed sorrow. My careless, rash, presumptuous soul has needed fears; and I have experienced some of these. Mercy deemed it good for me, as necessary to prevent my dangerous deceptions and lapses.

O that in the hour of sensual temptations I had feared more and turned away from evil! Yet it is holy love that must be my life; otherwise I am dead despite my fears.

Oh, come then, and study the life of love. It is more a holy nature than an art, yet study must do much to prepare you to receive it. This is the great purpose of a heavenly conversation.

The contemplation, belief, and hope of the glorious state of love hereafter must make us like it and kindle it within us here.

Reasons Arising from My Will

The burning glass must be directed straight at the sun if you want it to ignite anything. There is a carnal or common love for God kindled in people by carnal pleasures; but a holy love, like that in heaven, must be sought from heaven and kindled by the foresight of what is there and what we shall be there forever.

Faith must ascend and look beyond the veil. You must not live as a stranger to your home—your God and Savior—and your hopes. The fire that must warm you is in heaven; draw near to it or open yourself to its influence if you wish to feel its power.

It is night and winter for carnal minds, while it is day and summer for those who set their faces heavenward.

Although all my receptions will come from God, they will not come from Him alone. We must also live in perfect union with one another and with all the heavenly society. As we must love them all, so shall we be loved by them all. This will be a subordinate part of our blessedness. God will use secondary causes in communicating His love and glory.

The Lord Jesus Christ will not only be the object of our delightful love, but He will also love us with an effective, operative love forever. His love will be like the vital heat and motion of the heart to all its members—the root of our life and joy. The love of our Redeemer will flow into us like vital spirits. His glorious face will be the sun of the heavenly Jerusalem, shining upon us and revealing God to us; and in His light we see light.

Did His tears for dead Lazarus make people say, "See how He loved him!" Oh, then, what will the reviving rays of heavenly life make us say about that love which fills us with the pleasures of His presence and turns our souls into joy itself? He comforts us now through the teaching of His word; but surely the fruition of salvation will be more joyful than the news of it. When He who told us of glory in His gospel gives it to us, we shall not only believe but feel that He loves us.

Believe, O my soul, in your Savior's love so that you may foretaste it and be prepared to feel it. In sinful flesh we were incapable of seeing Him except as clothed in flesh, and His consolations were given through promises suitable to His appearance. But when He withdrew His bodily presence, the Comforter was sent with fuller consolation. Yet all that was merely the earnest and firstfruits of what He will be to us forever.

Do not be infrequent, unbelieving, or dismissive in your thoughts of your Savior's love, for He is the way to infinite love. Let your belief be such a part of your daily work that you may say that "that Christ may dwell in your hearts through faith;" (Eph. 3:17) and that while you live here, it is Christ who lives in you. Know also that your life in the flesh is not a fleshly life, but by the faith of the Son of God "who loved me and gave Himself for me." (Gal. 2:20)

And though you do not see Him, yet, believing, you love Him with unspeakable joy, as you believe in the unspeakable perfect joy which His love will communicate to you forever.

Look upon the sun and think to yourself: How wonderful is the emanation of this sun—its motion, light, and heat communicated to so many millions of creatures all over the earth and in the seas. What if all these beams of light and heat were proportionate beams of perfect knowledge, love, and joy; and if all creatures under the sun had, from its influx, as much wisdom, love, and joy as they have light, heat, and motion? Would not this earth then be like a world of angels, a heaven? Oh, what a blessed world that would be, and what a benefactor the sun would be to the world!

Even so, Jesus Christ will be to the celestial world. He is the sun of glory. His influence will send forth life, light, and joyful love upon all the blessed, from the face of God, just as the sun sends forth its motion, light, and heat upon this world. Therefore begin and live upon Him: live upon the influence of His grace — His teaching, love-kindling, and quickening grace — so that you may bear His name and mark, and that He may find in you something of Himself when you come to His righteous judgment.

His grace is not under my control or at my command. It ought not to be so; and He has not bade me to seek and beg in vain. If He had only told me that He would give it when I asked, that would already be like a promise. But He has given me more. He teaches me to pray. He frames my prayers. He writes a prayer-book on my heart. He gives me desires, and He delights to be importuned by them.

His Spirit is first a spirit of supplication and then a spirit of consolation, and in both He is a Spirit of adoption. He is so far from being displeased by my requests that He invites me to seek His grace, and He is offended when I do not ask for more.

All this is true. Yet why does my soul remain so low, so dark, so bound to this wretched flesh and world, and so reluctant to go home and dwell with Christ? A taste of heaven on earth is a mercy too precious to be squandered by those who have long grieved and quenched the Spirit and are not prepared to receive it through diligent and patient seeking.

He who proclaims a general peace will grant peace only to the sons of peace.

If, after such unkind neglect and willful sins as I have committed, I were to expect suddenly to be in my Savior's arms and to be feasted immediately with the firstfruits of heaven, I would expect the Most Holy to manifest too little hatred of my sin. My conscience recalls the follies of my youth and many later detestable sins. It reminds me that, if heaven were wholly hidden from my sight and I never saw the face of that glorious, eternal love, it would be just.

I look upward day by day. I groan to see His pleased face and to know my God and my home better. I cry to Him daily, "My God, this little is better than all the pleasures of sin. My hopes are better than all the possessions of this world. Your gracious looks have often revived me, and Your mercies have been immeasurable to my soul and body."

But oh, how far short am I of what, even fifty years ago, I hoped to have attained sooner! Where is the peace that surpasses understanding, which should keep my heart and mind in Christ? Where are the seeing, the longing, the rejoicing, and the triumphant faith? Where is that pleasant familiarity above, that should make a thought of Christ and heaven sweeter to me than thoughts of friends, health, or all the prosperity and pleasure of this world?

Do those who dwell in God, and God in them, who have their hearts and conversations in heaven, attain no clearer and more satisfying perceptions of that blessed state than I have yet achieved? Is no fuller acquaintance above to be expected here? Is there no livelier sense of future joys, no sweeter foretaste, no fuller silencing of doubts and fears?

I am not so reluctant to go to a friend, nor to the bed where I often spend the night in restless pain, as I have too often been to come to You. Alas, how many of Your servants are less afraid to go to prison than to their God, and would rather be banished to a land of strangers than sent to heaven.

Lord, must I—who am called Your child, an heir of heaven, and a co-heir with Christ—have no more acquaintance with my glorified Lord and no more love for You, my portion, before I depart and come before You? Shall I have no more of the heavenly life, light, and love?

Reasons Arising from My Will

Alas, I have scarcely enough in my meditations to call them truly heavenly meditations. I have scarcely enough in a prayer to make it indeed a heavenly prayer, or in a sermon to make it a heavenly sermon. Shall I have no more when I come to die? Must I depart this life so much like a stranger to my home? Will You take strangers into heaven and recognize them as Yours who do not better know You here?

O my God, grant a sinner yet more of Your Spirit — the same Spirit that came down to earth to call earthly minds to God and to open heaven to all believers! What do I beg for so frequently and earnestly, for the sake of my Redeemer, but the spirit of life and consolation? Grant me that spirit which may show me the pleased face of God, unite all my affections to my glorified Head, and draw up this dark and drowsy soul to love and long to be with You.

But alas, though these are my daily groans, how little do I yet ascend. I dare not blame the God of love; He is full and willing. I dare not blame my blessed Savior; He has shown He is not reluctant to do good. I dare not accuse the Holy Spirit; it is His work to sanctify and comfort souls.

If I knew no reason for my low and dark state, I would have to conclude that it is something within myself. But my conscience abundantly points out the cause. Sinful resistance to the Spirit and ungrateful neglect of grace and glory are undoubtedly the reasons. Yet are these not causes that mercy can forgive and grace can overcome? May I not still hope for such a victory before I die?

Lord, I will lie at Your doors and groan. I will pour out my moans before You. I will beg, and whatever You will, do with me.

You described the dogs' kindness to Lazarus who lay at a rich man's gate in sores. You commended the neighborly pity of the Samaritan who cared for a wounded man. You condemned those who will not show mercy to the poor and needy. And You command us to be merciful, just as our Father in heaven is merciful.

If we see our brother in need and withhold compassion from him, it is because Your love does not dwell in us. And shall I then wait at Your doors in vain and go away empty from such a God, when I ask only for that which You have commanded me to seek—and without which I cannot serve You, or come to You, live or die as becomes a member of Christ, a child of God, and an heir of heaven?

O give me the wedding garment, without which I shall only dishonor Your bounteous feast. Let me wear a livery that befits Your family, as a child of God. How often have You commanded me to rejoice—yes, to rejoice with exceeding and unspeakable joy—and how eager would I be to obey!

O that I had more faithfully performed other preparatory duties, in ruling my senses, my fancy, my tongue, and in diligently using all Your talents! Then I might have more easily obeyed You in this.

You know, Lord, that love and joy are duties that require more than a command. O speak an effective word and bid me to do them. How can I rejoice in death and darkness? When the bridegroom is absent, I must fast and mourn. While I look toward heaven only through the crevices of this dungeon of flesh, my love and joy will be only commensurate with my light.

How long has it been since I hoped I had been translated from the kingdom of darkness, delivered from the power of darkness, and brought into that light which is the entrance to the inheritance of the saints? Yet, alas, darkness is still my misery. There is light all around me in Your word and works, but darkness is within me. If my eye is dark, the sun will be no sun to me.

Reasons Arising from My Will

Alas, my Lord, it is not all the learning in the world—even in theology—that amounts to true, heavenly light. Knowing what You have written in the sacred book is not enough to know my glorified Savior, my Father, and my home. It must be a light from heaven that shows me heaven. And it must be a light accompanied by vital heat that turns to love and joy within me.

O let me not have only a dreaming knowledge of words and signs, but quickening light to show the things those words signify to my mind and heart. Surely the faith by which we must live must be a living faith, reaching beyond words, however true they may be.

Can faith live in the dark? What is it but an effect of Your illumination? What is my unbelief but the darkness of my soul?

Lord Jesus, scatter all these mists! Make Your way, O Sun of Righteousness, into this benighted mind. O send Your Advocate to silence every temptation against Your truth and against You. Send Your agent to prosecute Your cause against Your enemies and mine, and to be the abiding witness of Your truth, and of my sonship and salvation. Hearing about You is not satisfactory to me. It must be the real presence and operation of Your light and love, shed abroad by Your Spirit on my heart, that will quiet and content my soul.

I confess, with shame, that I have sinned against heaven and before You, and am unworthy to have any glimpse or taste of heaven. Yet many who were once like me are now entertained and feasted by Your love in glory.

My Lord, I know that heaven is not far from me. I believe it is not a day's, or even an hour's, journey for a separated soul. How quickly my eyes can commune with the sun, which seems far off — could You not show it to me in a moment? Is not faith a seeing grace? It can see the invisible God, the unseen world, the new Jerusalem, the innumerable angels, and the spirits of the perfected just, if it is animated by Your influence. Without that influence it can do nothing and is nothing. You, who often healed the blind in the flesh, told us that it is even more Your work to illuminate souls. If You would but forgive all my sins and remove the film that sin has gathered, my illuminated soul would see Your glory.

I know that the veil of flesh must also be torn before I shall see You with an open face and know my fellow citizens above as I am known. I am not begging for heaven on earth, but that I may see it from Mount Nebo and have the bunch of grapes — the pledge and the first fruits — that faith and hope which kindle love and desire. Let these make me run my race with patience, and live and die in the joy that befits an heir of heaven.

But if my part on earth must be no greater than it is, let it make me wearier of this dungeon. Let it make me groan more fervently to be with You, longing for the day when all my longing shall be satisfied and my soul filled with Your light and love.

Undoubtedly, as I shall love the angels and saints in heaven, I shall, in subordination to Christ, receive from them. Our love will be mutual. In whatever way I owe duty, I shall expect some corresponding return of benefit. The sun shines upon the stars as well as upon the earth, and the stars shine upon one another. If angels are greatly useful to me here, they will be far more useful there, where I shall be a more capable receiver.

It will not diminish Christ's honor that He makes use of my fellow creatures for my joy, no more than it does here. The whole creation will still be one interconnected frame. The heavenly society will forever retain relationships to one another, along with the aptitude and disposition for the duties and benefits of those relationships. As we shall be far more fit for them than we are here, so shall we have far more comfort in them. How gloriously will God shine in the glory of the blessed! How delightful it will be to see their perfection in wisdom, holiness, love, and concord!

What voices they use, or what communication instead of voices, we shall shortly know. Surely there is a blessed harmony of minds, wills, and practices. All are not equal, but all harmonize to love and praise their glorious God, readily obey Him, and perfectly love one another. There is no jarring or discordant spirit out of tune; no separation or opposition among them. As God's love in Christ is our full and final happiness, so nature, which has made us sociable, teaches us to desire to be loved by one another, especially by the wise and worthy. Saints and angels in heaven will love incomparably better than our dearest friends on earth can, and better than those friends did when we were on earth; for they will love what is best, where most of God appears — otherwise it would not be intellectual love.

Therefore they will love us much better when we come to heaven, because we shall be better. If we leave behind loving friends on earth, we shall go to those who love us far more. The love of those here only pities us in our pains and weeps with our carcasses to the grave; but the love of those above will joyfully escort or welcome our souls to their triumphant society. All the holy friends we thought we had lost, who went before us, we shall find rejoicing there with Christ.

Oh, what a glorious state that common, uniting love will be! If two or three candles joined together make a greater flame and light, what would ten thousand stars united do? When all the love of angels and saints in full perfection is so united as to make one love — to God who is one, and to one another, who are all one in Christ — oh, what a glorious love that will be! That love and joy will be the same thing, and that one universal love will be one universal joy.

Little do we know how great a mercy it is to be commanded here to love our neighbor as ourselves, and much more to be effectually taught by God to love one another. If we all lived here in such unfeigned love, we would be like heaven, bearing the image of the God of Love. But alas, our societies here are small; our goodness, which is our amiableness, is woefully imperfect and mixed with loathsome sin and discord. There, however, a whole heaven full of blessed spirits will flame forever in perfect love to God, to Christ, and to one another.

Go then, go willingly, O my soul! Love joins with light to draw up your desires. Nature inclines all things toward union: even the lifeless elements have an aggregative motion, so that when their parts are violently separated they hastily return to their natural adhesion. Are you a lover of wisdom, and would you not be united to the wise? Are you a lover of holiness, and would you not be united to the holy, who are made of love? Do you hate enmity, discord, and division, and love unity on earth — would you not be where all the just are one?

This union is not unnatural to your advantage; nothing shall be taken from you by it. You shall receive more than you can contribute. It shall not be forced against your will; it is but a union of minds and wills, a perfect union of loves. Let not natural or sinful selfishness make you think suspiciously or harshly of it, for it is your happiness and end. What did the angels who fell into selfishness gain from their separation? And what did Adam, who followed them, gain? The further any person moves from unity through selfishness, the deeper they fall into sin and misery away from God. What does grace do but call us back from sin and selfishness to God's unity again?

Do not dwell on this dark, divided world. Is not your body, while its parts are kept together by a uniting soul, in a better state than when it is crumbled into lifeless dust? Does not death creep upon you by gradual dissolution? Away, then, from this sandy, incoherent state; the further from the center, the further from unity. There is indeed a unity of all things, but it is one heavenly life, light, and love — the true felicitating union.

We dispute here whether the aggregative motion of separated parts (as in descent by gravity) comes from a motive principle in the part, from the attraction of the whole, or from some external impulse. It is likely that some aspect of all these is true. Surely the greatest cause will contribute most to the effect. The body of the earth has more power to attract a clod or stone than the intrinsic principle has to move it downward; yet intrinsic gravity is also necessary. The superior attractive love and loveliness of God must do more to draw my mind up to Him than my intrinsic holiness can do to move it upward; but without that holiness the soul would not be capable of feeling that attractive influx. Every grace comes from God to fit and lead my soul to Him. Faith, therefore, believes in the heavenly state; love, with some delight, desires it; and hope reaches after it, that I may at last attain it.

Those who have argued against propriety and who would have all things common in this world forget that there is a rightness in our present individuality and natural constitution that makes some accidental propriety necessary. Each person has bodily parts and inherent accidents that belong to them. Each person needs their own food, their own place, clothing and possessions, their own children, and therefore their own spouse, and so on.

But the highest perfection is most for community, insofar as nature allows. God showed this when the first recipients of extraordinary outpourings of His Spirit sold all and voluntarily made all things common—none saying, "This or that is my own"—not by any law of compulsion but by the law or power of uniting love. They were first all of one heart and soul (Acts 4:32). Do not take your inordinate longing for propriety as if it were health; treat it as a sickness. Do not cherish it, do not fear losing it, and do not measure heavenly happiness by it. Spirits are penetrable; they claim no propriety of place as bodies do.

Your present weakness and imperfection make it seem desirable that your house, your land, your clothes, your books — even your knowledge and grace — should be yours and no one else's. How much more excellent a state would be, if we were capable of it, where we could say that all these are like the common light of the sun — yours and everyone else's at once. Why do we long to speak all languages, if not so we might understand all people and be understood by them, making our thoughts as common as possible?

Why are people so given to talkativeness if not because nature inclines us to make our thoughts and passions as common as possible? And why else are learned people eager to spread their learning and godly people so intent on making others wise and holy? One of the greatest sorrows of this life is that after the longest, hardest study a person may attain much knowledge yet cannot bequeath it, or any part of it, to an heir at death — everyone must acquire it for themselves. When God has sanctified parents, they cannot communicate their holiness to their children (though God promises to bless them on their account). Much less can anyone make their grace or knowledge entirely common: both nature and grace incline us to desire it, but we cannot accomplish it.

For this reason we talk, preach, and write. For this reason we study — to be as plain, convincing, and moving as we can, so that our knowledge and affections may be as common to our hearers and readers as possible. Oh, what a blessed work preaching and writing would be if we could make everyone know what we know and love what we urge them to love! Then there would be no need for schools and universities: a few hours would accomplish more than they do in an age. Yet, how rare it is for a father of excellent learning and piety to have even one son like himself after all his industry.

Is not the heavenly communion therefore desirable, where each person will have their own and yet their own will be common to all? My knowledge will be mine and others' as well; my goodness will be mine and theirs; my glory and happiness will be mine and theirs; and theirs will be mine in the same way. The knowledge, goodness, and glory of the whole heavenly society shall be mine according to my capacity. Grace is the seed of such a state: it makes us one in Christ. There will be neither Greek nor Jew, circumcised nor uncircumcised, barbarian nor Scythian, slave nor free. Grace gives us to love our neighbors as ourselves, to love both our neighbors and ourselves for Christ, and to see Christ in all. Paul rightly said, "All things are yours:"

But here it is only as in the seed; the perfect union and communion belong to the world to come. Earth and heaven must be distinguished; we must not extend our hopes or our pretensions here beyond the capacity of our natures. Just as perfect holiness and knowledge belong to heaven, so too perfect unity and concord belong there and are not to be expected here. The papal claim of an impossible union under one ruler of all the earth hinders the union that is possible. The state of perfection is the state of perfect union and communion.

Hasten then upward, O my soul, with fervent desires. Breathe after that state with the strongest hopes. There you will not be rich while your neighbors are poor, nor poor while they are rich; you will not be well while they are sick, nor sick while they are well. Their riches, health, and joy will be yours, and yours will be theirs, like the common light. No one will be diminished by sharing with others; indeed, communion will be part of everyone's happiness and will constitute the very being of the city of God. This celestial communion of saints in one holy church, beyond what is attainable here, is now an article of our faith; but believing will soon end in seeing and enjoying.

9. Reasons Drawn from Heavenly Living

Seeing and loving will be the heavenly life. But besides these, there will also be executive powers and corresponding practice. There are good works in heaven, and they are far more numerous and better than those on earth.

1. There will be more vital activity, and therefore more exercise for it; the power exists for action.

2. There will be more love to God and to one another; and love is active.

3. There will be a greater likeness to God and to our Redeemer, who is communicative and does good because He is good.

4. Our union with Christ—who will be everlastingly beneficent as well as benevolent—will make us beneficent in our respective places as well.

5. Our communion in the city of God will mean that we all play our part, like members of one body, contributing to the welfare of the whole and offering common returns to God.

But what are the heavenly works we must fully know when we arrive there? In general, we know:

1. That they will be works of love toward God and toward His creatures; that is, actions to which love inclines us.

2. They will be works of obedience to God; that is, actions we perform to please His will, and because He wills them as our duty.

3. They will be useful works to others.

4. They will be pleasant to ourselves, and part of our happiness.

5. And they will direct all to God, our end.

Some of them are particularly described in the Holy Scriptures:

We shall, in concord with the holy society or choir, give thanks and praise to God and our Redeemer (Revelation 19:5; 1 Peter 4:11; Revelation 7:4; 4:7, 11; 5:13; 7:12; 19:1; Philippians 4:20). Whether there will be any voice at all, or only such spiritual activity and exultation as belongs to men in the flesh, is not clearly understood. It is not fitting for us here to presume to determine. Whatever the form, it will be higher and more excellent than our vocal praise and singing, of which this bears some analogical resemblance or signification.

As all passions earnestly desire vent and exercise, so especially do our holy affections — love, joy, and admiration of God Almighty. We also desire communion with many in such affections and expressions. When I sing or speak God's praise in large assemblies with joyful and fervent souls, I have the liveliest foretaste of heaven on earth.

I could almost wish that our voices were loud enough to reach through the whole world and to heaven itself. Nor could I ever be offended (as many are) at the organs and other suitable music, soberly and seasonably used, which excite and help to tune my soul for such a holy work. No true assistance in this is to be despised.

No work comforts me more in my greatest sufferings; none seems more congruous and pleasant to me while I wait for death than psalms and words of praise to God. Nor is there any exercise in which I would rather end my life. Should I not then willingly go to the heavenly choir, where God is praised with perfect love, joy, and harmony? Had I a more praising frame of soul, it would make me long more for that life of praise.

For I never find myself more willing to be there than when I most joyfully speak or sing God's praise. Though the dead do not praise God in the grave, and dust does not give Him thanks, yet living souls in heaven do so joyfully while their fleshly clothing turns to dust.

Lord, tune my soul to Your praises now, that this sweet experience may make me long to be where I shall do it better! I see that wherever there is excellent music, people naturally flock to it, and those who are yet only hearers join by a shared fancy and delight. Surely, if I had once heard the heavenly choir, I should echo their holy songs, though I could not imitate them; and I should count it the truest blessedness to be there and bear my part.

My God, the voice of Your comforting Spirit, speaking Your love effectually to my soul, would make such holy music in me that it would incline me to the celestial consort; and without it, all these thoughts and words will be in vain. It is the inward melody of Your Spirit and my conscience that must tune me to desire the heavenly melody.

O speak Your love first to my heart, and then I shall joyfully speak it to my brethren, and shall earnestly seek that communion of those who praise You better than sinful, groaning mortals can. Though my sins here make a loathed jar and discord in my songs, I hope my groans for those sins and their effects will make no discord: sighs and tears have had the honor to be accepted by You, who will not despise a contrite and broken heart.

Reasons Drawn from Heavenly Living

But if Your Spirit sings and speaks within me and helps me against the discordant murmurs of my unbelieving heart and my pained flesh, then I shall offer You something more fitting to Your love and grace. I confess, Lord, that daily tears and sighs are not unsuitable for one so great a sinner under Your correcting rod. What better could I expect, when I grieved Your Spirit, than that it should share my grief? Yes, this is far better than the plain effects of sin.

But this is not what is most fitting to be offered to the God of love: he who offers praise glorifies You; and is not this "to offer up spiritual sacrifices acceptable to God through Jesus Christ" (1 Peter 2:5)? I do not refuse, Lord, to lie in tears and groans when You require it, and I do not ask You to reject those tears and groans. But O give me something better, that I may have of Your own to offer You. By this prepare me for the far better which I shall find with Christ. That which is best for us, Your creatures, will be accepted as best by You, who are glorified and pleased in the perfection of Your works.

It is, at least, very probable that God makes glorified spirits His agents and ministers of much of His beneficence toward the creatures below them.

1. We see that when He endows any creature with the noblest qualities, He commonly uses that creature most for the benefit of others. In heaven we shall be most equipped to do good, and that equipment will not be unused.

2. Christ tells us we shall be like the angels — equal to them in certain respects; though this does not mean in every particular, it signifies more than merely being above carnal generation. It points to a similarity in nature and state as the ground for other benefits. That the angels are God's ministers for the good of His chosen in this world, and administrators of many affairs on earth, is beyond doubt.

3. The Apostle tells us that the saints will judge the world and that we shall judge angels; and in Scripture to "judge" often means to rule. It is therefore at least probable that devils and the damned will be placed under the saints, and that, together with the angels, they will be employed in some ministerial oversight of the inhabitants and affairs of the promised new earth.

4. When even the more noble superior bodies, such as the stars, are of great use and influence to inferior bodies, it is likely that superior spirits will also be of use to the inhabitants of the world below them.

However, I think it is inappropriate to venture here into uncertain conjectures beyond the revelation of God's Word; therefore I shall add no more. I conclude that God knows what use to make of us hereafter as well as here, and that if there were nothing for us to do in heaven but, with perfect knowledge, love, and joy, hold communion with God and all the heavenly society, that would be enough to draw a sensible and considerate soul to fervent desire to be at home with God.

Here I must also reject the harmful opinion of too many philosophers and divines who exclude all sense and affection from heaven and acknowledge nothing there but intellect and will. This error arises from their seeing sense and affection in animals and concluding that the souls of animals are merely some quality or perishing temperament of matter; therefore they suppose that sense and affection in us are no better.

1. What happiness can we conceive of without any affection of delight or joy? Certainly, bare volition without these seems no happiness to us; nor does knowledge have value if there is no delight in knowing.

2. I leave it to people's experience to judge whether there is any proper act of willing in us that is not also accompanied by some internal sense of, and affection for, the good we will. If it is complacency, the

pleasedness of the will, this signifies some pleasure. Love, in its first act, is nothing else but such an appetite. If it is desire, it contains a pleasedness in the thing desired as it is thought of by us. What is love without all sense and affection?

3. Why does Scripture ascribe love and joy to God and the angels if there were not some reason for it? Doubtless, there is a great difference between heavenly love and joy and ours here in the body; and likewise between their knowledge and ours, and their will and ours. Yet it is not that theirs is less or lower than ours, but rather more excellent, of which ours gives some analogical or imperfect notion.

4. And what if animals have sense and affection? Does it follow that we have none now or that we shall have none hereafter? Animals have life; must we therefore have no life hereafter because it is common to animals? Rather, just as we now possess all that animals have and more, so shall we then have life, sense, and affection of a nobler sort than animals, and more. Is not God the living God? Shall we say that He does not live because animals live? Rather, animals live a sensitive life, and man a sensitive and intellectual life, because God is essential, transcendent, infinite life, which makes them live.

5. If they claim that there is no sensation or affection except through bodily organs, I have answered that before: the body feels nothing; the soul in the body feels. The soul unites itself most closely to the fiery, airy parts called the spirits; and in them it feels, sees, tastes, smells, etc. The soul that feels and sees also inwardly loves, desires, and rejoices; and the soul which does this in the body has the same power and faculty outside the body.

If they judge by the cessation of sensation when the organs fail or die, they might as well conclude against our future intellection and will, whose operation in an apoplexy we no more perceive than that of sense. But I have already shown that the soul will not lack exercise for its essential faculties for want of objects or bodily organs. Men conclude basely about the souls of animals, as if they were not enduring substances, without any proof or probability. They tell us idle dreams, calling them mere vanishing temperaments, which rest on another dream — that fire (or the motive, illuminative, calefactive cause) is not a substance either. Thus our unnatural materialists know none of the most excellent substances, which actuate all the rest, but only the more base and gross, which are actuated by them. They think they have acquitted themselves well by speaking of subtle, active matter and motion, without understanding what any living, active motive, faculty, or virtue is. Since no one knows what God does with the souls of animals — whether they are merely one common sensitive soul of a common body, or whether they remain individuate and transmigrate from body to body, or what else — they make ignorance a plea for error and claim they are not substances or that they are annihilated.

I have no doubt that sensation (as mentioned earlier) is an excellent operation of the essential faculties of real substances called spirits, and that the highest and noblest creatures have it in the highest excellence. Although God, who fits everything to its use, has given, for example, a dog a more perfect sense of smell than a man, yet man's internal sense is far more excellent than that of animals, and thus gives an advantage to our intellection, volition, and joy here in the flesh. In heaven we shall have not less, but more — more excellent sense and affections of love and joy, and more excellent intellection and volition — though in ways we cannot now clearly conceive.

Therefore, there is great reason for all those analogical collections I mentioned in my book called The Saint's Rest, drawn from the present operations and pleasures of the soul in the flesh, to help our conceptions of its future pleasures. Although we cannot rule out that they may differ in manner from what we now feel, I have no doubt that we shall feel and rejoice, as certainly as we live, and that the soul is essential life, and that our life, feeling, and joy will be incomparably better.

10. How God Makes Us Willing to Depart

I am convinced that it is far better to depart and be with Christ than to remain here. Yet conviction alone is not enough to raise my soul to such desires. Still, there resist:

1. The natural aversion to death which God has placed in every animal, now made inordinate and too strong by sin.

2. The remnants of unbelief, which take advantage of our darkness here in the flesh and our excessive familiarity with this visible world.

3. The lack of more lively foretastes of a heavenly mind and love, due to weakness of grace and the fear of guilt. These oppose all that is said, and words alone will not overcome them. What then must be done? Is there no remedy?

There is a special way in which God teaches us to "number our days, That we may gain a heart of wisdom." Without this understanding we will never truly learn this or any of the most common and obvious lessons. Even after we have read, heard, spoken, and written the most sound truths and certain arguments, we often know as if we do not know, and believe as if we do not believe, with only a vague, dreamlike apprehension.

This changes when God, by a special illumination, brings these truths clearly to our minds and awakens our souls with a distinct prompting. Then we truly feel what we know. He brings our souls into accord with revealed truth by an influx of His love, giving us a pleasing sense of the beauty and harmony of the things presented.

Since we have separated ourselves from God, a barrier exists between our senses and our understanding, and between our understanding and our wills and affections. This division disrupts the communion among our faculties and causes a schism within ourselves. Everyone can see demonstrations of divine perfection in the world and in every part of it; yet, how little is God truly known. People can easily acknowledge that there is an almighty, omniscient God, who is goodness itself, eternal, omnipresent, the Maker, Preserver, and Governor of all, and who deserves our complete trust, love, and obedience. Yet this knowledge is often not reflected in their hearts or lives.

Everyone knows that the world is vanity, that we must die, that riches will be of no use then, that time is precious, and that we have only this brief period to prepare for what we will face afterward. Still, how little do people seem to genuinely understand these truths, which no one doubts. When God comes with His awakening light and love, all these truths take on a new reality and affect us differently than before, as if we are just beginning to know them. Words, doctrines, people, and things then appear to us as if newly known.

All my best reasons for our immortality and future life are like the newly formed body of Adam before God breathed into his nostrils the breath of life. It is He who must make them living reasons. To the Father of lights, therefore, I must still look up, and for His light and love I must still wait, as I wait for His blessing on the food I have eaten, which must be digested into my living substance. Arguments are but undigested food until God's effectual influx digests them.

I must learn both as a student and as a beggar. After thinking a thousand times, I must beg Your blessing, Lord, upon my thoughts, or they will be mere dullness or self-distraction. If there is no motion, light, and life here without the influx of the sun, what can souls do, receive, or feel without Your influx? This world, without Your grace, will be like a grave or dungeon where we lie in death and darkness. The eye of my understanding, and all its thoughts, will be useless or vexatious to me without Your illuminating beams. O shine the soul of Your servant into a clearer knowledge of Yourself and Your kingdom; love him into more divine and heavenly love, and then he will willingly come to You.

And why should I struggle against the natural course of life and my only hopes of happiness because of the fear of death? Is it not appointed for men to die once? Would I have God change His ordained course and make sinful man immortal on earth?

When we are freed from sin, we shall be immortal. The love of life was given to teach me to preserve it carefully and to use it well, not to torment me with a constant, troubling awareness of death. Shall I make myself more miserable than plants and animals? Neither they nor I grieve that flowers must fade and die, that sweet and pleasant fruits must fall, or that trees lose their leaves until spring. Birds, beasts, fish, and worms have a self-preserving fear that drives them to flee danger; but few, if any, suffer a tormenting dread from knowing they must die. To the body, death is less troublesome than sleep; in sleep I may have pains or unsettling dreams, yet I do not fear going to bed. I will address this further below.

If it is the misery after death that is feared, what should I do but accept the free, reconciling grace offered to me from heaven, to save me from such misery, and devote myself entirely to Him who has promised that those who come to Him He will never cast out?

But this fear arises from my selfishness. Had I focused on my duty and remembered that I do not belong to myself, and that it is God's role, not mine, to determine the length of my life, I would have been free from these fruitless fears. When I turn inward, away from God, I begin to care for myself as if it were my responsibility to measure out my days; and then I fail to trust God with what is His.

If my resignation and devotion to Him had been more complete, trusting Him would have been easier. But, Lord, You know I truly desire to be Yours, wholly Yours; it is to You that I wish to live. Therefore let me quietly die to myself and fully trust You with my soul.

And why should my lack of clear conceptions about the future state of separated souls, and my unfamiliarity with their existence and operations, lead me to doubt those general truths that are evident and beyond rational dispute? I have no doubt that souls are substances and are not annihilated, and that they remain essentially the same when they leave the body as they were before. Otherwise, neither the resurrection of Christians nor the transmigration of souls, as the Pythagoreans believed, would be possible. If the soul ceases to exist, it cannot enter another body nor return to this one. If God raises this body, it must be by another soul. For the same soul to be annihilated and then to begin to exist again is a contradiction; the second beginning would be a creation, which would produce a new soul, not the same one that existed before.

The invisible things are the most excellent, active, operative, and permanent. The visible things (except light, which makes all else visible) are, in themselves, lifeless dross. It is the unseen part of plants and flowers that causes all their growth and beauty, their fruit and sweetness. Passive matter is merely moved up and down by invisible active powers, just as chess pieces are moved by the player's hand. What a loathsome corpse the world would be without the invisible spirits and natures that animate, actuate, and move it. To doubt the existence or continuation of the most excellent, spiritual parts of creation, when we live in a world animated by them and where everything demonstrates their effects, is more foolish than doubting the existence of the gross materials we see.

How often have I been convinced that there are good spirits with whom our souls have a certain communion, though not as tangible as our life with the sun or as our fellowship with one another? And that there are evil and envious spirits that fight against our holiness and peace, as certain accounts of apparitions and witches and as the sad experience of temptations shows. The marvelous diversity of creatures on earth, in kind and number; indeed, the diversity of stars in heaven, and the various angels and devils, partly tell me that although all are one, and through one, and to one, absolute unity is the divine prerogative. We must not presume to expect such perfection that we lose our specific or numerical diversity through any union that may occur to our souls. Nor can I reasonably doubt that so noble and active a nature as souls dwelling above in the bright regions, in communion with their kind and with their betters, shall be without activity, pleasure, and happiness suitable to their nature, their region, and their company. My Savior has entered the Most Holy Place and has assured me that in His Father's house there are many mansions; and that when we are absent from the body, we shall be present with the Lord.

Organic sight is given to me for use here in the body; a serpent or a hawk has as much or more of it than I do. Mental knowledge reaches further than sight and is the act of a nobler faculty, serving a higher purpose. Although it is the soul itself, embodied in the fiery spirits, that sees, it is through a higher and more useful faculty than mere understanding; and faith is not an act of understanding. Faith knows things unseen because they are revealed. Who can think that all believing, holy souls who have departed from this world since the beginning have been deceived in their faith and hope? And that all the wicked, worldly infidels, whose hope was only in this life, have been the wisest and have been right? If virtue and piety are faults or follies, and brutish sensuality is the best, then why are laws not made to command sensuality and forbid piety and virtue? To say this is to deny humanity, the wisdom of our Creator, and to pretend that the world is governed by a lie—taking the perfection of our nature for its disease and our greatest disease for our perfection. But if piety and virtue are better than impiety and vice, then the principles and necessary motives for them are certainly true, and their practice is not in vain. What abominable folly and wickedness it would be to say that the wicked alone attain their ends, and that those who seek to please God in hope of a better life to come live and die in miserable deceit, believing that He is a rewarder of those who diligently seek Him. Would not this justify the foolish Manicheans, who thought a bad God created this world? It would imply that He not only made us for mischief but rules us to our deceit and harm, and gives us both natural and supernatural laws, out of ill will, to mislead us to our misery and fill our lives with needless troubles. Shall I not abhor every suggestion that contains such inhuman absurdities as these?

It is wonderful that Satan can maintain so much unbelief in the world while he must make men such fools to turn them into unbelievers and ungodly.

That my soul is no more heavenly, and that my foretaste of future blessedness is so small, is partly the result of the many willful sins by which I have quenched the Spirit that should be my comforter. It is also partly due to our common state of darkness and strangeness while the soul is in the flesh, operating as the body's form according to its interests and capacity. Affections are more easily stirred by things seen than by things that are unseen and known only very imperfectly, through general rather than clear, distinct perceptions.

And yet this, O this, is the misery and burden of my soul! Though I can say that I love God's truth and graces, His work and His servants, and whatever of God I see in the world, and that this is a love of God in His creatures, word, and works; yet the fact that I have no more desiring and delightful love for heaven — where His loveliness will be more fully revealed — and that the thought of my soon appearing there is no more joyful to me than it is, is my sin, my calamity, and my shame. If I did not see that it is the same with other servants of Christ as with me, I would doubt whether affections so disproportionate to my profession did not signify unsoundness in my belief. It is strange and shameful that one who expects to quickly see the glorious world and enter the holy celestial society should be no more joyfully affected by these hopes, and that I should make any great matter of the pain, languishing, and perishing of the flesh when it is the common road to such an end. O hateful sin that has so darkened and corrupted souls as to estrange and disqualify them from the only state of their hoped happiness. Alas! what did man do when he forsook the love and obedience of his God? How just that this flesh and world should become our prison, which we would make our home and would not use as our Lord appointed us, as our servant and way to our better state. Though our way must not be our home, our Father would not have been so strange to us on the way if we had not ungratefully turned away from His grace and love.

To those of us who do not know the mysteries of infinite wisdom, it is the saddest thought that ever occupies our minds to consider that there is so little grace and holiness, so little knowledge of God, and so little communion with Him in this world. That so few are saints, and those few so lamentably defective and imperfect. That when the sun shines on all the earth, the Sun of Righteousness shines on so small a part of it, and so few live in the love of God and the joyful hopes of future blessedness; and those few have such a low measure of it and are troubled with so many contrary affections. Infinite goodness is not unwilling to do good. He who made us capable of holy and heavenly affections did not give us that capacity in vain; and yet, alas! how little of God and glory occupies the hearts of men!

But man has no cause to resent God. The devils, before their fall, were not made indefectible; divine wisdom delights in the diversity of His works and does not make them all of equal excellence. Free will was meant to act its part; hell is not to be as good as heaven: so much sin, so much hell. What is sin but a willful forsaking of God? And can we forsake Him and still love Him and enjoy His love? God's kingdom is not to be judged by His prison or gallows. We willfully forsook the light and made the world a dungeon for ourselves. And when recovering light shines upon us, how ungratefully do we usually receive it? We cannot have the guidance and comfort of it while we shut our eyes and turn away.

And what if God does not give all men an overwhelming measure, nor to the best as much as they desire? The earth is but a spot, or a print, of God's creation; not so much as an anthill compared to a kingdom, or perhaps to all the earth. Who is scandalized because the world has a heap of ants in it, or even a nest of snakes that are not men? The vast, immeasurable worlds of light above us are inhabited by beings suitable to their glory. A window, a crevice of light, or a candle in this dark world is an unspeakable mercy; indeed that we may hear of a better world and may seek it in hope. We must not resent that in our prison we do not have the presence of our King and the pleasures of the kingdom, as innocent and free subjects do; hope of pardon and a swift deliverance are great mercies to malefactors.

If my lack of knowledge and love for God, along with my absence of joyful communion with the heavenly society, is my prison—akin to the outskirts of hell—shouldn't it make me long for the day of my redemption and the glorious freedom of the children of God? My true desires for deliverance, holiness, and perfection are evidence that I shall obtain them. Just as the will is the sinner, so a stubborn persistence of a will to sin constitutes bondage and the cause of ongoing sin. A continued hell is, at least in part, continued sin. Therefore those who remain in hell continue with a will to sin and thus maintain a love and willingness for that portion of hell.

To the extent that God makes us willing to be freed from sin, we are delivered; our initial, imperfect deliverance is the pathway to greater freedom. If pain makes me groan for relief and sickness makes me yearn for health, why should not my remnants of ignorance, unbelief, and estrangement from God compel me to long for the day of my salvation? This is my greatest trouble, and should it not also be the most burdensome weight from which I should earnestly desire to be freed?

Grace never effects harm in itself, although it can be misused and cause harm objectively, particularly to those who are proud of it. Conversely, sin never does good in itself, yet it may serve as an object of grace, and using it in that way is not sin. My unbelief, darkness, disaffection, and excessive love for this life hinder my desires for deliverance and a better life. Objectively, what could be more fitting to make me weary of such a grievous state? If my unbelief and earthly mindset were dominant, they would chain my affections to this world. Conversely, if I were begrudgingly weary of a miserable life, I would have no comforting hopes for a better one.

As it is the nature of my sin to draw my heart away from God and glory, so it is the nature of my faith, hope, and love to elevate it and desire heavenly perfection—not to love death, but to love what lies beyond it. After spending so many years in the school of Christ, learning how to live and die, pleading for this grace, and practicing it against this sinful flesh, shall I now, after all this, find the flesh more powerful in drawing me downward than faith, hope, and love are in lifting my desires upward to God?

O God forbid! O You who freely gave me Your grace, maintain it to the end against its enemies, and make it ultimately victorious! It came from You; it has been preserved by You; it is on Your side and wholly for

You. O let it not now fail and be conquered by blind and base carnality, or by the temptations of a hellish, defeated enemy.

Without it, I would have lived like a beast, and without it I would die more miserably than a beast. It is Your image that You love; it is a divine nature and a heavenly light. What will a soul be without it but a dungeon of darkness, a devil in malignity, dead to holiness and heaven?

Without it, who will plead Your cause against the devil, the world, and the flesh? Without Your glory, the earth is just earth; without Your natural efficacy it would be nothing; without Your wise and powerful ordination it would be but chaos; and without Your grace it would be hell.

O deny me the light of the sun rather than the light of Your countenance! I would have been less miserable without life or being than without Your grace. Without You and my Savior's help, I can do nothing; I did not live without You; I could not pray or learn without You; I could never conquer a temptation without You; and can I die, or be prepared to die, without You?

Alas! I can only say, like Philip of Christ, "Lord, we do not know where You are going, and how can we know the way?" My Lord, having loved His own in the world, loved them to the end. You love fidelity and perseverance in Your servants; even those who forsook Him and fled during His sufferings are commended and rewarded by Christ for continuing with Him in His trials (Luke 22:28). Will You forsake a sinner in his extremity who consents to Your covenant and would not forsake You?

My God, I have often sinned against You, but You know I would gladly be Yours. I have not served You with the resolution, fidelity, and delight that such a Master should have received. Yet I would not forsake Your service, nor change my Master or my work. I can say, with Your servant Paul, that You are the God to whom I belong and whom I serve: O that I could serve You better!

For to serve You is to receive Your grace and to use it for my own and others' good, thus glorifying You and pleasing Your will. Your will, being love itself, is most pleased when we receive and do the greatest good (Acts 27:23).

I have not loved You as infinite goodness, love itself, and fatherly bounty should be loved; yet I would not forsake Your family. Nothing in this world grieves me more than that I do not love You more.

Do not forsake, then, a sinner who would not forsake You; one who looks to You every hour and feels it as a piece of hell to be so dark and strange to You. He gropes, groans, and gasps after You, feeling, to his greatest sorrow, that while he is at home in the body, he is absent from the Lord.

My Lord, I have nothing to do in this world but to seek and serve You. I have nothing to do with my heart and its affections but to long for You. I have nothing to do with my tongue and pen but to speak to You, for You, and to proclaim Your glory and Your will.

What have I to do with my reputation and my friends' interests but to increase Your church and propagate Your holy truth and service? What have I to do with my remaining time, even these last and languishing hours, but to look up to You and wait for Your grace and Your salvation?

O pardon all my carnal thoughts, all my ungrateful neglects of Your precious grace and love, and all my willful sins against Your truth and You. Let the fuller communications of Your forfeited grace now tell me by experience that You do forgive me!

Even under the terrible law, You proclaimed Your very nature by declaring Your name: "The Lord, the Lord God, merciful and gracious, longsuffering, and abundant in goodness and truth, keeping mercy for thousands, forgiving iniquity and transgression and sin." And is not the grace of our Lord Jesus Christ revealed in the gospel for our more abundant faith and consolation?

My God, I know that just as I cannot love You according to Your loveliness, I cannot trust You according to Your faithfulness: I can never be sufficiently confident in Your all-sufficient power, wisdom, and goodness.

When I have said, as in Psalm 77:7, "Will the Lord cast off forever? And will He be favorable no more? Has His mercy ceased forever? Has His promise failed forevermore?"

"Has God forgotten to be gracious? Has He in anger shut up His tender mercies?" Conscience has replied that this is my infirmity; I never lacked comfort because You lacked mercy, but because I lacked faith and fitness to receive and perceive it. But do You not also have mercy to give me that very fitness and that faith? My God, all is from You and through You and to You; when I attain blessedness, all glory forever will be Yours. None who trusts in You (according to Your nature and promise) shall be ashamed. If I can live and die trusting in You, surely I shall not be confounded.

Why, then, should it seem difficult to ask how I may willingly leave this world and have my soul depart to Christ in peace? The same grace that regenerated me must bring me to my desired end, just as the same principle of vegetation that causes the bud will bring the fruit to sweet maturity.

1. Believe and trust your Father, your Savior, and your Comforter.

2. Hope for the joyful reception of His love and for the blessed state He has promised.

3. Long, through love, for a closer union and communion with Him; and thus, O my soul, you may depart in peace.

How sure is the promise of God! How suitable to His love, to the nature of our souls, and to the workings of every grace. It is first fulfilled here, while our desires are turned toward Him, and the heavenly seed and spark are begotten in a soul that was once dead, dark, and estranged.

Is it strange for fire to ascend? Or for the fiery principle of growth in a tree to carry up earthy matter to great heights? Is it strange that rivers flow to the sea? Where else should spirits go but to the realm of spirits? And where should Christ's members and holy powers go but to Himself and the heavenly society?

Is not that a more holy and glorious state than this one below? Earth lies between heaven and hell. It is a place of gross and passive matter, where spirits act upon what needs them, and where they may be detained for a while in such action, or as incorporated forms, if not as imprisoned offenders. But it is not their center, end, or home. Even sight and reason persuade me that all the noble, invisible powers that work in this lower world primarily belong to a higher realm. What can earth add to their essence, dignity, or perfection?

But why, O my soul, are you so vainly anxious to have formal, clear, and distinct conceptions of the celestial world, or of the individuality and actions of separated souls—any more than of the angels? While you are the formal principle of an animated body, your conceptions must suit your present state and purpose. When you are in a better state you will know it as a possessor ought to; for the knowledge you now seek is part of that possession. To long to know and to love in full clarity and perfection is to long to possess.

It is your Savior, and His glorified ones, who are the comprehenders and possessors; and it is His knowledge that should now be your chief satisfaction. To seek His prerogative for yourself is vain and arrogant. Would you be a god and savior to yourself? Consider how much of the fall is present in this selfish care and desire to be like God — seeking to know good and evil that belongs to God alone.

You know, without doubt, that there is a God of infinite perfection who is a rewarder of those who diligently seek Him. Strive more to know your duty to this God, and absolutely trust Him about the particulars of your happiness and reward. You trusted your parents to provide food and clothing when you dutifully obeyed them. Though they might have forsaken or harmed you, you did not live in constant fear of that.

You have trusted physicians to give you unpleasant medicines without inquiring about every ingredient or fearing they willfully poison you. I trust a barber with my throat. I trust a boatman or shipmaster with my life. Yes, even my horse that might throw me — because I have no reason to distrust them except for their insufficiency and uncertainty as creatures. If a pilot undertakes to take you to the Indies, you can trust his guidance even though you know neither the ship nor navigation, nor the way nor the destination to which you are being taken.

Must not your God and Savior be trusted to bring you safely to heaven, even if He does not satisfy every inquiry about the individuality and actions of spirits? Leave unsearchable and useless questions to Him who can resolve them, and to those to whom that knowledge belongs. You only entangle yourself in sin and self-torment when you assume God's work and seek to know for yourself what He must know for you.

Your knowledge and your concern for it did not precede or prepare your birth, nor the motion of a single pulse or breath, nor the digestion of a single morsel, nor the continuance of your life for one hour—

provided you use the means God has appointed, avoid what is hurtful, and seek His blessing.

The command to be anxious for nothing, to make our requests known to God in everything by prayer and supplication with thanksgiving, and to cast all our care upon Him—for He cares for you—binds us in all things that are God's part, both for our souls and for our bodies. Truly, trusting Him with our greatest concerns is our chief duty, provided we do our part: use the means and obey His precepts.

To dispose of a departing soul is God's part, not ours. Oh, how much evil lies in this distrustful, self-providing care! If I could know what I want to know about my soul and myself, choose the condition it should be in, and be the final disposer of it, oh, what satisfaction and joy that would bring me! Is this not to be, in part, a god to myself? Is He not better fitted to know, choose, and dispose of me than I am?

I could easily trust myself—my wit and will—in such a choice if I had the power. But cannot I trust God and my Redeemer without all this care, fear, trouble, and these minute inquiries? If you are escorting your child in a boat or coach, by water or land, and he cries at every turn, "O father, where are we going?" or "What shall I do?" or "I shall drown or fall," is it not rather his trust in you, rather than the satisfaction of his ignorant doubts, that must calm and reassure him?

Do not be foolishly distrustful and inquisitive. Do not make yourself your own disquieter or tormentor by an excessive concern for your own security. Do not be cast down, O departing soul, nor let unbelief disturb you within.

"Why are you cast down, O my soul?
And why are you disquieted within me?
Hope in God;

For I shall yet praise Him,
The help of my countenance and my God." (Psalm 42:11)

Oh, what clear reason and great experience command me to trust Him absolutely and implicitly, and to distrust myself!

He is essential, infinite, perfection, power, wisdom, and love. In Him is all that should invite and encourage rational trust, and nothing that should discourage it.

There is nothing in any creature to be trusted, except God in that creature, or God working in and through it. Distrust Him, and there is nothing to be trusted—not the earth to bear me, nor the air to breathe, much less any mutable friend. I am altogether His own—His by right, and His by devotion and consent. And shall I not trust Him with His own? He is the great benefactor of the world, giving all good to every creature, not by constraint or exchange, but as freely as the sun gives forth its light. And shall we not trust the sun to shine? He is my Father and special benefactor, and has taken me into His family as His child. And shall I not trust my heavenly Father?

He has given me His Son as the great pledge of His love. What then will He think too dear for me? Will He not with Him also freely give me all things? (Rom. 8:32.) His Son came to reveal the Father's unspeakable love and to save us. Shall I not trust Him who has proclaimed His love and reconciliation through such a messenger from heaven?

He has given me the Spirit of His Son—the Spirit of adoption—which is the surest mark of His child: the witness, pledge, and earnest of our inheritance; the name and mark of God upon me, holiness to the Lord. And yet shall I not believe His love and trust Him?

He has made me a member of His Son and already united me to Him. Will He not care for the members of His Son? Will He lose those given to Him? Is Christ not to be trusted with His members?

I am His interest, and the interest of His Son — freely beloved, dearly bought. For whom so much is suffered and done, that He is pleased to call us His peculiar treasure. May I not trust Him with His dear-bought treasure?

He has established me in relationship with the angels, who rejoice when a sinner repents, and with the heavenly company, which will not lose the least part. Angels will not lose their joy, nor their ministry.

He is in covenant with me — the Father, Son, and Holy Spirit. He has given me exceedingly great and precious promises; shall I fear that He will break His word or covenant?

My Savior is the Forerunner, who has entered into the Holiest, appearing and interceding for me. This followed His conquest of death, His resurrection to assure me of a future life, and His ascension into heaven to show us where we must ascend. And that after these comforting words, "say to them, 'I am ascending to My Father and your Father, and to My God and your God.'" (John 20:17.) Shall I not follow Him through death and trust such a Guide and Captain of my salvation?

He is there preparing a place for me and will receive me to Himself. May I not confidently expect it?

He told a criminal on the cross that he would be with Him that day in Paradise, thus assuring believing sinners of what they may expect.

The church, by the article of His descent into hell, has signified the common belief that His separated soul continued to exist and to act, and did not sleep or perish—an affirmation of the immortality of separated souls.

His apostles and other servants have served Him on earth with all these expectations.

The spirits of the perfected just now possess what I hope for. I follow those who, through faith and patience, inherit the promises. May I not trust Him to save me who has already saved multitudes in this way? Just as I would trust a ferryman to carry me across a river because he has safely ferried thousands before me, so would I trust a physician who cures all whom he undertakes with the same disease.

I must be at His disposal whether I will or not. I shall live while He wills, die when He wills, and go where He wills. I may sin and torment my soul with fears, cares, and sorrows, but I shall never prevail against His will.

Therefore there is no rest for souls except in the will of God. That will created us, governs us, and will be fulfilled in us. It was our efficient and governing cause, and it shall be our end. Where else should we find rest—in the will of men, angels, or our own wills? All creatures are but creatures, and our own wills have undone us. They have misruled us and are our greatest enemies—our disease, our prison, and our death—until they are brought into conformity with the will of God. Until then they are like a limb out of joint; like a child or subject in rebellion. There is no righteousness or health, no order, no peace, no true happiness, but in the conformity of our wills to God's. Shall I die in distrustful striving against His will, desiring to maintain my own?

What abundant experience have I had of God's fidelity and love? After all this, shall I not trust Him? His undeserved mercy gave me existence. It chose my parents and instilled in them a tender love for me and a desire for my well-being. It taught them to instruct me early in His

Word and to raise me in His fear. It provided me with suitable company and a good home. It gave me a teachable mind; it selected my teachers; it brought many excellent and appropriate books into my hands; it provided me with some beneficial public instructors; it placed me in the best land on earth, and, I believe, in the best age that land has seen.

It early destroyed all great expectations and desires of the world, teaching me to bear the yoke from my youth. It made me groan under my infirmities rather than fight against strong and powerful lusts. It chastened me early but did not destroy me. Great mercy has trained me all my days, since I was nineteen, in the school of affliction. It kept my sluggish soul awake in the constant expectation of my change, killed my pride and overvaluation of this world, and directed all my studies toward the most necessary things. It served as a spur to excite my soul to seriousness and saved me from careless neglect and the loss of time.

Oh, what unspeakable mercy a life of constant but gentle chastisement has shown me! It urged me, against all dull delay, to make my calling and election sure and to prepare my accounts as one who must quickly give them up to God. The face of death and the nearness of eternity convinced me what books to read, what studies to prefer and pursue, and what company and conversation to choose. It drove me early into the Lord's vineyard and taught me to preach as a dying man to dying men.

Divine love and mercy made sacred truth so pleasant to me that my life has been—despite all my infirmities—almost a continual delight in its discovery, contemplation, and practical use. How happy a teacher I have had! What excellent help and sweet illumination! How far beyond my expectations has divine mercy encouraged me in His sacred work! How fittingly has He chosen every place of my ministry and habitation to this day, without my foresight or seeking!

When, and where, since He first sent me, did I labor in vain? How many have gone to heaven, and how many are on the way, to whom He has blessed the word I delivered in weakness, by His grace and providence! Many good Christians are glad to have an hour now and then to meditate on God's Word and engage in His holy worship; yet God has allowed and called me to make that the constant business of my life. My library has provided both profitable and pleasant company and help at all times whenever I used it.

I have dwelt among the shining lights that learned, wise, and holy men of all ages have set up and left to illuminate the world. How many comfortable hours have I spent in the society of living saints and in the love of faithful friends! How many joyful days have I spent in solemn assemblies, where God has been worshipped in seriousness and joy by united (though imperfect) saints! There the Spirit of Christ has manifested His presence — helping me and my brethren in speaking, the people in ready, delightful hearing, and all of us in gladly receiving His doctrine, covenant, and laws.

How unworthy was such a sinful worm as I — who never had much academic help, nor much from the mouth of any teacher — that books should become so great a blessing to me; and that, beyond my own intentions, God should incline me to provide similar helps for others! How unworthy was I to be kept from the multiplied snares of sects and errors that reigned in this age, to be used as a means for the preservation and restoration of others, and to be kept in a love of unity and peace.

How unworthy was I that God should make known to me so much of His reconciling truth, while extremes prevailed all around and were commended to the churches by the advantages of piety on one side and of worldly prosperity and power on the other. And that God should use me for over forty years in so comforting a work — pleading and writing for love, peace, and concord—and grant me so much success therein, despite the general prevalence of the contentious military tribe.

Mercy I have had in peace, and liberty in times of violence; mercy I have had in wars. I lived two years in safety in the city of defense, in the very midst of the land (Coventry), and saw no enemy while the kingdom was in wars and flames—only hearing of the common calamities around. When I went abroad and saw the effects of human folly and fury, and of God's displeasure, He mercifully kept me from harming anyone and from being harmed by anyone. How many times has He preserved me by day and night, in difficulties and dangers, from the malice of Satan, from the wrath of man, and from accidents that threatened sudden death!

While I beheld the ruins of towns and countries, and fields covered with the carcasses of the slain, I was preserved and returned home in peace. Oh, how great was the mercy He showed me in a teachable, tractable, peaceable, humble, and united people! So many in number, and so exemplary in quality, who to this day maintain their integrity and unity, even though violence has separated me from them for over thirty years.

Yes, the same mercy of acceptance and success beyond my expectations He has shown me everywhere. I have had opportunities for free ministry; even where there were many adversaries, I have had an open door. In the midst of human wrath and rage, He has preserved my liberty beyond expectation and continued my acceptance and success. When I could not speak by voice to any single congregation, He enabled me to speak by writing to many. For the success of my plainest and most popular writings—which cost me the least—I can never be sufficiently thankful. Some of these He sent to preach abroad, in other languages, in foreign lands.

When my mouth, along with eighteen hundred or two thousand others, had been silenced for many years, He has since opened them to some degree; and the sufferings intended for us by men have been partly prevented and partly much alleviated by His providence. The hardness of our terms has not hindered the success of faithful labors as much as we feared, nor as others hoped it would. I have had the comfort of seeing some peace and concord, and the prosperity of truth and piety maintained under the utmost opposition of diabolical and human power, policy, and wrath.

When I was sent to the common jail for my service and obedience to Him, He kept me in peace there and soon delivered me. He made the mouths of my greatest enemies—those who plotted my defamation and ruin—become my witnesses and defenders, contradicting their own designs. How wonderful that I should dwell in so much peace for so long, amid those who seemed to lack neither power nor skill, nor will, to trample me down into contempt and misery!

Oh, how many dangers, fears, and pains has He delivered this frail and languishing body from! How often has He helped me when flesh, heart, and skill have failed! He has cured my consuming coughs and many times stopped my bleeding; He has eased my painful limbs and supported a weary, worn-out body. He has lifted me from the jaws of death and reversed the sentence that men had passed on me.

How many thousands of weary days have been sweetened by His pleasant work; and how many thousands of painful, weary nights have been followed by a comforting morning! How many thousands of strong and healthy persons have been taken away by death, while I have been upheld under all this weakness! Many times have I cried to the Lord in my trouble, and He has delivered me from my distress. I have had fifty years added to my days—since I would have gladly accepted Hezekiah's promise of fifteen years.

Since the day I first preached His gospel, I did not expect to live more than a year; yet I have lived for fifty years since then. When my own prayers were cold and lacked faith, how many hundreds have prayed for me! And what strange deliverances, encouraging fasting and prayer, have I often experienced upon their earnest requests! My friends have been faithful, and the few who proved unfaithful profitably taught me not to place confidence in man or be overly attached to anything on earth; for I was forsaken by none of them except those few whom I excessively valued and loved.

My relations have been a comfort to me, contrary to my deserts and far beyond my expectations. My servants have been faithful; my neighbors kind; my enemies powerless, harmless, or even beneficial. My superiors have honored me with respectful words; and though they have afflicted me, thinking me an obstacle to their designs, they have not destroyed me but protected me. To my inferiors, God has made me, in my low capacity, somewhat helpful.

I was protected in ordinary health and safety when the raging pestilence came near my home and consumed a hundred thousand citizens. My dwelling was safe while I saw the glory of the land in flames and afterward witnessed the dismal ruins. When violence separated me from my beloved library and forced me into a poor, smoky house, I never had more help from God, nor did more difficult work than there. What pleasant retreats and quietness in the country have been the fruits of persecuting wrath!

And I must not forget, when I had greater public liberty, how He delivered me and all my hearers — once even by a miracle — from being buried beneath the ruins of the building where we met. He preserved others from the calamities, scandal, and lamentations that would otherwise have followed.

It is no small mercy that, though the tongues and pens of all sorts of sects, proud self-exalters, and even some worthy but differing brethren have long and vehemently conspired against me; though my infamy has been pursued in abundance of volumes, by the backbiting of angry divisive men, and by calumnious accusations from those too high to be contradicted—who would not allow me to answer or defend my innocence—all these together have never been able to fasten their charges, procure general belief, or bring me under the intended contempt. Much less have they been able to break my comforts, encouragements, or labors.

All these things, and many more besides, are my experiences of that wondrous mercy which has measured my pilgrimage and filled my days. God never broke His promise with me; He never failed me or forsook me. Had I not provoked Him by rash and willful sin, how little interruption of my peace and comforts would I have likely suffered!

And shall I now distrust Him at the end? Shall I not trust—quietly and confidently—that infinite wisdom, love, and power whom I have so long trusted and found so good?

Nature teaches man to love most those creatures that are tame and tractable—those that trust us and show affection, that come to our hands and enjoy our company, that will be familiar with us and follow us, whether horse or dog, beasts or birds. Those that are wild, that live in the woods and flee from man, are taken as game and prey by anyone who can catch and kill them.

And shall my foolish soul thus wildly flee from the face of God? Shall His children be like the fearful hare, like a guilty Cain, or like an unbelieving Sadducee who either believes not, or hopes not for, the forgiveness of sin and the life everlasting? Does not the spirit of adoption incline us to love our Father's presence and make us loath to be long from home?

To distrust all creatures, even yourself, is not unreasonable; but to distrust God has no just excuse. Flee from sin, from Satan, from temptations, from the world, from sinful flesh and idol self; but do not flee from Him who is goodness, love, and joy itself. Fear your enemy, but trust your Father.

If your heart is reconciled to Him and His service by the Spirit, He is certainly reconciled to you through Christ. If He is for you, and justifies and loves you, who shall be against you, who shall condemn you, or who shall separate you from the love of Christ? If your unreconciled will makes you doubt His reconciliation, it is time to abhor and lay aside your enmity. Consent, and be sure that He consents. Be willing to be His, to serve Him in holiness, and to be united in joyful glory to Him; then be sure that He is willing to accept you and receive you to that glory.

O dark and sinful soul! How little do you know your friend, yourself, or God, if you can more easily and quietly trust your life, your soul, and your hopes to the will of a fellow man, or to your own will if you had the power, than to the will of God. Every dog would be at home with his master; much more every genuine child with his father. And though enemies distrust us, wives and children will not, while they believe us just. And has God ever shown Himself unfaithful or unmerciful to me?

I commit my soul to You, O Lord, as to a faithful Creator (1 Pet. 4:19). I know that the Lord your God is the faithful God who keeps covenant and mercy for a thousand generations with those who love Him and keep His commandments (Deut. 7:9). You are faithful, who have called me into the fellowship of Your Son, Jesus Christ our Lord (1 Cor. 1:9). Your faithfulness has upheld me in temptation (1 Cor. 10:13); it has established me and guarded me from the evil one (2 Thess. 3:3); and it will preserve my whole spirit, soul, and body blameless at the coming of our Lord Jesus Christ (1 Thess. 5:23–24). I know, O Lord, that Your judgments are right, and that in faithfulness You have afflicted me (Ps. 119:75). And shall I not trust You, then, to save me?

It is a faithful saying: For if we died with Him, we shall also live with Him. If we endure, we shall also reign with Him. (2 Tim. 2:11-12.) To You, O my Savior, I commit my soul: it is Yours by redemption; it is Yours by covenant; it is marked and sealed by Your Spirit as Yours, and You have promised not to lose it. This is the will of the Father who sent Me, that of all He has given Me I should lose nothing, but should raise it up at the last day. (John 6:39.) Therefore, in all things He had to be made like His brethren, that He might be a merciful and faithful High Priest in things pertaining to God, to make propitiation for the sins of the people. (Heb. 2:17.)

By Your blood we have boldness to enter the Holiest by a new and living way which You consecrated. Cause me to draw near with a sincere heart, in full assurance of faith, by You who are the High Priest over the house of God; for He is faithful who has promised life through You (Heb. 10:20-23). Your name is Faithful and True (Rev. 19:11), and all Your promises are faithful and true (Rev. 22:6; 21:5). You have promised rest to weary souls that come to You (Matt. 11:28; 2 Thess. 1:7). I am weary of suffering and weary of sin; weary of my flesh, and weary of my darkness, dullness, and distance, and of this wicked, blind, unrighteous, and confounded world. Where should I look for rest but home to my heavenly Father and to You?

I am a bruised reed, yet You will not break me; I am a smoking flax, yet You will not quench what Your grace has kindled. You, in whose name the nations trust, will bring forth judgment to victory (Matt. 12:20-21). The Lord redeems the souls of His servants, and none of those who trust in Him shall be condemned (Psalm 34:22). Therefore I will wait on Your name, for it is good, and will trust in the mercy of God forever (Psalm 52:8-9). The Lord is good, a stronghold in the day of trouble; He knows those who trust in Him (Nahum 1:7).

Sinful fear is a snare; but he who puts his trust in the Lord shall be safe (Prov. 29:25). Blessed is the man who makes the Lord his trust, and does not respect the proud nor those who turn aside to lies (Psalm 40:4). You are my hope, O Lord God; You are my trust from my youth. You have upheld me from the womb, and my praise shall be continually of You. Do not cast me off now in the time of old age; do not forsake me when my strength fails. O God, You have taught me from my youth, and hitherto I have declared Your wondrous works. Now also, when I am old and gray, O God, forsake me not (Psalm 71:5-9, 17-18). Do not leave me destitute; my eyes are toward You, and my trust is in You (Psalm 141:8).

I would have fainted unless I had believed that I would see the goodness of the Lord in the land of the living. The sun may cease to shine on man, and the earth may cease to bear us; but God will never cease to be love, nor to be faithful in His promises.

Blessed be the Lord who has given me this safe and comforting duty: to trust Him and cast all my cares on Him, as on One who has promised to care for me.

And blessed be God who has made it my duty to hope for His salvation. Hope is the ease and the life of our hearts; without it they would break and die within us. Despair is no small part of hell. God cherishes hope because He is the lover of souls.

Satan, our enemy, fosters despair when his road of blind presumption fails. Just as fear gives a foretaste of evil before the evil is felt, so hope anticipates and forefeels salvation before it is possessed.

It is the hope of worldly hypocrites that perishes; anyone who looks for true or lasting happiness only in the pleasures of this perishing flesh is bound to be deceived. But happy is he who has the God of Jacob for his help, whose hope is in the Lord his God, who made heaven and earth, who keeps truth forever (Psalm 146:5-6). Woe to me if my hope were only in this life (1 Cor. 15:19); yet the righteous has hope even in his death (Prov. 14:32). Hope does not disappoint, for the love of God has been poured out in our hearts by the Holy Spirit (Rom. 5:5). Blessed is the man who trusts in the Lord, and whose hope is the Lord (Jer. 17:7).

Lay hold then, O my soul, upon the hope set before you (Heb. 6:18). It is your firm and steadfast anchor (ver. 19); without it you will be like a shipwrecked vessel. Your foundation is sure: it is God Himself. Our faith and hope are both in God (1 Pet. 1:21).

It is Jesus our Lord, risen from the dead and reigning in glory, who is our hope of glory (1 Tim. 1:1; Eph. 3:17; Col. 1:27). In this hope, which is better than the law Moses gave, we draw near to God (Heb. 7:19). The Holy Spirit is both our evidence and the source of our hope (Gal. 5:5; Rom. 8:16, 23). By Him we hope for what we do not see, and therefore wait patiently for it (Rom. 8:24-25). By hope we are saved.

Hope is an encouraging grace that stirs us when despair would kill our efforts. It cures sloth and makes us diligent and constant to the end, helping us to full assurance (Heb. 6:11-12). It is a desiring grace that longs to obtain the glory hoped for, and a quieting, comforting grace (Rom. 15:4). The God of hope fills us with all joy and peace in believing, so that we may abound in hope by the power of the Holy Spirit (Rom. 15:13).

Shake off despondency, O my soul, and rejoice in the hope of the glory of God (Rom. 5:2). Believe in hope, even when dying flesh tells you it is contrary to hope (Rom. 4:18). God, who cannot lie, has confirmed His covenant by an immutable oath, that we who have fled to the hope set before us might have strong consolation (Heb. 6:18). What blessed preparations are made for our hope — shall we let the tempter shake or discourage it?

The abundant mercy of God the Father has begotten us again to a living hope through the resurrection of Jesus Christ, to an inheritance incorruptible, undefiled, and that does not fade away, reserved in heaven for us (1 Pet. 1:3). Grace teaches us to deny ungodliness and worldly lusts, and to live soberly, righteously, and godly in this present age as we look for that blessed hope and the glorious appearing of our great God and Savior (Tit. 2:12-13). We are renewed by the Holy Spirit and justified by grace so that we may be made heirs according to the hope of eternal life (Tit. 3:6-7).

We are enlightened to know the hope of His calling and the riches of the glory of His inheritance in the saints (Eph. 1:18-19). The hope laid up for us in heaven is the chief doctrine of the gospel, which brings life and immortality into clearer light (Col. 1:5; 2 Tim. 1:10). For this hope we keep a conscience void of offense and serve God in the world (Acts 24:15-16; 26:7). Therefore gird up the loins of your mind and put on the helmet—the hope of salvation (1 Thess. 5:8). Let not death seem to you as it does to those who have no hope (1 Thess. 4:13).

The love of our Father and our Savior has given us everlasting consolation and good hope through grace to comfort our hearts and establish them in every good word and work (2 Thess. 2:16-17). Keep the rejoicing of hope firm to the end (Heb. 3:6). Continue grounded and steadfast in the faith, and do not be moved away from the hope of the gospel (Col. 1:23; 1 Pet. 1:13).

And now, Lord, what do I wait for? My hope is in You (Psalm 39:7). Uphold me according to Your word, that I may live; let me not be ashamed of my hope (Psalm 119:116). Though my iniquities testify against me, yet, O You who are the Hope of Israel, the Savior in the time of trouble, be not as a stranger to my soul (Jer. 14:7-9). Your name is called upon by me; O forsake me not!

Why have our eyes beheld Your wonders, and why have we had Your covenant and mercies, but that we might set our hope in God? Remember the word to Your servant upon which You have caused me to hope (Psalm 78:5, 7; Psalm 119:49). If You, Lord, should mark iniquities, who could stand? But there is forgiveness with You, that You may be feared. I wait for the Lord; my soul waits, and in His word I do hope. I will hope in the Lord, for with Him there is mercy and abundant redemption (Psalm 130:3-5, 7). He takes pleasure in those who fear Him, in those who hope in His mercy (Psalm 147:11).

Though flesh and heart fail, the Lord is the strength of my heart and my portion forever; "The Lord is my portion," says my soul, "Therefore I hope in Him!" The Lord is good to those who wait for Him, to the soul who seeks Him. It is good to hope and quietly wait for the salvation of the Lord. It was good for me to bear the yoke in my youth, to keep silence and put my mouth in the dust, if perhaps there might be hope (Psalm 73:26; Lam. 3:24-27, 29).

God does not flatter such worms as we are, nor promise what He never intends to perform. He has laid the foundations of our hope in a nature capable of desiring, seeking, and thinking of another life. He has called me by grace to actual desires and endeavors, and has granted some foretaste. I look for no heaven but the perfection of divine life, light, and love in endless glory with Christ and His holy ones. He has begun this in me already; shall I not boldly hope when I have the capacity, the promise, and the earnest and foretaste? Is it not God Himself who has caused me to hope? Were not nature, promise, and grace from Him? Can a soul miscarry and be deceived that departs this life in a hope God Himself has caused and encouraged?

Love is the perfection of all your preparations. It desires to please God and therefore seeks the most pleasing state, free from all that is displeasing to Him—something not entirely possible on earth. Love longs for nearness, acquaintance, union, and communion. It grows weary of distance, estrangement, and alien affairs. It seizes every notice, intimation, or mention of God to renew and exercise these desires. Every message and mercy from Him fuels love and, while we remain imperfect, stirs up our longing for more.

When love tastes the sweetness of the grapes, it yearns for the vine. When it savors the fruits, it longs to dwell where they grow and possess the land. Thoughts of closeness and fulfillment are sweet; no other person or thing can satisfy them. The soul resides where it loves. If a friend dwells in our hearts through love, and if fleshly pleasure, riches, and honor dwell in the hearts of the indulgent, the greedy, and the proud, then surely God—our Redeemer—the heavenly society, holiness, and glory dwell in the heart that loves them fervently.

If heaven dwells in my heart, should I not desire to dwell in heaven? Light with light, fire with fire, are not more inclined to union than love with love—gracious love and glorious love. If divine, original, universal love were to pour itself more abundantly into my heart, how easy it would be to leave this flesh and this world and to hear the sentence of my departure to my God! Death and the grave would be a triumph for victorious love. It would be easier to die in peace and joy than to rest at night, to return home from travels to beloved friends, or to go, when hungry, to a feast.

A little love has made me study willingly, preach willingly, and write willingly; would it not compel me to go more willingly to God? Shall the imagination of houses, gardens, walks, libraries, views, meadows, orchards, hills, and rivers entice the desires of deceived minds? And shall not thoughts of heavenly mansions, society, and delights allure and elevate my desires even more?

The reading of a known fiction—such as a City of God, an Utopia, or an Atlantis—has pleased many. But if I were to hear of a place in the world where men never die, never suffer sickness, weakness, or sadness; where the prince is perfectly just, pious, wise, and peaceable, devoted to God and the public good; where the teachers are all wise, judicious, and universally knowledgeable, all of one mind, heart, tongue, and practice; where they love each other and the people as themselves, leading the flocks heavenward through all temptations with triumphant hopes and joy; where all the people perfectly obey God, their leaders, and their teachers, living in perfect love, unity, and peace, engaged daily in joyful praises of God and hopes of glory, doing all possible good to one another, contending with none through ignorance, uncharitableness, or pride, nor ever reproaching, injuring, or hurting one another — if I knew or heard of such a country, should I not love it before I ever see it and earnestly desire to be there?

Nay, do I not over-love this distracted world, where tyranny sheds streams of blood, lays waste to cities and countries, and exposes inhabitants to lamentable distress and famine? Where tyranny elevates the wicked, reproaches and oppresses the just, hinders the gospel, and sustains idolatry, infidelity, and wickedness across the earth? Where Satan often chooses pastors for the churches of Christ — those who, through ignorance, pride, sensuality, worldliness, and malignity, become thorns and thistles, devouring wolves to those they should feed and comfort? Where no two people are of one mind in all things; where evil is commended and truth and goodness are accused and oppressed because people are unacquainted with them or unsuitable to them; where the greatest pretenders to truth most eagerly contend against it — almost all the world is scolding or scuffling in the dark, with little hope for remedy.

Can I love such a world as this? Should I not think more delightfully of the inheritance of the saints in light, the uniting love and joyful praises of the church triumphant, and the heavenly choir?

Should I not love a beautiful and loving world far more than one with comparatively little beauty or love? All that comes from God is good and lovely, yet His glory does not shine here in full measure. I am taught to look upward when I pray, saying, "Our Father in heaven." God's works are admirable, even in hell; yet, though I would know them, I would not want to be there.

Alas, much of what man does is mixed with the works of God. Here is God's wisdom manifest, but here is also man's stubborn folly. Here is God's governance, but here is man's tyranny and disorder. Here is God's love and mercy, but here are men's malice, wrath, and cruelty — worse to one another than wolves and tigers, depopulating countries and filling the world with bloodshed, famine, misery, and lamentation. Proud tyrants are worse than raging plagues; they make men choose calamity rather than pursue their enemies, as David did when he chose the pestilence over pursuit.

Here is much of God's beautiful order and harmony, but also much of man's madness, deformity, and confusion. There is historical truth and some civil and ecclesiastical justice; but, alas, how much odious falsehood and injustice is mixed in. There is much precious theological truth, yet much of it remains dark to blind, negligent, and corrupted minds that abound everywhere.

Wise and judicious teachers and companions can be found; but, alas, how few they are compared to the many, and how hard to recognize by those who most need them. There are sound and orthodox ministers of Christ; yet how few who most need them know who they are, how to value them, or how to use them. How many thousands of seduced or sensual sinners are led to believe that they are only deceivers, or, as some called Paul, pestilent fellows and instigators of sedition among the people?

In many parts of the world they are like the prophets whom Obadiah hid in caves, or like Micaiah or Elijah among the lying prophets and followers of Baal. Though they are those of whom the world is not worthy, is that world then more deserving of our love than heaven? There are worthy and religious families that honor God and are honored by Him; but, alas, how few. Usually, through the temptations of wealth and worldly interests, such families become filled with the sins of Sodom—pride, excess, and idleness—and often unmercifulness to the poor.

How are they tempted to justify their sins and snares by calling opposing views rustic ignorance? How few pious families of the higher sort do not quickly degenerate in posterity through false religion, error, or sensuality, growing contrary to the minds of their devout ancestors. Many educate their children wisely in the fear of God and find comfort in them; but how many, having devoted them in baptism to God, train them up in the service of the flesh, the world, and the devil—which they themselves renounced?

They never understood, or at least never intended for themselves or their children, what they professed. How many parents think that when they offer their children to God in baptism, without sober and due consideration of the nature and meaning of that great covenant, God must accept them and certainly regenerate and save them? Too many religious parents forget that they themselves are sponsors in that covenant and are bound to use the means on their part to make their children fit for the grace of the Son and the communion of the Spirit as they grow.

They suppose God should absolutely sanctify, keep, and save their children simply because they are His and were baptized, though they do not protect them from great and unnecessary temptations, nor teach them plainly and seriously the meaning of the covenant made for them—its nature, benefits, or conditions. How many send their children to others to be instructed in grammar, logic, philosophy, the arts, or even divinity before the parents themselves have taught what they did with God in baptism, what they received, and what they promised and vowed to do?

They send their children into trades or secular callings, or send them to travel in foreign lands among a multitude of snares: tempting company, alluring baits, and dangerous business. They do this before the children have been instructed, armed, and grounded at home against the temptations they will face.

Too often, if the children are not prepared at home, they are undone by what they encounter. Yet when parents have first neglected this great duty of fortifying them, they will plead some necessity for thrusting them, utterly unarmed, into temptation — for trivial reasons of honor or conformity to the world. They fear the contempt of worldly men, or they hope to adorn their still-naked souls with a few plumes or painted trifles, ceremonies, or compliments. Those things will never serve in place of heavenly wisdom, mortification, and the love of God and neighbor.

As if a child were likely to learn the fear of God in a crowd of distracting, tempting company, baits, and bustling business — when they never learned it under the nurture, teaching, and daily oversight of their religious parents in a safer environment!

As if it were better to send them to sea without a pilot or anchor and presume God must save them from the waves. As if it were wiser to place them in Satan's school or army and risk their damnation rather than forgo preferment, wealth, fashions, or the favor of the times.

Then, when parents hear that their children have forsaken God and true religion — given themselves to lust and sensuality, and perhaps, as enemies of God and good men, have destroyed what their parents labored to build up — they wonder at God's judgments and lament their misfortune with broken hearts.

They would do better to lament their own neglect. Best of all would have been to lament it earlier and to have acted.

Thus families, churches, and kingdoms fall into blindness, ungodliness, and confusion. Self-undoing and serving the malice of Satan for fleshly lust is the common employment of mankind. What is truly wise, good, and sweet—what God prescribes in nature or by supernatural revelation—is rejected. Instead, folly, sin, and misery are mistaken for wit, honesty, and prosperity.

Most people rage against that which they nominally pretend to and profess. When we try to deliver them from their deceit and misery, it is well if we are not tempted to imitate them, partly infected by their disease, or at least reproached and oppressed as their enemies. Much of the world has become a Bedlam, where madness passes for wisdom. The bravest man is he who can sin and be damned with reputation and renown, and who can lead the greatest number with him to hell. The world resembles that state well: it has forsaken God and is, in turn, largely forsaken by Him.

This world competes with the spiritual, blessed world for my love. I have known much of God's mercies and comforts here, but their sweetness has only given me a taste of divine love and a longing for heavenly perfection.

What, then, was the purpose of all the good I have seen, of all God has done for my soul and body, if not to teach me to love Him and to desire still more? How many experiences of weaning have I had? How often have I held bitter or contemptuous thoughts about the glory and pleasures of this world? How many tokens of God's love have called me to believe and to taste His goodness?

Wherever I go and whatever direction I look, I see vanity and vexation written upon all things in this world, as far as they compete with God and seek to be the end and portion of a fleshly mind.

At the same time I see "Holiness to the Lord" inscribed upon whatever declares God and leads me to Him as my ultimate end. God has not engaged me in a war against this world for nothing, nor commanded me to treat it as an enemy without reason. The emptiness, danger, and bitterness of the world—contrasted with the all-sufficiency, trustworthiness, and goodness of God—have been the substance of my life's experience.

Shall a worldly, backward heart overcome the teachings of nature, Scripture, the Spirit of grace, and all my experience? Far be it from me.

But, O my God, love is Your great and special gift; all good comes from You. Love is the godlike nature, life, and image. It is given to us from the love of the Father, the grace of the Son, and the quickening, illuminating, and sanctifying work of the Holy Spirit.

What can the earth return to the sun but its own reflected beams? Just as man is a medium in generation and nature, so whatever part man has in the mediate work of believing and repenting—though not without Your Spirit and grace—must be accomplished by the blessed Regenerator. He makes us new creatures by imparting this divine nature: holy love, the soul's holy appetite and drive.

Come down, Lord, into this heart, for it cannot rise to You. Can the plants that need life, or the eye that needs light, ascend to the sun? Dwell in me by the Spirit of love, and I shall dwell in love with You.

Reason is weak and thoughts are unstable; without love to guide the soul, a person will be slippery and uncertain. By Your grace I feel that I love Your Word, I love Your image, I love Your work, and how heartily I love to love You and long to know and love You more! If all things are from You, through You, and to You, then my love for the beams of Your glory here on earth is especially so. It is You, Lord, that it means; to You it looks; it serves You; it mourns, seeks, and groans for You; in You it trusts. The hope, peace, and comfort that sustain me are in You.

When I was a returning prodigal in rags, You saw me afar off and met me with embracing, feasting love. Shall I doubt that He who has clothed me and dwells within me will entertain me with a greater feast of love in the heavenly mansions — the world of love?

The suitability of things below to my fleshly nature has held my affections too much to the earth. Should not the suitability of things above to my spiritual nature draw my love far more to heaven?

There is the God whom I have sought and served. He is present here, veiled and little known; there He shines to heavenly spirits in full glory. There is the Savior in whom I have believed. He walked in flesh on earth, clothed in meanness and humbled to a life and death that were a stumbling block to the Jews and a reproach to the Gentiles. But now He shines and reigns in glory, above the malice and contempt of sinners. I shall live there because He lives; and in His light I shall have light.

He loved me here with redeeming, regenerating, and preserving love; there He will love me with perfecting, glorifying, joyful love. Here I had some rays of heavenly light, but interpositions caused eclipses and long winter nights.

There I shall dwell in the city of the sun — the city of God, the heavenly Jerusalem — where there is no night, eclipse, or darkness. There are the heavenly hosts whose holy love and joyful praises I would gladly share. I have felt some of their loving assistance here, though unseen because above our fleshly mode of converse. There I shall be with them, of the same nature, in the same sphere, and part of the same triumphant church and choir.

There are perfected souls gathered home to Christ. They are not, as here, striving like Esau and Jacob in the womb; nor like John who leaped in the womb at his mother's joy; nor like wrangling children scarcely kept in the same house in peace. They are not like Abraham's or Lot's servants, nor like Paul and Barnabas, Luther and Carolostadius, or Ridley and Hooper—nor like the many striving parties among us.

They are not like the disciples contending who should be greatest; not like Noah's family in a wicked world, nor Lot in a wicked city, nor Abraham in an idolatrous land. They are not like Elijah left alone; nor like those who wandered in sheepskins and goatskins, destitute, afflicted, and tormented—hid in dens and caves of the earth; nor like Job on the dunghill, nor Lazarus at the rich man's door.

They are not like the African bishops whose tongues were cut out, nor like the preachers silenced by Popish imposers; not like Tzegedine, Peucer, and many other worthy men whose maturest years were spent in prisons. They are not like we poor bewildered sinners, feeling evil and fearing more—confounded in folly and mad contention. Some hate the only way of peace; others grope for it in the dark, wandering and lost in the clearest light. The illuminated can only pity the blind, but they cannot make them willing to be delivered.

What is heaven to me but God? God—who is life, light, and love—communicates Himself to blessed spirits, perfecting them in the reception, possession, and exercise of life, light, and love forever. These are not accidents but the very essence of God, who is my heaven and all to me.

Should I fear death, which passes me into infinite essential life? Should I fear a dark passage into a world of perfect light? Should I fear to go to love itself? Consider, O my soul, what the sun's quickening light and heat are to this lower, corporeal world. Much more is God — infinite life, light, and love — to the blessed world above.

Does this not lift your desires toward a world of love? There love will be our region, our company, our life — more to us than the air for our breath, more than light for our sight, more than food for our life, more than friends for our solace, and more to us than we are to ourselves. O excellent grace of faith that foresees, and blessed word of faith that foreshows, this world of love!

Shall I fear to enter where there is no wrath, no fear, no strangeness, nor suspicion, nor selfish separation — where love will make every holy spirit as dear and lovely to me as myself, and me to them as lovely as they are, and God to us all more amiable than ourselves and all? There love will have no defects or distances, no dampness or discouragement, no discontinuance or mixed disaffection. As life there will be without death, and light without darkness — a perfect, everlasting day of glory — so will love be without hatred, unkindness, or alloy.

As many coals make one fire, and many candles joined produce one light, so will many living spirits make one life; many illuminated, glorious spirits will make one light and one glory. Many spirits, naturalized into love, will become one perfect love of God and be loved as one by God forever.

For all the body of Christ is one. Even here it is one in initial union of the Spirit and relation to one God, Head, and Life (1 Cor. 12 throughout; Eph. 4:1-17). It shall be presented as beloved and spotless to God when the great marriage day of the Lamb arrives (Eph. 5:24, 25; Rev. 21 and 22).

Had You not given me the life of nature, O Lord, I would not have conceived of a glorious, everlasting life. But if You do not give me the life of grace, I shall have no sufficient, delightful inclination for it. Had You not given me sight and reason — the light of nature — I would not have thought how desirable it is to live in glorious light and vision. But unless You give me the spiritual illumination of a seeing faith, I shall not long for the beatific vision. Had You not given me a will and love, which are part of my very nature, I could not taste how desirable it is to live in a world of universal, perfect, endless love. Yet unless You also shed abroad Your love in my heart by the Spirit of Jesus — the great medium of love — and turn my very inclination into divine and holy love, I shall not long for that world of love.

Desire follows nature. Do not give me only the appearance or outward acts of godliness, or occasional efforts; grant me the true divine nature — holy love — so my soul will run after You and cry out, "How long, O Lord, how long! O come, come quickly; make no delay."

Surely the fear of dying indicates some contrary love that inclines the soul another way; it reveals some shameful unbelief and a great failure to apprehend the attractive glory of the world of love. Otherwise, no frozen person longs for the fire, nor anyone in a dungeon desires light as we should long for heavenly light and love.

God's infinite, essential self-love — by which He is eternally delighted in Himself — is the most amiable object and is heaven itself to saints and angels. Next to that stands His love for all His works, for the world, and for the church in heaven. That love reveals His loveliness even more plainly than His love for any one of us.

Yet due self-love in me is His work and part of His natural image. When this self-love grows excessive through sin — when a contracted, narrow soul withdraws from union and proper love toward fellow creatures and toward God — I must examine God's love for me and let my desires be moved. I am not capable now of ascending above self-interest and self-love as I shall be in the state of glorious union.

I am glad to perceive that others love God, and I love those most whom I find love Him the most. But it is not other men's love for God that will be accepted by Him instead of mine. Nor is it God's love for others (which yet rejoices me) that will satisfy me without His love for me. But when all these are still before me—God's essential self-love and delight, His love for His creatures, especially the glorified, and His love for me, even for me, a vile, unworthy sinner—what then should hinder my ascending love or discourage my desires to be with God?

And do you doubt, can you doubt, O my soul, whether you are going to a God who loves you? If the Jews discerned the great love of Christ for Lazarus by His tears, can you not discern His love for you in His blood? It is not less, but more, obliging and amiable that it was not shed for you alone, but for many. May I not say, as Paul does (Gal. 2:20), "I live by faith in the Son of God, who loved me and gave Himself for me." Yes, it is not so much I that live, as Christ lives in me. Will He forsake the habitation which His love has chosen and which He has so dearly bought? Oh, read often that triumphant chapter, Rom. 8, and conclude, "Who shall separate us from the love of Christ?" If life has not done it, death shall not do it. If leaning on His breast at meat was a token of Christ's special love for John, is not His dwelling in me by my faith and His living in me by His Spirit a sure token of His love for me?

If a dark saying—"If I will that he remain till I come, what is that to you?"—raised a report that the beloved disciple should not die, why should not plain promises assure me that I shall live with Him who loves me forever? Be not so ungrateful, O my soul, as to question, doubtingly, whether your heavenly Father and your Lord love you. Can you forget the sealed testimonies of it? Did I not just repeat so many that should shame my doubts? A multitude of your friends have loved you so entirely that you cannot doubt of it. Did any of them signify their love with the convincing evidence that God has done? Have they done for you what He has done? Are they love itself? Is their love so full, so firm, and so unchangeable as His?

My thoughts of heaven are sweeter because an abundance of my ancient, lovely, and loving holy friends are there; and I am more willing, through death, to follow them. Should I not think of it more joyfully because my God and Father, my Savior, and my Comforter are there? And not alone, but with all the society of love. Was not Lazarus in the bosom of God Himself? Yet it is said that he was in Abraham's bosom, and the promise runs that we shall sit down with Abraham, Isaac, and Jacob in the kingdom of heaven. What makes the society of the saints so sweet is holy love.

It is comforting to read that we are commanded to "You shall love the Lord your God with all your heart, with all your soul, and with all your strength," and that the second is like it: "You shall love your neighbor as yourself." For God's commands proceed from His will, which is His very nature or essence, and they tend to the same end as their objective. Therefore, He who has made love the great command tells us that love is the great conception of His own essence, the spring of that command; and that this commanded, imperfect love tends to perfect, heavenly love, even to our communion with essential, infinite love.

It would be strange if the love and goodness equal to the power that made the world and the wisdom that orders it should be scant and backward to do good, and to be suspected more than the love of friends. The remembrance of the holiness, humility, love, and faithfulness of my dearest friends of every rank, with whom I have conversed on earth in every place where I have lived, is so sweet to me that I am often ready to recreate myself with the naming of such as are now with Christ. But in heaven, they will love me better than they did on earth, and my love for them will be more pleasant. Yet all these sparks are little compared to the sun.

Every place that I have lived in has been a place of divine love, which has set up its obliging monuments. Every year and hour of my life has been a time of love; every friend, every neighbor, and even every enemy have been messengers and instruments of love. Every state and change of my life, notwithstanding my sin, has opened to me treasures and mysteries of love. After such a life of love, shall I doubt whether the same God loves me? Is He the God of the mountains and not of the valleys? Did He love me in my youth and health, and does He not love me in my age, pain, and sickness? Did He love all the faithful better in their life than at their death?

If our hope is not chiefly in this life, neither is our state of love, which is principally the heavenly, endless grace. My groans grieve my friends, but do not diminish their love. Did He love me for my strength? My weakness might be my fear; as those who love for beauty loathe those who are deformed, and those who love for riches despise the poor. But God loved me when I was His enemy, to make me a friend, and when I was bad, to make me better. Whatever He takes pleasure in is His own gift. Who made me to differ? What do I have that I have not received? And God will finish the work, the building, the warfare that is His own.

Oh, the multitude of mercies to my soul and body, in peace and war, in youth and age, to myself and friends — the many great and gracious deliverances that have testified to me the love of God! Have I lived in the experience of it, and shall I die in the doubts of it? Had it been love only for my body, it would have died with me and not accompanied my departing soul.

I am not much in doubt of the truth of my love for Him; though I have not seen Him, I love Him as one sees in a mirror, dimly. I love my brethren whom I have seen, and those most who are most in love with Him. I love His word, and works, and ways, and I would gladly be nearer to Him and love Him more; and I loathe myself for loving Him no better.

Shall Peter say more confidently, "You know that I love You," than "I know that You love me?" Yes, he may; because, though God's love is greater and steadier than ours, our knowledge of His great love is less than His knowledge of our little love. And as we are defective in our own love, so are we in our certainty of its sincerity. Without the knowledge of our love for God, we can never be sure of His special love for us. Yet I am not utterly a stranger to myself; I know for what I have lived and labored in the world, and whom I have desired to please. The God whose I am, and whom I serve, has loved me in my youth, and He will love me in my aged weakness. My flesh and my heart fail; my pains seem grievous to the flesh; but it is love that chooses them, that uses them for my good, that moderates them, and will shortly end them.

Why then should I doubt my Father's love? Shall pain or dying make me doubt? Did God love none from the beginning of the world but Enoch and Elijah? What am I better than my forefathers? What is in me that I should expect exemption from the common lot of mankind? Is not a competent time of great mercy on earth, in order to the unseen felicity, all that the best of men can hope for? O for a clearer, stronger faith, to show me the world that excels this one, more than this excels the womb where I was conceived! Then I should not fear my third birthday, whatever pangs may precede it, nor be unwilling for my change.

The grave, indeed, is a bed that nature abhors; yet there the weary find rest. But souls newly born have a double nature that is immortal and go to the place that is agreeable to their nature, even to the region of spirits and the region of holy love. Even passive matter, which has no other natural motion, has a natural inclination to uniting, aggregative motion. And God makes all natures suitable to their proper ends and uses.

How can it be that a spirit should not incline to be with spirits? Souls that have the divine nature in holy love desire to be with the God of love. Arts, sciences, and tongues do not become a nature to us; otherwise, they would not cease at death. But holy love is our new nature, and therefore does not cease with this bodily life. Shall accidental love make me desire the company of a frail and mutable friend? And shall not this engrafted, inseparable love make me long to be with Christ? Though the love of God for all His creatures will not prove that they are all immortal, nor oblige them to expect another life if they never had the capacity or faculties to expect it, yet His love for those who, in nature and grace, are made capable of it does warrant and oblige them to believe and hope for the full perfection of the work of love.

Some comfort themselves in the love of St. Peter, as having the keys of heaven. How many could I name that are now with Christ, who loved me so faithfully on earth, that were I sure they had the keys and power of heaven, and were not changed in their love, I could entrust my departing soul into their hands and die with joy. Is it not better in the hands of my Redeemer, and the God of love, and Father of spirits? Is any love comparable to His, or any friend so boldly to be trusted? I would consider it ungrateful unkindness in my friend to doubt my love and trustworthiness if I had given him all that he has and maintained him constantly by my kindness. But oh, how odious is sin! By destroying our love for God, it makes us unfit to believe and sweetly perceive His love; and by making us doubt of the love of God and lose the pleasant relish of it, it increases our difficulty of loving Him.

The title that the angel gave to Daniel—"you are greatly beloved"— should be enough to make one joyfully love and trust God, both in life and death. Will Almighty love ever hurt me or forsake me? And do not all saints have that title in their degrees? What else signifies their mark and name, "HOLINESS TO THE LORD"? What is it but our separation to God as His peculiar, beloved people? And how are they separated but by mutual love, and our forsaking all that alienates or is contrary? Let scorners deride us as self-flatterers who believe they are God's darlings; and woe to the hypocrites who believe it on false presumption! Without such belief or grounded hopes, I see not how any man can die in true peace. He who is no otherwise beloved than hypocrites and unbelievers must have his portion with them. He who is no otherwise beloved than as the ungodly, unholy, and unregenerate shall not stand in judgment, nor see God, nor enter into His kingdom. Most upright souls are to blame for groundless doubting of God's love, but not for acknowledging it, rejoicing in it, and, in their doubts, being most solicitous to make it sure.

Love brought me into the world and furnished me with a thousand mercies. Love has provided for me, delivered me, and preserved me until now; and will it not entertain my separated soul? Is God like false or insufficient friends, who forsake us in adversity?

I confess that I have wronged love by sin; by many and great unexcusable sins. But all, save Christ Himself, were sinners whom love purified and received to glory. God, who is rich in mercy, because of His great love with which He loved us, even when we were dead in trespasses, made us alive together with Christ — by grace you have been saved — and raised us up together, and made us sit together in the heavenly places in Christ Jesus (Eph. 2:4-6). O that I could love much, having so much forgiven! The glorified praise Him who loved us and washed us from our sins in His own blood and made us kings and priests to His God and Father (Rev. 1:5-6). Our Father who has loved us gives us consolation and good hope by grace (2 Thess. 2:16).

I know no sin of which I do not repent with self-loathing; and I earnestly beg and labor that none of my sins may be unknown to me. I dare not justify even what is uncertain; though I dare not call all that my sin which siding men of different judgments on each side passionately call so. While both sides do it on contrary accounts, not to go contrary ways is a crime. O that God would bless my accusations to my illumination, that I may not be unknown to myself! Though some think me much better than I am, and others much worse, it most concerns me to know the truth myself. Flattery would be more dangerous to me than false accusations; I may more safely be ignorant of other men's sins than of my own.

"Who can understand his errors? Cleanse me from secret faults. Keep back Your servant also from presumptuous sins; let them not have dominion over me."

I have an advocate with the Father, and Your promise that he who confesses and forsakes his sins shall have mercy.

Some men count as my greatest sins the very things my most serious thoughts judged to be my greatest outward duties. I performed those duties under the greatest difficulty, and they cost me dearly in the flesh. They demanded the largest measure of self-denial and patience from my reluctant mind.

Where I have erred, Lord, make it known to me, so that my confession may prevent others from sinning. Where I have not erred, confirm and accept me in the right.

And seeing an unworthy worm has had so many testimonies of Your tender love, let me not be like those who, when You said, "'I have loved you,' says the Lord. 'Yet you say, "In what way have You loved us?"'" Heaven is not more spangled with stars than Your word and works are with the refulgent signatures of love.

Your well-beloved Son, the Son of Your love, undertaking the office, message, and work of the greatest love, was full of that Spirit which is love. He pours that love into the hearts of Your elect, that the love of the Father, the grace of the Son, and the communion of the Spirit may be their hope and life.

His works, His sufferings, His gifts, as well as His comfortable word, say to His disciples, "As the Father loved Me, I also have loved you; abide in My love." And how, Lord, shall we continue in it but by the thankful belief of Your love and loveliness, desiring still to love You more and, in all things, to know and please Your will, which You know is my soul's desire.

Behold then, O my soul, with what love the Father, Son, and Holy Spirit have loved you, that you should be made and called a son of God, redeemed, regenerate, adopted into that covenant state of grace in which you stand.

"Therefore, having been justified by faith, we have peace with God through our Lord Jesus Christ, through whom also we have access by faith into this grace in which we stand, and rejoice in hope of the glory of God."

He has loved His own to the end, and without end. His gifts and calling are without repentance. When Satan and your flesh would hide God's love, look to Christ. Read the golden words of love in the sacred gospel, peruse your many recorded experiences, and remember the convictions which secret and open mercies have often afforded you.

But especially draw nearer to the Lord of love. Do not be seldom and slight in your contemplations of His love and loveliness. Dwell in the sunshine, and you will know that it is light, warm, and comfortable. Distance and strangeness nourish your doubts; acquaint yourself with Him, and be at peace.

Yet look up, and often and earnestly look up after your ascended, glorified Head, who said, "I am ascending to My Father and your Father, and to My God and your God." Think where and what He is, what He is now doing for all His own, and how humbled, abased, and suffering love is now triumphant—reigning, glorified love; no less in heaven than in all its tender expressions upon earth.

As love is nowhere perfectly believed but in heaven, so I can nowhere so fully discern it as by looking up by faith to my Father and Savior, who is in heaven, and by conversing more believingly with the heavenly society. Had I done this more and better, and as I have persuaded others to do, I would have lived in more convincing delights of God's love. Those delights would have turned the fears of death into more joyful hopes and more earnest desires to be with Christ, in the arms and life of love, which is far better than to be here in a dark, doubting, fearing world.

But O Father of infinite love! Though my arguments are many and strong, my heart is bad, my strength is weakness, and I am insufficient to plead the cause of Your love and loveliness to myself or others. Oh, plead Your own cause—what heart can resist? Let it not be my word only, but Yours, that You love me, even me, a sinner; speak it as Christ said to Lazarus, "Lazarus, come forth!" If not by that, yet as You tell me the sun is warm, and as You have told me that my parents and my dearest friends loved me—much more powerfully than so—tell it to me by the consciousness and works of life. Let the experience "You who know all things, know that I love You" include "therefore I know that I am beloved by You." Then I may come to You in the confidence of Your love, and long to be nearer in the clearer sight, the fuller sense, and the joyful exercise of love forever.

Father, into Your hands I commit my spirit. Lord Jesus, receive my spirit! Amen.

11. Divine Revelation and the Truth of Christianity

"And without controversy great is the mystery of godliness: God was manifested in the flesh, justified in the Spirit, seen by angels, preached among the Gentiles, believed on in the world, received up in glory." (1 Timothy 3:16)

These are the creed, or six articles of the gospel which the apostles preached.

God manifested in the flesh of Jesus is the first and greatest article. Believe this, and you will believe all. It is no wonder that believing Jesus Christ is the Son of God is so often described in Scripture as saving faith, the title to baptism, and the basis for pardon and salvation, as well as the evidence of the Spirit.

He who truly and practically believes that God came in flesh to man, and that Christ is the Father's messenger from heaven, must also believe that God has great value for the souls of men and for His church. He must believe that God does not despise even our flesh, that His word is true and fully to be trusted, and that He who so wonderfully came to man will certainly take man up to Himself.

Who can doubt the immortality of souls, or that Christ will receive the departing souls of the faithful to Himself, who believes that He took on man's nature and has glorified it now in heaven in union with the divine? Who can ever have low thoughts of God's love and mercy who believes this? And who can prostitute his soul and flesh to wickedness, who firmly believes that He took the soul and flesh of man to sanctify and glorify it?

The Holy Spirit is the justification of the truth of Jesus Christ. He is Christ's advocate and witness to the world. He proves the gospel by these five ways of evidence:

1. By all the prophecies, types, and promises of Christ in the Old Testament, before Christ's coming.

2. By the inherent impress of God's image on the person and doctrine of Christ, which, in its own light, shows itself to be divine.

3. By the accompanying miracles of Christ: read the history of the gospel for this purpose, and observe each account.

4. By the subsequent gift of the Spirit to the apostles and other Christians, through tongues, wonders, and multitudes of miracles, to convince the world.

5. By the undeniable and excellent work of sanctification on all true believers throughout the world, in all generations to this day.

These five are the Spirit's witness, which fully testifies to the certain truth that Jesus Christ is the Son of God.

How can we, who have never seen Christ's person, miracles, resurrection, or ascension, be sure that the accounts of these events are true?

We can be sure the original spectators were not deceived.

We can be sure those spectators did not deceive the people to whom they reported.

We can be sure the historical record that has reached us is not corrupted.

Men who were in their right minds, with normal eyes and ears, would not have believed for three and a half years that they saw the lame walk, the blind see, the deaf hear, and every disease healed. Nor would they have believed that the dead were raised and thousands miraculously fed — among crowds that still followed Christ — unless those things were real.

A single person's senses might fail once through some trick, but for multitudes to be mistaken so often, over so many years, in broad daylight, would be the same as saying no one can trust sight or hearing at all.

The disciples who accepted the apostles' and evangelists' report were plainly not misled. They did not rely on hearsay. They heard firsthand from eyewitnesses who knew exactly what they proclaimed. These reports came from men of the same era, land, and language, so anyone could investigate and expose falsehood if it existed.

The apostles appealed to crowds — and to thousands who had seen many of Christ's miracles — people who would have exposed the story if it had been a lie. They openly rebuked the rulers for persecuting Christ, which gave those rulers strong motive to disprove the apostles for their own defense.

Christ chose plain, uneducated men, not masters of rhetoric or trickery, so no one could accuse them of fabricating wonders by clever art.

Before His death He revealed little more to them than the daily facts they witnessed — that He was the Christ and that His moral teaching was true. They knew almost nothing beforehand about His death, resurrection, ascension, or the kingdom of heaven; later experience and the sudden coming of the Spirit taught them the rest.

They did not teach one another by collusion; each was personally taught by God. Yet, scattered throughout the world, they all agreed on the same doctrine and never differed in a single article of faith.

They sought no wealth, power, or earthly status. They renounced every worldly interest and sealed their testimony with suffering and blood, hoping for a heavenly reward they knew lies could never secure. Had they conspired to deceive, the crime was so great that at least one would have recanted — especially when facing death — but none did. They died joyfully, as men convinced of the truth.

Paul, once a persecutor, was converted when a light from heaven shone around him and he heard a voice. Those who journeyed with him saw the light.

Finally, the doctrine they delivered bears a divine stamp, just as light proves itself by shining.

For still firmer conviction, those who testified of Christ's miracles also did similar works themselves to confirm their testimony. They spoke with other tongues; they healed all kinds of sickness and all kinds of disease among the people. Even Peter's shadow and garments from Paul brought healing. They raised the dead. Those who turned whole nations in every place by such works — thereby attesting Christ's miracles and resurrection — must have compelled spectators to believe.

Yet more than all this, those who believed were immediately enabled to perform like acts in one form or another. The same extraordinary gift of the Spirit was received by the common multitude of believers through the laying on of the apostles' hands, so much so that Simon Magus sought to buy that power with money. When men had seen Christ's miracles and then wrought the same themselves, and when converts likewise did the same—whether in healing, speaking with other tongues, prophesying, or some wonder—it was an indisputable testimony.

When heretics quarreled with the apostles and sought to draw disciples away by disparaging them, the apostles still appealed to the miracles performed by their disciples or witnessed by them, as seen in Galatians 3:1-5. When the Jews accused Christ of casting out demons by Beelzebub, He asked them, "By whom do your sons cast them out?" If that accusation had been false, it would have turned all the people against them.

Their adversaries were so far from producing any refutation of their testimony that they confessed the miracles. They had no other recourse but either to blaspheme the Holy Spirit—claiming the miracles were done by the devil—or to resort to persecution and violence to suppress the truth. That supposes the devil could control the world and deceive it contrary to God's will. It would imply God Himself would permit a whole course of miracles to mislead the world, making God akin to the devil. It is as if the devil were so skilled that he could use miracles to promote so holy and just a doctrine as Christianity, which aims to make men wise, good, and just, and to destroy their sin. Thus this blasphemy against the Holy Spirit amounts to making Satan out to be God, or God to be Satan.

All the cruelty, power, learning, and strategy of their adversaries could not halt the progress of this testimony, far less prevail against it.

It is certain that the first witnesses were not deceived by Christ, nor were the believers deceived by them. The next question is whether we ourselves are deceived by a false historical tradition of these events. If we had seen everything ourselves, we would surely believe; but at this distance we cannot know what misreports may have intervened. For them, eyesight and hearing were primary; for us, it is tradition. The question, then, is whether the fact and doctrine they received are certainly the same as what we receive.

Let it be noted that there is no other means of assurance than what God has provided for us, and that is all that reason can rightly desire.

If we demand to see God, heaven, and hell with our own eyes, this is not a suitable requirement for those living in a state of probation on earth. Angels live by vision and the enjoyment of glory; animals live by sense and tangible things; rational beings must live by reason and by believing certain revelations.

If God sends His Son from heaven to assure us, yet we will believe no more than what we ourselves see, then Christ must remain on earth until the end of the world, and be in all places at once so that everyone may see Him. He would have to die and rise again before all men of every age. What an unreasonable expectation!

If every person who delivers the history must perform miracles before our eyes, or else we will not believe, the demand is utterly absurd. Will you not believe that the laws of the land are genuine, or that there ever were kings who made them, unless the teller works miracles? Should children not believe their parents, or students their teachers, unless those adults perform wonders?

I must preface that there are three types of tradition:

1. Those that depend on the common wit and honesty of mankind. This is highly suspect, for wickedness, folly, and lying are common in the world.

2. Those that depend on the extraordinary skill and honesty of some proven individuals. This deserves much belief, though it remains an uncertain human faith.

3. Those that depend on natural necessity and cannot possibly be false. We have both of these last types to assure us of the gospel history.

This rests on a distinction in the acts of man's will. Some acts are freely changeable and give no certainty. Others are naturally and immutably necessary, so that a man cannot act otherwise. These necessary acts provide natural, infallible certainty. Examples include loving oneself, desiring happiness, hating torment and misery, and knowing what is fully manifest to our sound senses.

When persons with opposing interests and temperaments all confess the truth about known matters, their agreement serves as tangible evidence of truth.

For that reason, popular agreement about natural observations carries infallible authority.

It seems strange that, from the time of Adam, the whole world has agreed on which day is first, second, third, and so on, without losing a day up to now. This could not be otherwise. Since the reckoning of days is a matter of shared, natural interest and observation, if any kingdom had lost a day by oversleeping or had conspired to falsify it, the rest of the world would have exposed and shamed them.

Thus Greeks, Latins, Englishmen, and others agree on the meanings of words. If some attempted to distort those meanings, the rest would quickly detect and expose the corruption.

Therefore we can be confident that the laws of the land are genuine. People with conflicting interests depend on those laws for their property and lives; if some had forged them, the others would have been driven by their interests to reveal the falsity.

Argument 1: There can be no effect without an adequate cause. In nature, there is no cause that could make all people agree on a known falsehood or deny a known truth against their own interests. Hence such an effect cannot exist.

Argument 2: A necessary cause will necessarily produce its effect. When people's evident interests compel them to concur about a known truth, that concurrence functions as a necessary cause of credibility, and therefore produces the corresponding effect.

You know who your parents are and when and where you were born by such tradition, albeit in a lesser degree. This knowledge does not rest on supposed authority or mere honesty, but on natural necessity.

Having established this point, I will show that we possess such a tradition of physical, infallible evidence. The faith held by the present church, in its essential matters, is the same faith the first churches received infallibly from the apostles.

The world knows that, ever since Christ's ascension, all who professed belief in Him were baptized, just as Abraham's covenant children were circumcised. Baptism is a profession of belief in Jesus Christ—who is dead, risen, and glorified—and a pledge to enter covenant with God the Father, the Son, and the Holy Spirit. All who have been Christians by solemn vow have professed this same faith. This represents a Christian tradition that has passed down through human generations from Adam, since all share the same humanity.

Those who were baptized were first catechized. During that instruction the three articles associated with baptism—especially Christ's death, resurrection, and ascension—were explained. This has been an undeniable tradition of the same faith.

From the beginning the Christian faith has been summarized in certain articles called the creed, which set forth the three baptismal articles. Churches everywhere have held the same understanding, and most have used similar wording. Those baptized at a proper age professed this creed. Thus there is a continuous tradition of the same belief in Christ's birth, death, resurrection, ascension, and glory—just as speaking is a tradition of our common human nature.

Before His ascension, Christ instituted the office of sacred ministry, an institution acknowledged by both friends and foes to have continued ever since. This ministry is the office dedicated to proclaiming the gospel of Christ—His life, death, miracles, resurrection, grace, and so on. That has been its role in every age, and so it stands as an undeniable tradition.

Christ and His apostles established the weekly remembrance of His resurrection on the Lord's Day. Friends and foes alike acknowledge that the first day of the week has been observed for this memorial ever since, throughout all Christendom. This uninterrupted practice demonstrates the widespread, practical tradition of belief in Christ's resurrection.

Since His resurrection, Christ and His apostles instituted solemn assemblies of Christians to be held on those days and at other times. At least once a week was the minimum throughout the Christian world. What did they gather for, if not to preach, to hear, and to profess the same Christian faith?

Christians consistently sang hymns of praise to Jesus Christ in their assemblies and homes, commemorating His resurrection among other things. Pliny told Trajan that this practice identified Christians to their persecutors; that testimony is a practical tradition.

Jesus Christ instituted the sacrament of His sacrifice, the Eucharist, and Christians have observed it ever since. They celebrate it to remember His death till He comes and to profess their belief that He is our life. Just as the continual celebration of the Passover—with all its ceremonies—kept alive the memory of the Egyptians' plagues and Israel's deliverance more vividly than written history alone, so the Lord's Supper has remained a continuous tradition of belief in our redemption through Christ.

From the beginning the church used firm discipline to keep itself distinct from heretics who denied any essential article of the faith. That discipline serves as a trustworthy witness to a single, unbroken belief.

Christians faced persecution from the start. When compelled to confess their creed before persecutors, both persecutors and confessors alike became witnesses to the same faith.

Whenever opponents wrote against believers, the Christians' replies show that they defended this very faith.

Most heretical groups, though hostile, still conceded the same basic facts.

The Jews long possessed the Old Testament books that foretell Christ. The New Testament books have been handed down to us by an unbroken chain. These books preserve the facts, the teaching, and every essential, integral, and incidental point of the faith.

No enemy has produced any solid writing that refutes those facts. Even Jews and other fierce adversaries concede much concerning Christ's miracles.

Martyrs gladly gave up life and all else to confess this faith.

God's providence has preserved it. The devil and all wicked people stand as its chief foes. Yet the Holy Spirit continues to bless this faith, forming the same holy, heavenly life in every sincere believer.

Tradition clearly proves that the essentials have remained the same. But how do we know the Scriptures themselves remain uncorrupted?

The entire Bible was not copied without minor slips. Scribes alone produced the manuscripts, so some errors inevitably crept in. Hundreds of variant readings exist in the New Testament; many cannot be settled with certainty. None, however, affect any article of faith or practice.

Words matter only as they convey the facts. Several safeguards have preserved them:

Every church and every minister has used the same Scriptures, publicly and privately, as God's Word, which made changes difficult.

All knew God's solemn warning that anyone who adds to or takes from the words of the book will have his part taken away from the Book of Life; this restrained tampering.

They regarded Scripture as the charter of their salvation.

Ministers were charged to expound it and to guard it from corrupters.

Those ministers and churches were spread throughout the world; if some altered the text, others would expose them.

Heresies and disputes soon arose, so rival sides watched one another closely and would expose any corrupter.

A few heretics tried to add to or pervert the text; the church swiftly condemned them and exposed their attempts.

In every debate, both sides appealed to the same Scriptures.

Early translations into many languages present the same books with no serious divergence.

Even today, though sin and tyranny have fractured the church into many factions, all accept the same canonical books. Some groups add the Apocrypha, yet that addition does not change the gospel faith.

Does appealing to tradition bolster Roman Catholic claims?

No. The difference is clear.

Roman Catholics treat tradition as a supplement to Scripture, as though Scripture were only part of God's word, and they claim a special authority to guard and judge that extra tradition.

We rely on the practical, infallible tradition of Christianity's essentials, as expressed in the creed; that tradition is less than Scripture. We also affirm that Scripture itself has been preserved — uncorrupted in every matter on which faith depends. Scripture is the full record of God's will, containing more than the essentials alone.

Angels were the observing and admiring servants of this great mystery:

They announced Christ at His incarnation.

They ministered to Him during temptation, in agony, and through other trials.

They proclaimed and testified that He is risen.

They rolled back the stone and made the guards shake for fear.

They told those who watched that He will come in like manner as they had seen Him go into heaven.

They opened prison doors to free the apostles and later freed Peter alone.

They rejoice in heaven over one sinner who repents.

They gladly guard even the least of Christ's little ones.

They act as guardians over churches and over kingdoms.

They brought messages and conveyed revelations to the apostles.

They have been instruments of miracles and of judgment upon the church's enemies.

They will escort departing souls to Christ.

They will attend Christ when He comes in His glory and help separate the wicked from the righteous.

They will be our companions in heaven's choir forever.

Therefore:

We ought to love the angels.

We must thank God for giving them to us.

We should think more cheerfully about heaven because they are there.

We should pray to receive the benefit of their ministry on earth, especially in times of danger.

The fourth article is "Preached to the Gentiles." The Jews, possessing a covenant of uniqueness, were proud of their privilege and often abused it. They despised the rest of the world and would not even eat with them, as if they alone were God's people. Indeed, the rest of the world was so corrupted that we find no nation, as such, renouncing idolatry and devoting itself in covenant to the true God alone as the Jews did. That God should be manifested in the flesh to reconcile the heathen world to Himself, and to extend greater privileges indefinitely to all nations than the Jews ever had in their state of uniqueness, was a mystery of godliness the Jews found hard to believe.

What makes this wonder more remarkable is that the Gentile world was filled with idolatry and unnatural wickedness, as Paul describes. That God should suddenly and freely send them a message of reconciliation, and be found by those who did not seek Him, is a wonder that obliges us Gentiles — who once lived as if we were without God in the world — to be thankful to Him. (Rom. 1:2; Eph. 2; 3:18, etc.) The fifth article is "Believed on in the world." The effect of the gospel on men's souls, through their genuine faith, is one of the evidences of Christian truth.

I mentioned earlier that the fifth witness of the Spirit in the souls of all believers would be considered here. It is part of the wonder that Christ should be believed on in the world, even by a common faith. To believe that a humble man is the Mediator between God and men and the Savior of the world — yes, one who was crucified as a criminal — is surely a difficult thing.

The Jewish nation was as contemptible to the Romans — one of their poorest, subdued provinces — as the Gentiles were to the Jews. And Christ was, by birth, a Jew.

The greatness of the Roman Empire then, ruling much of the world, was such that bringing its peoples to be subjects of a crucified Jew by preaching, and not by war, was a marvelous work. It was equally remarkable to bring conquered nations to become Christ's voluntary subjects.

Roman and Greek learning were then at the height of their perfection, and Christians were despised by them as unlearned barbarians. That learning, arts, and empire should all submit to such a King and Savior was certainly a work of supernatural power. Christ did not raise armies to overcome the nations, nor did victory compel them. Rather, the victors and lords of the world—men skilled in the greatest human wisdom—were conquered by the gospel preached by a group of inferior men.

This gospel that conquered them was still opposed by many, and Christians were persecuted and hated until the gospel overcame the persecutors.

It is true that heathenism holds the greater part of the world, and Muslims have as much as Christians; but one obtained it by the sword, while the other gained it through the doctrine and holy lives of a few unarmed, inferior men.

However, I offer this about the extent of faith as a probable, not a compelling, argument. The main argument rests on the sanctifying effect of faith.

I know some will say that many, or most, Christians are as bad as other men.

But it is one thing to belong to a professed religion because it is the religion of the king and country, which benefits one's worldly advantage and meets with little opposition. This is true of most people in the world—Christians, Muslims, and heathens alike. It is another thing to be a serious believer who, after trial and consideration, chooses Christianity.

It is well known that such serious Christians are holy, sober, and just, and they greatly differ from the corrupt world. This fully proves that God approves the gospel, which He makes so effective in producing such a great change.

Here consider: 1. What that change is; 2. How difficult and great a work it is; 3. That it is certainly a work of God; and 4. That the gospel is the means by which God accomplishes it.

The nature of His holy work in all serious, sincere Christians is to set all their hopes and hearts on the promised glory of the life to come. It transforms the very nature of their wills into a prevailing love of God and of men, and of heaven and holiness. It mortifies fleshly lusts and subjects sense to reason and faith, the body to the soul, and all to God. It directs the heart to the sincere study of doing all the good they can to friends, neighbors, and enemies, especially for the public good. Their delight is to deny ungodliness and worldly lusts and to live soberly, righteously, and godly in the present age. Sin becomes their chief hatred, and nothing grieves them more than the inability to reach greater perfection in faith, hope, obedience, patience, and in heavenly love and joy. It causes them to disdain wealth, honor, fleshly pleasure, and life in comparison to God's love and everlasting life. This change wrought by God's Spirit is found in all true believers.

Those who are ungodly have only the name of Christians; they never truly understood what Christianity is, nor have they received it by true faith. But all who understand and seriously believe in Jesus Christ are sanctified by the Spirit of our God.

This is a work greater than miracles, both in excellence and in difficulty.

It is the very health of the soul; it is salvation itself. It makes a person, in measure, like God and reflects His image. It is a heavenly nature and serves as the earnest and preparation for heaven. It delivers a person from the greatest evil on earth and grants the firmest peace and joy — peace with God, the pardon of sins, and the hope of everlasting glory.

It is easy to see how great this work is by observing the deep roots of contrary vices in the corrupted nature of man. Experience shows that man, by his corrupt nature, is proud and ignorant, and cares little beyond fleshly and worldly things. He is a slave to his appetites and lusts; bodily prosperity alone truly captures his heart. Indeed, unless God restrains them, all wicked men are bitter enemies of all that is truly wise and holy — even among heathens and infidels. If anyone is better than the rest, the wicked become their deadly enemies. There is such visible enmity between godliness and wickedness — between your seed and her Seed — that this greatly confirms the Scripture which describes it. It is not merely the name of Christians that changes men's nature. We, who have peace from the world, are under such implacable hatred from wicked men who call themselves Christians that even many bears or wolves would be less harmful to us.

The widespread prevalence of this wickedness across all ages and nations shows how great a work it is to cure.

The failure of all other means highlights this as well. Until the Spirit of God applies the gospel to the heart, children will grow up in wickedness despite all a parent's counsel, love, and correction. No words or reasoning will prevail with them any more than with drunken men or beasts.

We find it extremely difficult to cure a person of even one deeply rooted sin, much less all.

The common misery of the world proclaims man's vice and the difficulty of the cure. How else do people live in self-seeking falsehood, fraud, malice, and in bloody wars — worse than wolves and serpents against one another?

Finally, where God cures souls through true faith, it is accomplished only after the pangs of sharp repentance and a great conflict, before God's Spirit prevails.

It is therefore evident that this sanctification of souls is an eminent work of God Himself.

1. It is done in so many of His chosen ones across all ages and places.

2. As difficult as it is, He often turns sinners' hearts to Himself in a very short time, sometimes by a single sermon.

3. It is a work that none can accomplish but God, who holds power over souls.

It is a work so good that it bears God's own image. It is the writing of His law and gospel on men's hearts. None is more for it than God. Satan clearly fights against it with all the power he can muster in the world. Observe, and you will find that most of the turmoil in the world — caused by false teachers, tyrants, and private malice — is merely Satan's war against faith, holiness, and love. Certainly, it is not he who promotes them.

4. It is evident, through experience, that it is the gospel of Christ which God uses and blesses to accomplish this great sanctifying work on souls. Among Christians, none are converted by any other means. God would not bless a word of falsehood and deceit to such great and excellent effect.

All who are made holy, heavenly, and truly conscientious among us are made so by Christ's gospel. The wicked are either enemies of the serious practice of it or rebels who despise it. The effects we see daily prove that God Himself endorses it as His word.

If you say there are as good men among the heathen and Muslims as there are holy, heavenly, and just individuals, I respond:

1. I have lived over seventy-seven years, and I have never known one serious, holy person in England who was made such by the writings of heathens or Muslims.

2. Many excellent things can be found in the writings of some heathen authors — Plato, Cicero, Hierocles, Plutarch, Antoninus, Epictetus, and many others. Yet in them I find a lack of the expressions of that holy and heavenly frame of mind and life, and that victory over the flesh and the world, which Christianity contains.

3. Christ is like the sun, whose rays provide some light before it is seen at its rising and after it has set. The light of Jews and heathen was like the dawn of the day before the sun rises. The light among Muslims is akin to the light of the sun after it has set.

Certainly, the same God who has used Muslims as a dreadful scourge against wicked Christians — those who have abused the gospel through false professions — has also used them to accomplish much good against idolatry in the heathen world. Wherever they go, idolatry is destroyed.

Indeed, corrupt Christians, Greeks, and especially Catholics, who worship images, angels, and bread, are justly rebuked and condemned by Muslims. But oh, that those who have conquered so far by the sword would be conquered by the sacred word of truth, and truly understand the mystery of redemption and the doctrine of the gospel of Jesus Christ!

Objection: They consider us idolaters for saying that Christ is God and for believing in the Trinity.

Regarding the Trinity: it is not contradictory for one fire or sun to have the essential ability to move, light, and heat; nor is it contradictory for one soul to possess the powers of vegetation, sense, and reason; nor for a rational soul to have a unique power of vitality, intellect, and free will. Why then should the Trinity seem incredible?

We do not believe that the Godhead undergoes any change, nor that the divine nature becomes flesh, or that the human nature becomes God. Rather, we believe that the Godhead is incomprehensibly united to human nature by assumption, in a way that it is united to no other creature, for those unique operations on the humanity of Christ that make Him our Redeemer.

Those who truly understand that God is everything, more essential than the soul to the world, and as close to us as our souls are to our bodies — in whom we live and move and have our being — will realize that it is more challenging to comprehend how God can be further from any soul than how He is so intimately united with Christ. This is evident because the different ways in which God interacts with His creatures are clear to us.

From all this, we see that every sanctified Christian has the inward witness that Christ is true. He is indeed a physician who heals and a Savior who saves all who seriously believe and obey Him. The Spirit of God, in a new, holy, and heavenly nature of spiritual life, light, and love, serves as this witness.

The sixth article in my text is "Received up into glory."

The fact that Christ was taken up into heaven after forty days on earth, in the sight of His disciples, is a matter attested by the infallible proofs already given, which I shall not repeat here.

If Christ were not glorified now in heaven, He could not send down His Spirit with His word on earth, nor could He have enabled the first witnesses to speak in all tongues, heal the sick, raise the dead, and perform all the miracles they did. A dead man cannot send down the Holy Spirit in the likeness of cloven tongues like as of fire, nor enable thousands to perform such works. Nor could He accomplish what is done in the souls of serious believers in all ages and nations to this day. He is surely alive who makes men live; and, from heaven, He draws hearts to heaven.

This is our hope and joy: heaven and earth are in His power. The suffering and work He performed for us on earth were brief; His heavenly intercession and reign are everlasting. Guilty souls cannot have immediate access to God. All is through a Mediator. Everything we receive from God comes through Him, and our services are presented by Him and accepted for His sake. As the Mediator between the Father and us, His Spirit intercedes between Him and us. By His Spirit He gives us holy desires and every grace. And by that same Spirit we exercise them in our returns to Him.

Our glorified Savior has Satan and all our enemies under His power. Life and death are at His command, and all judgment has been committed to Him. He who has redeemed us is preparing us for heaven, and for our sakes He receives our departing souls into His own joy and glory. He has promised that we shall be with Him where He is and shall see His glory. He who is our Savior will be our Judge. He will come with thousands of His angels to bring confusion to the wicked and to be glorified in His saints. He will create a new heaven and a new earth in which righteousness shall dwell. Angels and glorified saints will, with Christ our Head, form one city of God, one holy society and choir, in perfect love and joy to praise the blessed God forever.

The differences between this world and the one I am going to: This world is God's footstool. That world is His throne.

Here are His works of inferior nature and of grace. There, He shines forth in perfect glory.

Here is gross, receptive matter moved by invisible powers. There are the noblest, efficient, communicative powers moving all.

This is the inferior, subject, governed world. That is the superior, regent world.

This is a world of trial, where the soul belongs to whoever can win its consent. That is a world where the will is perfectly determined and fixed.

Satan, by winning men's consent, has a large dominion over fools here. There, he is cast out and has no possession.

Here, he is a tempter and a troubler of the best. There, he has neither the power to tempt nor to trouble.

This world is like the dark womb where we are regenerated. That is the world of glorious light into which we are born.

Here, we dwell in a world of sordid earth. There, we shall dwell in a world of celestial light and glory.

Here, we live in a troublesome, tempting, perishing body. There, we are delivered from this burden and prison into glorious liberty.

Here, we are under a troublesome cure for our maladies. There, we are perfectly healed, rejoicing in our Physician's praise.

Here, we are using the means in weariness and hope. There, we obtain the end in full fruition.

Here, sin makes us loathsome to ourselves and brings us annoyance. There, we shall love God in ourselves and our perfect selves in God.

Here, all our duties are defiled with sinful imperfection. There, perfect souls will perfectly love and praise their God.

Here, Satan's temptations are a continual danger and source of distress. There, perfect victory has ended our temptations.

Here, there is still a remnant of the curse and punishment of sin. Pardon and deliverance are perfected there.

Repentance, shame, sorrow, and fear are part of my necessary work here. There, all the troublesome parts are past and utterly excluded.

Here, we see in a mirror, dimly, the invisible world of spirits. There, we shall see them face to face.

Here, faith, alas, is too weak and must serve in place of sight. There, presence and sight will remove the need for such believing.

Desire and hope are here our very life and work. But there it will be full felicity in fruition.

Our hopes are here often mixed with grievous doubts and fears. But there, full possession will end them all.

Our holy affections are here corrupted with carnal mixtures. But there, all are purely holy and divine.

Here, the coldness of our divine love is our sin and misery. There, its perfection will be our perfect holiness and joy.

Here, though the will itself is imperfect, we cannot do what we would. There, will, deed, and attainment will all be fully perfect.

Here, by ignorance and self-love, I have desires which God denies. There, perfect desires shall be perfectly fulfilled.

Here, pinching wants of something or other, and troublesome cares, are daily burdens. Nothing is lacking there, and God has ended all their cares.

Here, our senses rebel against faith and reason and often overcome them. There, our senses will be only holy, and no discord will be found in our faculties or actions.

Pleasures and contentments here are short, narrow, and twisted with their contraries. There, they are objectively pure and boundless, and subjectively complete and absolute.

Here, transitory things are called vanity and vexation. Above, things are called reality, perfection, and glory.

This world is but a point in God's creation—a narrow place for a few passing travelers. Above are vast, capacious regions, ample for all saints and angels.

This world is like Newgate, and hell like Tyburn; from here some are saved and others condemned. The other world is the glorious kingdom of Jehovah with the blessed.

Here Christ was tempted, scorned, and crucified. There he reigns in glory over all.

Here the spiritual life exists only as a spark or a seed. There it becomes a glorious flame of love and joy, producing perfect fruit and bloom.

Here we have only the firstfruits, the earnest, and the pledge. There is the full, glorious harvest and perfection.

Here we are like children under guardianship, little different from servants. There we will receive full possession of our inheritance.

Here the prospect of pain, death, the grave, and decay tarnishes every pleasure. There is no death, nor any fear of the end of happiness.

Here God's Word is often imperfectly understood, and errors abound even among the best. There, in the world of light, all mysteries of nature and of grace are unveiled.

Many of God's promises remain unfulfilled here, and our prayers go unanswered. There the truth shines in their full performance.

Here our grace is so weak and our hearts so dark that our sincerity is often questioned. There, the flames of love and joy leave no place for such doubt.

Because of our inconstancy, here one day is joyful and the next sad. There, our joys will be uninterrupted.

Here we live among sinful companions like ourselves, in the flesh. There, holy angels and redeemed souls, together with Christ, are our company.

Here even our best friends and helpers, through sin, hinder us in part. There, all contribute to the harmony of active love.

Our errors and corruptions make us hurtful and burdensome to our friends here. There, Christ and they will forgive us, and we will trouble them no more.

Selfishness and conflicting interests here disrupt and mar our conversations. There, perfect love will make the joy of every saint and every angel mine.

Here the militant church, imperfectly sanctified, lives in scandal and sad divisions. There the glorious church, united in God by perfect love, has no contention.

Here sin and error turn even our public worship into discord. The celestial harmony of joyful love and praise is, to mortal minds, inconceivable.

Here weak, blind, and wicked teachers keep most people in delusion and division. There glorious light has banished all lies, deceit, and darkness.

Here the wills of blind tyrants serve as law for most people. In heaven, the wisdom and will of the Most Holy God are the law of the heavenly society.

Here lies cloud the innocence of the just and make truth and goodness seem odious. There all false judgments are reversed, slander is silenced, and the righteous are justified.

Here government is exercised through terror and violence. There God rules with light, love, and perfect joy.

Here enemies reproach us and persecution harasses and tempts us. There all storms are past, and the conquerors are crowned and rest in joy.

Here the glory of divine love and holiness is obscured by abundant sin and by the vastness of Satan's kingdom on earth. But the great and glorious heavenly kingdom — of which this earth is only a point and a prison — will banish such false thoughts and glorify God's love and goodness forever.

This world, corrupted, is an enemy to God and to us; we renounce it in baptism and must be delivered from it. The heavenly world is what we seek, pray for, and wait for all our lives, and for it we must forsake all the tempting vanities of this present world.

This body and world are like our riding clothes, our horse, our way, our inn, and our traveling company — merely instruments for our journey home. The other is our city of blessedness and everlasting rest, toward which every grace inclines the soul and every present means and mercy leads.

Our ignorance of nature and of sensible things makes this life a labyrinth. Our studies, sciences, and learned conversations seem like a dream or a puppet show — a childish bustle about mere words. In heaven, however, a universal knowledge of God's works will be among the least of the glories by which He shines to the saints.

Here the distance and darkness of souls in the flesh — those who long to know more of God and the heavenly world but cannot — make life a burden because of unsatisfied desires. There, glorious presence and immediate knowledge provide full satisfaction.

Here our sin and imperfection make us incapable of being the objects of God's full, complacent love, though we share His benevolence that will lead us to it. There, to our various degrees, we will perfectly please God and be perfectly satisfied in Him forever.

All things here are short and transitory from their beginning, hastening toward their end, which is near, certain, and always before our eyes. Time is so brief that beings here are almost nothing; the bubble of worldly prosperity, pomp, and fleshly pleasure swells and bursts so quickly that it seems both to be and not to be at once. But the heavenly substances, their works, and their joys are crowned with duration and are assuredly everlasting.

Such, O my soul, is the blessed change that God will make.

My belief and hope in this perfection are supported by natural reason. It tells me that God made every creature suited to its intended use; even animals are more fit for their various offices than man is. He does not give any creature its faculties in vain. Whatever a wise creator makes, he equips for the purpose for which he made it. Man's faculties enable him to think of God—our relation to Him, our duty to Him, our hopes from Him, and our fears of Him; to consider the state of our souls in relation to His judgment; to ponder what will happen to us after death, whether reward or punishment, and how to prepare for it. This nature, with its faculties and powers, is not made in vain.

Reason assures me that every person is bound by nature to prefer even the smallest probability of everlasting joy over all the prosperity of this world, and to suffer the loss of all fleeting vanity to escape the least possibility of endless misery. Nature gives such indications of rewards and punishments after death that no one can claim certainty there is no such thing. Therefore, by the law of nature, all are obliged to be religious and to seek first and foremost their salvation in the life to come. If not, God would have made human nature to deceive itself, causing people to spend the chief part, indeed all, of their lives in labor and suffering for that which is not—making their greatest duty their greatest deceit and misery, and leaving the worst men least deceived. But this cannot be attributed to our wise and good Creator.

The universal sense of moral good and evil in all mankind is strong evidence of another life. Even the vilest atheist cannot bear to be considered a knave, a liar, or a bad man; nor will he equate a vicious servant with another. Everyone wishes to be thought good, even if they will not be good. And does not God make a greater distinction than man? Will He not show it?

Human society is largely governed by the hopes and fears of another life, and by human nature it cannot be well governed without them. But the Almighty — most wise and most holy — does not need to, and will not, rule the world through mere deceit.

The gospel of Christ has made life and immortality much clearer than nature alone could. It is by believing in Christ that we find our full satisfaction. Oh, what God has accomplished in the wonders of redemption to assure us!

When answering doubts that may arise from certain difficult passages of Scripture, we must consider the following:

1. Christ and His apostles confirmed the truth of the gospel by many undeniable miracles. The gospel was proclaimed and validated eight years before any part of the New Testament was written, and nearly seventy years before the last book was completed.

2. Moreover, Christ did not speak in the language in which the gospel is now presented to us; what we have is a translation of His original words, and it is the substance of the message that is chiefly sealed.

Moses and Christ, the two great legislative mediators, came with a great stream of undeniable miracles. People need full proof that a law or doctrine comes from God before they accept it. But the priests and prophets after Moses — and the preachers and pastors of the Christian church, who were not sent to introduce new laws or a new gospel but to proclaim and teach what they received — did not need fresh miracles to confirm their ministry.

The personal belief of each priest or prophet after Moses, or of every pastor after Christ and His apostles, was not as essential for salvation as belief in the law and the gospel themselves. Therefore, although all Holy Scripture is true, the law and the gospel must be distinguished from the rest.

The history of the law and the gospel is supported by full, confirming historical evidence — evidence unmatched elsewhere in the world. Therefore, the doctrine must be true.

The fulfillment of prophecies demonstrates the truth of the gospel and the divine imprint upon it as a whole.

The sanctifying work of the Spirit, wrought through the gospel among sincere believers in all nations and ages, serves as a constant divine attestation.

My faith, grounded in God's work through His Word and His Spirit, gives me hope and urges me to seek a higher state of fulfillment. Any change in my heart and life must come from God; He would not give a grace that leads to falsehood or is ultimately wasted. His Spirit is the sure pledge of future glory.

All the course of religious and moral duty that He has commanded me, and in which He has engaged my life, was never imposed to deceive me. I am sure, by nature and by Scripture, that it is my duty to love God and my neighbor, to seek protection, to serve God, and to do good with all my time and power. I trust God for my reward, believing that all this shall not be in vain and that what is best will not be made my loss. O blessed be God for commands and holy duty; for they are equal to promises. Who can fear that he shall lose by seeking God?

As God has sealed the truth of His word, He has, through instituted offices and ordinances, sealed and delivered to me His covenant with the gift of Christ and of life in baptism and in the Lord's Supper.

He has given me such a love for holy things and persons that I greatly long to see His church in perfect light, love, and harmony. Oh, how sweet it would be to see all men wise, holy, and joyfully praising God. Every Christian longs for this; therefore, such a state will surely come to pass.

I have experienced the great benefit of the love and ministry of angels, as described in Psalm 91. They have kept me day and night, which confirms my hope that I shall dwell with them. I love them more than men because they love and serve God better.

The humble communion I have here with God through Christ and the Spirit — seen in His answers to my prayers — supports and comforts me, and leads me to expect still more.

The joy I find in love, when I think of the blessedness of my many holy departed friends and of the glory of Christ and of the heavenly Jerusalem, is surely a hopeful indication of their state.

When I see fire rise upward, and consider that spirits are of a far more sublime and excellent nature than fire, and observe that much of what is done in this world is accomplished by unseen spiritual powers moving this gross and drossy matter, I have no doubt that my soul, being a spirit, has a vast and glorious world of spirits to ascend to. God has, by nature, instilled in all things an aggregative, uniting inclination; earth has no other natural motion. The ascent of fire indicates that its element is above, and spirits naturally incline toward spirits, holy spirits especially toward the holy.

I am certain of my own understanding and will because I actively use these abilities. These actions confirm that I possess the faculties to perform them, for doing the impossible is not feasible. Thus I know a substance with such powers exists, since that which does not exist cannot produce any effect.

My soul, then, being certainly an intellectual, volitional, vital substance, I have no reason to think that God — who does not annihilate even the smallest grain of sand — will annihilate so noble a substance. Nor do I believe that He will destroy those powers which are its essential form and turn it into something else. Nor do I think that such essential powers shall lie dead and inactive, as if they continued in vain. Therefore, to natural reason nothing remains uncertain except the continuance of individuation for separate souls.

1. Apparitions and witches have removed any doubt regarding this, notwithstanding many fables and delusions.

2. Christ has further clarified this matter.

3. While substance, faculties, and acts continue, it is the error of our selfish, fleshly state that makes any fear of too close a union seem threatening, as if it would end our individuation. In truth, the greatest union will lead to the greatest perfection and will not result in any loss for souls.

God's wonderful providences for the church and for individual saints on earth reveal His love and care, and these providences will ultimately bring them to Him.

The nature of God greatly lessens the terror I feel about my departure.

I am sure I shall die at the will of, and into the hands of, infinite essential love and goodness; whose love will draw up my longing soul.

I am going to a God whose mercies have long assured me that He loves me better than my dearest friend does, better than I love myself, and is a far better chooser of my lot.

As He has absolute right to dispose of His own, the fulfillment of His will is indeed the ultimate end of all things, and therefore most desirable in itself; and His will shall be fulfilled in me.

I go to a glorified Savior, who came down to fetch me up, has conquered and sanctified death, made it my birthday for glory, takes me as His dearly bought own, and is in glory ready to receive His own.

I go to that Savior who, on the cross, committed His spirit into His Father's hands, and taught me, with dying Stephen, to say, "Lord Jesus, receive my spirit."

I do not go a solitary, untrodden way, but follow all the faithful since the death of Abel to this day (except for Enoch and Elijah), who all went by death into that glorious world, where I shall find them.

I have long groaned under a languid body, in a blind, distracted, and (by man) incurable world, where Satan reigns through lies, malice, and murder—alas! how many are affected. I am especially weary of my own darkness and sinful imperfection, which gives me great reason to desire deliverance.

I have already received a large share of mercies in this world, in time, and manifold comforts from God, so reason commands me to rest in God's timing for my removal.

I shall leave some fruits, not useless, to serve the church when I am gone; and if good is done, I have achieved my purpose.

When I am gone, God will raise up and use others to do His appointed work on earth. A church shall continue to praise Him, and the spirits in heaven will rejoice in it.

When I am gone, I shall not wish to be back on earth.

Satan, through his temptations and all his instruments, would not have done so much in the world to keep us from heaven if there were not a heaven that conquerors obtain.

When the darkness and uncertainty of the manner of the action and fruition of separated souls daunt me, it is enough to know explicitly what is revealed and implicitly to trust Christ with all the rest. Our eyes are in our head; who knows for us? Knowledge of glory is part of fruition; therefore, we must expect here no more than is suited to a life of faith.

All I can do is my own duty, and then trust God — obeying His commanding will and fully and joyfully resting in His disposing and rewarding will. There is no rest for souls but in the will of God. To repose our souls in life, and at death, is the only way to ensure a safe and comfortable departure.

The glorious marriage day of the Lamb cannot be far off when the number of the elect shall be complete. When the Son of Man comes in His glory, and all the holy angels with Him, He will be glorified in His saints and admired in all believers. I expect a new heaven and a new earth, for the first heaven and the first earth will pass away; and therein dwells righteousness. In that kingdom will be what God has prepared for those who love Him — eye has not seen, nor ear heard, nor has it entered into the heart of man—and therefore we cannot form a full, formal conception of it.

Even so, come, Lord Jesus!

Fear not then, O my soul, to lay down this flesh. Mercy has kept it up for my preparing work; but, oh, what a burdensome and chargeable companion it has been! Is it better than the dwelling place of perfect spirits? Oh, what are my groans, and all my cold and faint petitions, and my dull thanksgiving, compared to their harmonious, joyful praise? If a day in Your courts is better than a thousand, what is a day, or even everlastingness, in the heavenly society and work?

Oh, how hateful is darkness and unbelief, when the remnants of them thus stop poor souls in their ascent and make us half unwilling to go home! What—unwilling to be with my glorified Lord? Unwilling to be with saints and angels, who are all life, light, and love? Unwilling to see the glory of Jehovah? O foolish, sinful soul! Has Christ done so much to purchase heavenly glory for you, and now are you unwilling to enter into its possession?

Have you been seeking, praying, laboring, and suffering for so many years for that which now you seem scarcely willing to obtain? Do you not judge yourself unworthy of eternal life when you no longer desire to enjoy it? All this is due to your too much adherence to self and sense. You are still desiring sensitive satisfaction, and, not content to know your part, you want to know for yourself what Christ knows for you, as if you could better trust yourself than Him.

Fear not, weak soul; it is your Father's good pleasure to give you the kingdom. Trust in infinite power, wisdom, and love. Trust that faithful, gracious Savior who has so wonderfully merited to be trusted. Trust that promise which has never deceived anyone, confirmed by signs and wonders, by the oath, and by the Holy Spirit.

Whenever you depart from this house of flesh, the arms of mercy are open to embrace you. Essential, transcendent love is ready to receive you. The Spirit of love has sealed you with the Holy Spirit of promise. Christ will present you justified and accepted. Most of my old, holy, familiar friends have gone before me, and all the rest who died since the world began. The few imperfect ones left behind are hurrying after them, and if I go before, they will quickly overtake me. Though they weep as if it were for a long separation, it is their great mistake. The gate of death stands open all day, and my sorrowful friends are quickly following me, as I am now following those for whom I sorrowed.

Oh, pity those who are left for a while under the temptations, dangers, and fears that have long been your own affliction! But do not be afraid of the day of your deliverance, the bosom of everlasting love, the society of the wise, just, and holy, the end of all your troubles, the entrance into the joy of your Lord, and the place and state of all your hope.

Oh, say not notionally only, as from argumentative conviction, but confidently, and with glad desire and hope, that to depart and be with Christ is far better than to be here.

But, O my God, I have much more hope in speaking to You than to myself. Long may I plead with this dark and dull, yet fearful soul before I can plead it into joyful hopes and heavenly desires, unless You shine on it with the light of Your countenance, and You, whom my soul must trust and love, will give me faith and love themselves.

I thank You for convincing arguments; but had this been all the strength of my faith and hope, the tempter might have proved too subtle for me in dispute. I thank You that some experience tells me that a holy appetite for heavenly work and a love for the heavenly company and state do more to make me willing to die and think with pleasure of my change than ever bare arguments would have done.

Oh, send down the streams of Your love into my soul, and that will powerfully draw it up by longings for the near and full fruition! Oh, give me more of the divine and heavenly nature, and it will be natural and easy for me to desire to be with You. Send more of the heavenly joys into this soul, and it will long for heaven, the place of joy!

I must not hope on earth for any such acquaintance with the world above as is proper to the enjoying state. But if the sun can send its illuminating, warming rays to such a world as this, according to the various disposition of the recipients, doubtless You have Your effectual, though unsearchable, ways of illuminating, sanctifying, and attracting souls.

One such beam of Your pleased face, one taste of Your complacential love, will kindle my love, draw up my desires, and make my pains and sickness tolerable. I shall then put off this clothing with less reluctance and willingly leave my flesh to the dust, singing my nunc dimittis when I have thus seen Your salvation.

O my God, let not Your strengthening, comforting grace now forsake me, lest it overwhelm me with the fears of being finally forsaken. Dwell in me as the God of love and joy, that I may long to dwell in love and joy with You forever. But where sin abounded, grace abounded much more; let Your strengthening and comforting mercy abound when weakness increases and my necessities abound.

My flesh and my heart fail; but God is the strength of my heart and my portion forever. This short life is almost at an end, but Your lovingkindness is better than life. I know not with what pains You will further try me, but if I love You, You have promised that all things shall work together for my good.

The world that I am going to by death is not apparent to my sight, but my life is hidden with Christ in God. Because He lives, we shall live, and we shall be with Him where He is. When He appears, we shall appear with Him in glory and enter into our Master's joy, and be forever with the Lord. Amen.

What a tangible manifestation of His kingdom Christ provided in His transfiguration.

Our Lord, who brought life and immortality to light, understood the difficulty of believing such great unseen realities. Therefore He chose to give some tangible aids by way of demonstration. In Matthew 16 and Matthew 17:1-2, Mark 9:1, and Luke 9:28 He promised some disciples a vision of His kingdom as it would come in power, or a glimpse similar to what Moses experienced when he saw the back of God's glory. He fulfilled that promise first in His transfiguration, and later in His resurrection, ascension, and in sending the Holy Spirit to empower them to preach, perform miracles, and convert the nations.

By the kingdom of God we mean God's government of His holy ones, conveyed by a heavenly communication of life, light, and love—beginning on earth by grace and perfected in heaven by glory. This is a special theocracy.

To understand this, we must remember that when God made man good, in His image, He spoke to him in a heavenly manner—either immediately or by an angel—revealing His will. But man, as a free, self-determining agent, was left to choose whom he would follow. By listening to Satan and turning from God, he became a slave of Satan, who thereby gained the advantage to deceive and rule him.

This rebellion did not nullify God's power or governing purpose, nor did it remove man's obligation to obedience. Yet by forsaking God, man was largely, though not entirely, abandoned by God's special fatherly approval and left to Satan and his own will. The eternal Word intervened for man's reprieve and redemption, undertaking to break the serpent's head and to conquer him who had deceived and captivated mankind.

Choosing a special seed, God made them a peculiar people and set up a heavenly, prophetical government over them—revealing Himself by heavenly truth, making their laws, and choosing their chief governors under Him from time to time. He would not leave it to blind, sinful men to make laws or select princes for themselves, but kept them in special dependence upon heaven.

However, the carnal Israelites, having provoked God by odious idolatry, sought to remedy this by choosing a king like other nations, thus ending their dependence on heavenly revelation and choice for government. Consequently, theocracy became a more human regime, and God was more cast off—though He did not completely abandon them. The rest of the world remained under Satan's sway and under their own corrupted minds and wills, so that Satan maintains both an internal kingdom in wicked souls and a visible political government over the wicked nations, ruling them through men who are themselves ruled by him.

As Christ came to cast him out of men's hearts by His sanctifying, conquering Spirit, He also came to cast him out of the political governments of the world and to bring those governments under the laws, officers, and Spirit of Christ—ruling them by heavenly power and love as His own, and bringing them at last to perfection in one celestial kingdom. In this sense, we pray, "Your kingdom come."

To make men believe that He is the heavenly King sent from God to overthrow Satan's realm was the main aim of the gospel's preaching. He would demonstrate this both by miracles, which showed His victory over devils and His lordship over life, and by visible manifestations of glory.

It is said in 1 John 5:7-8 that there are three witnesses in heaven and three on earth. Here, Christ had three heavenly and three earthly witnesses to His transfiguration. From heaven He had the witness of a voice proclaiming, "This is My beloved Son, in whom I am well pleased. Hear Him!"

He also had the witness of Moses, the chief lawgiver, and of Elijah, the chief prophet, to show that the law and the prophets bear witness beforehand. But "Hear Him!" notifies us that Christ and His gospel are to be heard above the law and the prophets, teaching what they could only foreshadow. The law was given through Moses (with its types and shadows), but grace and truth—the substance they typified—came through Jesus Christ.

Light and glory are often of the same signification. Christ was transfigured into a luminous, glorious appearance of body. He teaches by this that He would have us form some idea of His kingdom from sensible experience. Many apparitions of angels have been accompanied by light. Christ appeared to Saul in a visible light (Acts 9). He appeared to John in Revelation 1. The glory of God illuminates the New Jerusalem, and the Lamb is its light. It is the inheritance of the saints in the light.

Some seem to think too lowly of sense and too eager to separate it from intellectual spirits, both as to power, act, and object—simply because sense is found in lower creatures. They might, on that basis, deny substantiality to spirits because brutes are substances.

Higher beings possess, either formally or eminently, all the perfections of the lower. It is not a perfection of a spirit to be insensible or to have nothing to do with sensible things, but to be eminently receptive of sense and to be superior agents over lower sensibles. God is love, and love is complacency. A high degree of complacency is delight or joy.

Thus God is essential, infinite joy—without the drossy qualities proper to souls in flesh and without the imperfections belonging to creatures.

Can we imagine what it is to enter into our Master's joy or to love and praise Him joyfully without any sense? I rather think that as vigorous youth enables greater delight than decrepit, languid age and sickness, so heaven will, by perfecting our natures, make us capable of inconceivably more joy than any earthly scene can provide.

And just as we will have heightened senses in power and action, we will also have tangible objects. God Himself delights in all His works, and so shall we. We must not, under the pretense of viewing the heavenly Jerusalem as merely spiritual, deprive ourselves of the sensory ideas it offers through God's descriptions.

Light is tangible; the glorified Christ is tangible. Moses and Elijah were tangible to Peter, James, and John, and Lazarus and Abraham were tangible to the rich man in his torment (Luke 16). Stephen saw the heavens opened and Jesus standing at the right hand of God. All eyes shall see Him at His glorious return.

Heavenly glory is not experienced solely through mere thought or knowledge, nor as if in a dream. Rather it is perceived by a most elevated intellectual sensation, enhanced and invigorated.

Do not say, O my soul, that this kingdom of glory is so far beyond you that you cannot conceive it. Do not think it unworthy of your desires and joyful hopes simply because you cannot fully understand it.

Do you not know the difference between light and darkness? If you had been kept in absolute darkness for a year, would you not long for light? The blind often feel half dead while they live. The faculty and its object must be compatible. Light may be too intense for weak eyes, just as heat can be tormenting at an unsuitable level. But when our souls are perfected, they will be capable of receiving a far more glorious light than we can endure now.

Moses was not hidden away in the cleft of the rock because he could only see the back part of God's glory. Here we see in a mirror, dimly; there we shall see face to face. Although our present physical eyes, like spectacles, will be set aside, we shall have more fitting means suited to our perfected state.

Just as I can envision heaven as a realm of glorious light, I can also think of it as a place and state of life and love. I know the difference between life and death, and that a living dog is better than a dead lion. I have known the delight of loving my friends, and from that I desire their close communion as my joy. Can I then have no idea of that world where life, light, and joyful love are the very essence of souls, as water is to fish?

If I can have some general understanding of that state, I can also comprehend the perfected condition of the spirits of the just. They are naturally at home in their element. They embody essential, created life, light, and love. They do not lack substance as the foundation for those powers, nor do they lack objects on which to exercise them.

Do not think, then, that heaven is so far beyond comprehension that it cannot be thought of at all. If we have no conception of it, we cannot desire it, nor can we have any joyful hope about it. What can we conceive more certainly than life, light, and love; a realm; and beings who embody these qualities? Do we not know what knowledge is, see what light is, and feel what life and love are?

It is true that our understanding of these things is sadly imperfect, and it will remain so until we possess, experience, and exercise them fully. Who knows what light or sight is except by seeing? Or what knowledge is except by knowing? Or what love and joy are except by loving and rejoicing? Who knows what perfect sight, knowledge, love, and joy are except by perfectly seeing, knowing, loving, and rejoicing?

No one can grasp these concepts by immediate perception alone. Still, we can form some abstract understanding of them by reasoning from the limited experience we have here in the kingdom of grace.

Can I regard the dark, earthly appearances—mere mutable, lifeless matter stirred and used by invisible powers—as more substantial than spiritual substances? Shall I think those unseen, powerful substances are less real because they are spiritual, or that they are not objects of knowledge? Are the stars I see less substantial than a carcass in a dark grave?

The Lord who appeared in shining glory has members like Himself and has promised that the righteous will shine forth in His kingdom. If some degree of this is already shown in those called children of light and lights of the world, how much more will they shine in the world of light? Those who call light merely a quality or an act must admit that it proceeds from a substance.

Alas for the deceived sensual unbeliever who spends life chasing fleeting shadows, walking in a vain show, and treating spiritual, glorious substances as if they were mere illusions or dreams.

Christ, Moses, and Elijah appeared as three distinct, individual persons. This refutes the false notion that death eliminates individuality and merges all souls into one. Perfect, indivisible, infinite unity belongs to God; multiplicity proceeds from that unity. Reason forbids us to imagine that the countless individuals on earth and the numerous stars above have so much divine perfection that they exist as one undivided substance without many inhabitants.

Some of the Sadducees thought the stars were inhabited worlds like the earth. Why, then, should they think souls lose their individuality when they join other persons? Christ has refuted such ideas even through sensible experience. Moses is still Moses, Elijah is still Elijah, and all our friends who have gone to Christ remain the same and can be called by the same names. Abraham, Isaac, and Jacob are the same in heaven; Lazarus was Lazarus in Abraham's bosom.

When we put off our flesh and are unclothed, we do not lose our personality. Each will receive his own reward according to what he has done in the body, and each must give an account of his own works and talents.

Why, then, should I not, with clear conception and joyful desire, seek after the souls of my departed friends now in the celestial kingdom? Some have scorned me for naming a few in my Saints' Rest, those individuals the despisers hated. I do not refrain from naming more, not because it is improper, but because there are more than can be numbered.

In every place I have lived, many excellent souls—though imperfect here—have gone to Christ. How sweet is the memory of communion with them: in Shrewsbury and other parts of Shropshire; in Dudley and its neighborhood; among multitudes in Kidderminster, Bewdley, and other parts of Worcestershire; in Coventry and other parts of Warwickshire; and in many other places where I have sojourned, above all in London and its vicinity. As Mr. Howe gracefully observed in his character of my dear friend Mr. Richard Fairclough, what a multitude of blessed saints will rise at the last day from London!

This earth is, as it were, hallowed by the dust and relics of so many blessed souls. Yet it is heaven that is adorned by these spiritual stars, the place honored by them and they by it, all through Christ. We are like infants or lambs who cry for their mothers when out of sight;

though the mothers are near, if unseen they cry as if lost. Just as Christ told His disciples He must depart and their hearts were sorrowful until the Holy Spirit came—better than His bodily presence—to prepare them joyfully to follow Him, so we think of our friends as almost lost by separation until the heavenly Spirit tells us where they are and prepares us to desire to be with them.

Elijah has a body now in heaven, and so does Enoch; but can we think only two or three there with Christ differ so much from all the rest that they have bodies while the others do not? Is there such dissimilarity among the saints in heaven? What are two or three in such a society?

Certainly their bodies are not corruptible flesh and blood, but spiritual bodies such as all saints will have at the resurrection. But are they in heaven the same visible, shaped bodies that appeared on the mount? The same difficulty arises with regard to Christ's risen body: He told Mary not to cling to Him because He had not yet ascended to His Father; He could appear and vanish at will; yet Thomas touched Him and felt that He had flesh and bones.

That body of flesh ascended visibly to heaven; yet in heaven it is not flesh and blood but a spiritual body, and it is not inferior to what He will make His members. We must acknowledge our inability to know these things fully, though we should be thankful for what we do know.

It seems likely that the bodies of Christ, Enoch, and Elijah were changeable according to the regions they were to inhabit. Christ could assume a body of flesh and blood and immediately transform it into a pure, incorruptible spiritual body when entering the spiritual realm. God did the same for Enoch and Elijah. As Paul says, we shall not all sleep, but we shall all be changed. If Elijah has business on the mount, he can take on a denser form to be seen by men and lay it aside or return to a more invisible, spiritual state when he goes back to the place from which he came. No wonder angels, and even Christ before His incarnation according to ancient testimony, have assumed bodies suited to their tasks on earth; they could eat and drink with men without dwelling in heaven in coarse attire.

But how did Moses come to have a body on the mount when it is said he was buried and thus took none with him into heaven? We must remember we are inquiring about matters beyond certain knowledge. Still, in humble conjecture, we may suggest it was no more impossible for Moses to assume the body he appeared in on the mount than for angels or departed souls to appear in human forms, as many apparitions have testified.

If wicked souls can appear, why not good ones when God wills it? The tradition that God kept Moses' body uncorrupted in the grave and that the devil contended about it with Michael seems merely a Jewish legend. Others say that at the transfiguration his body rose again. We need not embrace such speculations for our comfort. The soul of Moses could assume a body.

Yet the apparent dissimilarity of Enoch and Elijah from other saints in heaven remains a difficulty. If we knew God intended it so, that might satisfy us. There is a symmetry in the body of Christ, and it seems likely that the same realm has inhabitants of the same nature. Should we think Enoch and Elijah, upon entering those regions, laid aside their bodies and became like Abraham and the other holy souls? Why were they taken up to be laid aside? No doubt they laid aside corruptibility. God knows; much remains unknown to us.

Some fathers, Faustus Regiensis, Dr. More, and some recent thinkers, suggest that all spirits are souls and animate some bodies, so that all in heaven possess some bodies. If so, what bodies are they, and how do they differ from the resurrection state? Just as the soul here operates in and through fiery spirits in our bodies, it may be lodged in these so as to take some of them with it at death, like the life of a plant remaining in the seed. A person may be said to go unclothed to bed though they have not removed their shift, and to be clothed again when they put on the rest.

At the resurrection, as there will be a new heaven and a new earth, so spirits now in heaven may have more delightful tasks on that new, righteous earth than they do now and therefore may require additional bodies, differing from what they presently possess in heaven as their work on the new earth requires—just as the seed differs from the plant. Spirits, being communicative, will find greater happiness through more communication. Just as God delights in doing good to all His works, so the souls now in heaven will delight in being employed in doing good to the new earth and in animating bodies suited for such work; for now they only require spiritual, luminous receptacles appropriate to their present regions.

It is foolish to think, as some do, that departed souls will be as dormant and inactive as persons unconscious from apoplexy or sleep because they lack organized bodies. Spirits are inherently active, intellectual, and volitional. Will God continue such essential powers in vain?

Moses and Elijah did not lack bodies in those appearances. Those in heaven can praise Jehovah and the Lamb with holy, harmonious love and joy; whether they do so in ethereal forms or without visible bodies, we shall soon know.

That Moses and Elijah spoke with Christ shows Christ's close communion with the blessed. He who chose to come to earth in flesh, to live among humanity in humble condition, and who did not shrink from familiar conversation with the poor or from eating and drinking with tax collectors and sinners, will certainly not refuse everlasting, intimate fellowship with the glorified.

If the church is His dearly beloved spouse and, as it were, one with Him as His body, He will not be a stranger to even the least and lowest member.

Luke (9:31) states, "who appeared in glory and spoke of His decease which He was about to accomplish at Jerusalem." This was not to inform Christ—He came into the world to die for sin—so what was the purpose? Did Christ need to be told as if He did not know? That seems unlikely. Did He need their comfort, as angels ministered to Him and strengthened Him during His trials? The specific reasons for this conversation are unknown to us; however, it was in some measure preparatory for His great sufferings and death.

If Christ's sufferings and death required such preparation, must not mine also require forethought? Do I not need comforting messages from God? Carnal men prefer pleasant talk to discussions of suffering and death. Yet what must be endured and calls for the greatest strength must be contemplated and prepared for. It is worse than madness to be caught off guard by suffering and death without serious consideration beforehand. Such a sharp trial and significant change demand the greatest preparation.

He who can refuse to suffer and die may also refuse to think or talk about it. If Christ needed men from heaven to discuss His cross with Him, what reason have I not to study the cross? We should spend our lives anticipating it and, with obedient consent, submit to it—take it up to follow Christ—determining, with Paul, not to know anything among you except Jesus Christ and Him crucified; that is, to regard this as the only essential and excellent knowledge.

But, alas! How thoughtlessly death and suffering are discussed until they arrive. We are meant to learn how to suffer when suffering is upon us, and to learn how to die when nature, or the physician, pronounces the sentence of death. It is God's mercy to some to prolong their sufferings, giving ample time to learn. Just as we learn to write by writing, to converse by conversing, and every art and trade by practice, so through suffering we learn to endure. The lesson is severe.

Criminals suffer without learning, whether they will or not. But to suffer obediently, with childlike affection, is the lesson to be learned. How little many sincere Christians appreciate how much of their true obedience consists in childlike, holy suffering. They expect it too little, prepare inadequately, and are overwhelmed when it comes. Even under persecutions endured for righteousness' sake, how many shrink back, evade duty, or do unlawful things for safety because they were unprepared? The loss of possessions, imprisonment, and want seem unbearable trials to many. From some experience I can tell such people that physical pain and torment are far greater trials, which none escape, and require greater strength of faith to accept from God's hand.

Others will testify that the intensity of temptations, the terrors of God upon a wounded conscience, and a troubled soul are yet harder than these. These sorrows are the saddest because they make the mind unfit to use afflictions for holy ends. Christ, in all His agony — even when He cried on the cross, "My God, My God, why have You forsaken Me?" — had His intellect clear and perfect, knowing the nature, reason, use, and purpose of His sufferings. Many poor, distressed, and distracted souls lack that clarity. Oh, how central it is in Christianity to understand and rightly bear the cross! Most of our concern is to escape it rather than to submit to it.

Experiencing suffering and pain greatly deepens our understanding of the gospel. Hardship removes the offense of Christ's cross from me and helps me grasp its profound significance when I endure trials. How much I need the example of Christ! Every part of His suffering teaches endurance, just as the Ten Commandments teach what to do.

He fled proud, domineering Pharisees, false teachers, and worldly rulers, choosing instead to associate with the poor in deserts and obscure places. He was hated and persecuted for doing good and labeled a sinner for ignoring human ceremonies and traditions. Even those who saw His miracles found it hard to believe, and His own disciples were slow to learn. In His suffering they all abandoned Him, and one denied Him with oaths and curses. All these instances are instructive examples.

Christ's natural, though sinless, aversion to death and suffering, and His fear, were so intense they made His soul sorrowful even to the point of death. He experienced such agony that His sweat became like great drops of blood falling down to the ground, and He prayed three times that the bitter cup might pass from Him. The rulers, priests, soldiers, and the crowd all conspired to scorn Him—mocking, spitting on, beating Him, and making sport of Him—though He came to save them. They branded Him a sinner who never sinned, a deceiver and blasphemer, a rebellious usurper against Caesar, and even set up that charge above His cross to deny His innocence.

For the Lord and Savior of the world to endure all this is profoundly instructive for the suffering believer. That He should be reviled as a criminal on a cross, numbered with transgressors, have His side pierced, and cry out to His Father as if forsaken—then die, be buried, have His soul go to the place of departed spirits, and yet be in paradise—offers excellent lessons for us to learn.

I do not suffer for others, nor do I make God's justice a propitiatory sacrifice for sin as Christ did. Instead I must endure God's fatherly corrections and the discipline of paternal, healing justice. I must be saved as through fire and pass through this purgatory to be refined. I must suffer from Christ and for Christ, for my sin, and for the sake of righteousness. I must bear God's indignation with a childlike acceptance of His holiness and chastening justice because I have offended Him.

I am predestined to be conformed to Christ's image in suffering and sanctity. Indeed, I must "Yet indeed I also count all things loss for the excellence of the knowledge of Christ Jesus my Lord" (Romans 8:30, et cetera), for whom I must not hesitate to suffer the loss of all things and count them as refuse so that I may gain Him and be found in Him. I desire not only to know the power of His resurrection but also to share in "that I may know Him and the power of His resurrection, and the fellowship of His sufferings, being conformed to His death" (Philippians 3:8–10).

Paul rejoiced in such weaknesses and in his sufferings for the church, filling up what was lacking in the afflictions of Christ in his flesh (Colossians 1:24). Peter urges us, "But rejoice to the extent that you partake of Christ's sufferings, that when His glory is revealed, you may also be glad with exceeding joy" (1 Peter 4:13). And, "if indeed we suffer with Him, that we may also be glorified together" (Romans 8:17). It is a great gift to suffer for His sake (Philippians 1:29). Those who suffer for the kingdom of God are blessed (2 Thessalonians 1:5). It is a source of happiness and joy to suffer for righteousness' sake and for doing good (1 Peter 2:10; 3:14, 17; 4:15, 16, 19; Matthew 5:10, 11). The sufferings of Christ abound in such people, so that their consolations also abound (2 Corinthians 1:5).

But alas! I suffer far more for my own sins than for Christ and righteousness. Yet even this suffering, through the cross of Christ, is sanctified and becomes a powerful remedy against my sin. Just as Christ suffered for our sins and gained merit through His suffering, if we accept corrective punishment, exercise repentance and mortification while suffering, and submit obediently to the rod, God will regard this as acceptable service and bless it for our further good.

But how can it be said that Christ "though He was a Son, yet He learned obedience by the things which He suffered. And having been perfected, He became the author of eternal salvation to all who obey Him" (Hebrews 5:8–9)? Was He unlearned and imperfect before? He had no culpable imperfection. Yet His mediatorial work was incomplete until it was fully accomplished. When it was completed, He was thereby established as the perfect Mediator. As He declared on the cross, "It is finished!" (John 19:30).

Just as human nature receives additional acts of knowledge as it grows and encounters new objects—so Adam gained understanding when he first beheld the creatures—Christ's human nature acquired a fresh understanding of obedient suffering when He experienced it. In that sense He is said to have learned; He practiced it and so perfected it.

Should not my suffering be a school from God? Should I not learn obedience through it? Surely, as it sharply reminds me of the evil of past disobedience, it calls me to remember whose hands I am in, with whom I have to do, and what my duty is in such a state. God does no wrong to His own; He will not do anything ultimately harmful to His children. Scripture says of the people of old that "In all their affliction He was afflicted," which indicates He does not afflict willingly or without provocation.

Justice is good, and holiness is good; it is right for us to repent and detach ourselves from the flesh and the world. All good must be loved, including the means by which it is attained. Sharp, heart-penetrating sermons may be unpleasant, yet they should be valued for their usefulness. Afflictions are God's powerful sermons; even the proud and hardened are compelled to listen—those who scorn and persecute preachers for speaking the same truths. Should believers under suffering remain uneducated? Words are merely words, but stripes pierce the heart with forceful understanding. Obedient submission to great pains is a serious acknowledgment of God's dominion, wisdom, love, and the sure hope of a better life.

Impatience contains elements of atheism or blasphemy; it fails to acknowledge and honor God properly. Job's wife urged him to curse God and die, as if she were saying, "Do not hold fast to your integrity." Impatience shows a misunderstanding of God's dealings with the afflicted, while patience yields because it understands the source and the end of all things. A man who is bled for his life does not grow impatient with the surgeon; rather a beast will struggle, and a child will cry. Patience declares, "Therefore I will look to the Lord; I will wait for the God of my salvation; My God will hear me" (Micah 7:7).

Our burdens are heavy enough on their own; impatience makes them heavier and is often more painful than the suffering itself. Some have gone mad under their crosses, crosses that would have felt light to another. Patience is our comfort and relief, the health of the soul that enables it to endure infirmities. "By your patience possess your souls" (Luke 21:19). Whatever else we may lose, we need not lose ourselves. He who keeps faith, hope, and love through patience preserves his soul; the impatient lose themselves as if other losses were not enough.

A poor man sings while earning his living by day labor; yet a lord or knight would be tormented with sorrow if reduced to such a state. Struggling under our yoke and burden makes it more burdensome. We cannot pray for deliverance from the pain we bring on ourselves with the same hope or comfort as for that which God lays upon us. Still, we must pray for the grace that will save us from our own impatience.

Patience prevents many sins that impatience causes, such as harboring hard thoughts of God or speaking harsh and inappropriate words. "Job did not sin nor charge God with wrong." Impatience tempts people to believe that piety and prayer are in vain, to condemn the righteous, to abandon their duties, and to say, "Why should I wait on God any longer?" It can even lead them to resort to false and sinful means in hopes of finding relief and ease.

If it were up to men, we would have many devices to alleviate our impatience. However, impatience against God has no justifiable excuse. Infinite power, wisdom, and goodness can do nothing deserving of blame. We have God's promise that all things work together for good; can He not be trusted? Or should we accuse the means of our good?

Impatience is unbecoming for those who believe that heavenly rest and glory are imminent, where all pains and sorrows will cease. If a man were on the rack yet certain to receive all he desired afterward, he would endure it more readily. Why else did the martyrs suffer so patiently? It is incongruous to complain about anything that leads a person to heaven.

Christ himself was innocent and yet did not accuse God for His sufferings. We often suffer justly for our faults, and what we endure is far less than we deserve; the greatest punishments of sin are removed in mercy. Should we continue to sinfully please the flesh and not expect it to sting? Shall we grieve the Spirit of God and not feel grief ourselves? Shall we waste our time, neglect our duties, forget our true home, fall in love with the world, yield to temptations, and defile our souls with filth and vanity, and not expect correction to remind us of our foolishness? "For what credit is it if, when you sin and are beaten for it, you endure? But if when you do good and suffer for it you endure, this is commendable before God" (1 Peter 2:20). Our merciful Father often shames us for our impatience through the blessed outcomes of our afflictions. The conclusion God brought about for Job demonstrated the reasonableness of his patience. When our afflictions are over, do not all believers recognize reasons for gratitude and say, "It is good for me that I was afflicted"? The pain is past, and the benefits remain. If all that has passed was mercy to us, why should we fear what is to come? Heaven will end all and forever shame impatience.

Our patience is a significant part of our perseverance. How much labor do the impatient lose—people who learn, pray, and practice some religion, yet lack the patience to endure the final trial and fail just as they near the crown?

So hold on, poor desponding soul! Lift up your hands that hang down and your feeble knees. Run with patience the race set before you, looking to Jesus, the author and finisher of our faith, who, for the joy that was set before Him, endured the cross. God will not deceive your hopes. Sin has brought pain and death on humanity, but Christ has sanctified it and is the Lord of life. Just a little while longer, and the heavenly possession will turn your sorrows into everlasting joy, your moans and groans into praise, and there will be no more sickness, pain, or death. Oh, foolish, unbelieving hearts that cry out against suffering and yet long for deliverance; that desire freedom from all affliction and yet flee the only true freedom; that are impatient under their calamity yet dread passing into the only rest!

However, it is neither pain alone nor death alone that will adequately test our strength and exercise our faith and patience. The true trial combines great pain—often prolonged—with the certainty of death. Both elements were present in Christ's case: the torment of His agony, scourging, crucifixion, piercing, and abandonment, together with the inevitable death that followed. Great pains that leave hope of recovery and ease can be borne even by a worldly person, because the worldly hope of better days remains; thus such suffering is not a denial of all while life itself still appears possible.

We must accept the sentence of death within ourselves if we would find that we trust in God alone, relying on Him as the One who raises the dead to another and better life.

As long as a person has any hope of life and ease, their faith is not tested to the utmost by an actual forsaking of all. Yet an easy death alone does not fully test a person; those who know that all must die may submit to it, while they cannot endure prolonged pain beforehand. Therefore, prolonged and intense pains together with the sentence of death are the true trial.

If God chooses to test me in this way, why should I complain? The flesh may groan, but the mind can obediently submit. It is merely flesh — the very flesh that has tempted and imprisoned my soul. I have loved it too much and am too reluctant to leave it. Is it not merciful of God to make me weary of it? God is opposed to idols, which include anything loved and preferred before Him; and if anything resembles such an idol, it is the flesh. Its corruptibility reminds us that both its pleasures and pains are short-lived. Long pain is usually bearable, and intolerable pain will conquer nature but not last long. The grace of Christ is sufficient, and His strength is made perfect in our weakness even when He does not remove the thorn from our flesh, though, like Christ and Paul, we may pray three times or more.

To be impatient with death is to resent our mortal existence and to flee from heaven and all true hopes, along with the happiness purchased by Christ. Is this truly renouncing the world and trusting Christ for everlasting life? Why do we fear that which ends all our pains and fears? A true believer never suffers so much that his mercies do not far exceed his sufferings. His soul is united to Christ; his hopes of heaven have a sure foundation; he is sealed for glory. Rest and joy are near, and past mercies should not be forgotten. Should such individuals not endure patiently? What a shameful contradiction it is to choose heaven as our only portion, to believe in Christ for it, and to pursue it as the focus of life, yet be reluctant to die to obtain it and to flee in fear from that which we seek and hope for! What a contradiction to call God our Father and Christ our gracious Redeemer, yet avoid His presence with distrustful fear! Almighty love may correct us or even take our lives, but it cannot ultimately harm true believers.

So much of Moses and Elias' discourse concerned the sufferings and death of Christ.

It is certainly not true that the fathers' souls, before Christ's coming, did not enter heaven but lay in some inferior limbo. Moses and Elias came from heaven; their shining glory showed that, as did their discourse with Christ and the voice and glory that accompanied them. It should not be thought that they were separated from the rest of the faithful. Though God's house has many mansions and various degrees of glory, the blessed are all fellow-citizens of one society and children in one family of God. They will come from the east and the west, from the north and the south, and sit down in the kingdom of God. Lazarus has been carried to Abraham's bosom, and the believing thief is with Christ in Paradise.

It seems that Moses and Elias appeared to foreshadow the resurrection of Christ and of the faithful, making it easier for the three disciples to believe it. Why should they doubt that Christ would rise when they saw that Moses had risen before Him? And why should they doubt the resurrection of the faithful and the glory that follows when they saw these glorified saints? Some think this apparition was also for the strengthening of Christ Himself, whose human nature had need of such ministry from angels. However, it is more certain that it was for strengthening the disciples' faith, and ours through their testimony. As it is said, "Jesus answered and said, 'This voice did not come because of Me, but for your sake'" (John 12:30). Note how the glimpse of the kingdom was represented on the holy mount: a voice of God and a glimpse of His glory; our Redeemer in a glimpse of His glory; Moses and Elias in a glimpse of theirs; and three beloved disciples still in the flesh, struggling with weakness of faith, needing such confirmation. God our Father, our Savior, the saints of heaven, and those on earth are all part of one society or kingdom. There is a close relationship and communion among them all. When the eternal Word did not disdain to come to us in the form of a servant, even as a poor, despised, crucified man, it is less surprising that Moses and Elias should come down as His witnesses and servants (Heb. 12:23, etc.). The heavenly Jerusalem, the city of the living God, of which we are enrolled as citizens or heirs, has many parts: the assembly of the firstborn, innumerable angels, the spirits of the just made perfect, Jesus the Mediator of the new covenant, and God the Judge of all. Oh, what a holy, glorious, joyful company we shall have above! Christ and His angels will not despise the least of the saints.

But what was the introduction to this apparition and transfiguration? It was Christ's praying: "Now it came to pass, about eight days after these sayings, that He took Peter, John, and James and went up on the mountain to pray. As He prayed, the appearance of His face was altered, and His robe became white and glistening" (Luke 9:28-29). Surely this is written to invite and encourage us to pray. We are in greater need than Christ. It is folly for unbelievers to think prayers are in vain because God is unchangeable. We are not unchangeable; the exercise of faith, dependence on God, and true desires—being the conditions required in a proper receiver—make those blessings become ours, blessings we otherwise could not receive. God, who commands fervent prayer, has promised to answer it. Though we must not think we can rule the world or have whatever our flesh or folly desires simply because we ask earnestly, true prayer is the appointed way to obtain what we need and what is best for us, and it fits us to receive. Just as Christ had this wonderful response to His prayers, His servants have often found that their choicest mercies for soul and body came this way.

Though the three disciples were admitted to this glorious society, their case was very different from that of Christ, Moses, and Elias. At the beginning of this heavenly gathering they lay heavy with sleep, even while that glorious company stood near them.

Alas—such is our infirmity in the flesh, and such a burden are these earthly bodies to us—that when God is present, when heaven is before us, and when we have the greatest reason to watch and to pray, a heavy, weary, sluggish body chains an otherwise active spirit. We fall asleep or turn aside into wandering thoughts when we should be conversing seriously with Christ and attending to heaven.

Alas! What unworthy servants we are. Are such as these fit for his work, his love, his acceptance, or his kingdom? Yet how merciful is our Saviour, who does not treat his poor servants as they deserve but comforts them with a glimpse of heaven—for he died for his enemies.

It is crucial to understand in what cases this excuse will hold, and when our weakness does not make the willingness of the Spirit unacceptable to God.

If a drunkard, a fornicator, or any other sensualist should say, "My spirit is willing to leave my sin, but my flesh is weak, and temptation prevails," that excuse would not prove God's forgiveness. If a person habitually lives in known sin—sin they could refrain from if they were truly willing—and says, "for to will is present with me, but how to perform what is good I do not find; it is not I, but sin that dwells in me," this is a frivolous plea.

Yet for the sleepy disciples it was a valid excuse, and I believe the same applies to Paul in Romans 7. Where, then, is the difference? Some acts of man are not under the power of the will, while others are. The will cannot keep a sleepy person awake; that sleep may be purely of the flesh and involve no will at all, and so it excuses from guilt. Other actions require much strength and effort to resist. Perhaps, with extreme diligence, the disciples might have kept awake; in that case their sleep is a fault, but a pardoned fault of weakness.

Some people are constitutionally prone to excessive fear or grief, so that no degree of unwillingness will prevent them. Others could resist more than they do, but it is very difficult even with great effort; such cases are excusable to some extent. Paul would have perfectly obeyed God's law and never sinned, yet there is no perfection in this life; mere imperfection of true grace, when it predominates in the will, does not condemn a person.

But there are acts so subject to the will that a sincere will, though imperfect, can command them. He who repeatedly does these — or does the opposite — does not fail because he sincerely would and cannot, but because his wishes are ineffectual and his will is not truly set. This is especially true when he knowingly yields to great, material sins that true grace resists more strongly than it does an idle word, thought, or action.

In short, all omissions or commissions in which the will is positively or negatively guilty are sinful to some degree. But only those inconsistent with a soul's predominant love for God, for heaven, and for holiness finally condemn the sinner.

When the disciples awoke, they saw these glorious ones in conversation. Did they hear what was said, or did Christ tell them afterward? The latter is most probable.

Just as Moses tells us how God made the world — things no one could know except as God revealed them — the apostles wrote many things about Christ that they neither saw nor heard directly, but learned from Christ by word or inspiration. How else would they have known what Satan said and did to him in the wilderness or on the temple pinnacle? How would they have known what his prayer was in his agony? So here also it is likeliest that Christ reported the conversation.

Yet Christ's own testimony was enough to remove doubt, since they daily witnessed his confirming miracles.

How great the difference between Mount Sinai and this mount! When God gave the law to Moses, that mountain trembled with flame, smoke, and thunder, and the people were terrified and fled.

But here there was nothing but life, light, and love from heaven. A merciful Redeemer, whose face shone like the sun, appeared with heavenly company close to the disciples. He pitied and bore with their heaviness and infirmity, strengthened their faith and hope, and, by showing some of heaven's inhabitants, gave them visible proof of the resurrection and of a heavenly kingdom.

This was not a frightful sight but a confirming and delightful one. The law was given amid terror by Moses; grace, truth, peace, and pleasure are given by Christ.

This was an inviting and delightful, not an alarming, apparition.

Was it not a shameful infirmity and a sin that Peter denied Christ after such a sight as this, and that the other disciples forsook him and fled? After they had seen the kingdom of God come in power, and Christ's face shining like the sun, could they so soon forget? Could they doubt whether he or his persecutors were stronger and more likely to prevail in the end?

Oh, how frail, how uncertain, how wretched is depraved man!

Though Christ found them asleep and foreknew that they would forsake him, he did not forsake them or deal with them as they deserved. He comforted them with a glimpse of heaven—for he died for his enemies.

But this was only once during all the time he stayed with them. It was an extraordinary feast, not their daily bread. They still had Christ with them, but not transfigured in glory, nor did they continually see Moses and Elias.

We are too prone to think that if God gives us an extraordinary glimpse of heaven we must have it always, or that he has forsaken us when he denies it again. Oh, that we were as eager for holiness and duty as we are for the joy that is the reward! But our Father, not we, must choose both our food and our feast.

Moses did not dwell on Mount Nebo to keep seeing the land of promise; one sight before his death sufficed. Just as "flesh and blood cannot inherit the kingdom of God," so only a little of heaven enters into us now.

When the disciples awoke, they saw his glory and the two men who stood with him. It will not be a sleeping but an awakened Christian who will behold heavenly glory.

Just as we must love God with all our heart, with all our soul, and with all our strength, every part of us must be awake in seeking and attending him before we can enjoy a foretaste of his love. Carnal security, lazy neglect, and dull contempt make us incapable of such delights. Heavenly joy presupposes a heavenly disposition and heavenly desires.

Angels do not sleep, nor are they burdened with bodies of clay; earth has no wings. It must be holy vivacity that carries a soul to God, despite the fetters of flesh. While we are in these bodies we converse with each other's souls on earth. It is not sluggishness but lively faith and fervent desire that must converse in heaven with Moses, with Elias, and with our living Head.

But how did Peter know Moses and Elias, whom he had never seen? Perhaps glorified saints bear their identifying marks and need neither names nor speech to be known. Perhaps Christ told the disciples who those men were, or perhaps he made them know by inspiration, as the prophets knew. Any of these ways God could reveal them; it is not necessary for us to decide which. That they were known is certain.

We shall not be strangers to any saints in heaven, and therefore not to our old acquaintances. Whether we shall love them more because of prior acquaintance or because they were instruments of our good on earth I do not know. I do know that our love for those who gave us holy comfort here may make heaven feel more familiar and more suited to our desires.

Oh, how many godly friends I remember! They are so numerous I cannot catalogue their names, yet the memory of many delights me. When we meet there, we shall know one another far better than we did even to the most intimate on earth.

Oh, let Christians converse with one another, remembering that they must meet in heaven, where all that was secret will be brought to light.

If we wear a mask and pretend to be better than we are, if we hide any sin or base corruption, or if we deceive our friends by fraud or falsehood, all of this will be revealed when we meet in heaven. It grieves and shames me daily to think of the sins I committed against some who are now in heaven—sins I excused, minimized, or concealed—and to consider how much evil they will discover about me there that they did not know while on earth.

But God, who pardons, will cause his servants there to forgive one another; yet the revealed sin will remain an odious and shameful thing. Lying and hypocrisy will not be cloaks there but aggravations of our shame.

If we cannot confess and take shame upon ourselves through repentance while on earth, how shall we appear in the open light and look upon the faces of those we have wronged? I do not know how much this will lessen our joy, but it must surely dishonor us to have been false to God or man—especially when we meet in a place where sin is perfectly hated. To think how we sinned together or how we tempted and ensnared one another—that will affect us then in ways I cannot fully describe. Yet even now it grieves me more to think of anyone in heaven whom I have tempted or wronged than it did while they lived with me on earth.

I believe something of this nature is common to both good and bad: even the consciences of wicked men haunt them for notable injuries done to others, especially for concealed wrongs, and particularly for persecuting God's servants after those servants are dead.

Thus, though I do not doubt that some apparitions are real, I am inclined to think that many who claim to be haunted by the sight and voice of the deceased are really haunted by their own consciences, which present those persons vividly to the imagination.

On the other hand, it delights me to remember the good I received from many who are now in heaven. I recall the profitable sermons I heard from some and the enriching conversations with others. How often did we consult sweetly about matters of everlasting life! How many days, in public and in private, did we spend in preparation and hopeful expectation of the blessedness they now enjoy?

It is no small mercy to me that I can think of the multitudes now in heaven for whose conversion and salvation God used my weak efforts as a means.

Oh, what a mercy to reflect that while I remain beset by temptations, languishing in weakness, groaning in pain, and, worst of all, burdened with a dark and sinful heart, so many have passed all this with Christ thanks to the help he sent them through my labors. It has often humbled me greatly to read of men like John Janeway and Joseph Allen, who attributed much of their growth to my writings, and who surpassed me—leaving me behind in holy delights and praises of God. How much more am I humbled by the multitude now in heaven who once called me father on earth!

If here I must rejoice with those who rejoice and mourn with those who mourn, why should I not rejoice still more with the blessed society above, and more intimately with my old acquaintances, pupils, and dear friends? My love should be directed most toward the best; therefore I should love them more than any left behind.

Because my union with them is closer and their happiness far greater, I should think of them with more joy than of those who remain. They are safe in the harbor, past all our dangerous storms and waves. Though they may know—or will know—more of my sins than they did on earth and hate them more, those who feel the comfort of their own pardon will imitate God in pardoning me and will rejoice in God's forgiveness of me.

Though their vile bodies lie like common dust, how much better do they now know the love of God, the mysteries of grace, heavenly glory, and the state of spirits in the city of God than I do, who once preached these things to them. God, who sent down Moses and Elias to show that saints in heaven and on earth have communion, will bring me and my friends now in heaven together again into a far sweeter communion than we ever had here.

It is no great wonder that Peter was overwhelmed by this glorious sight and greatly delighted by this heavenly communion, saying, "Master, it is good for us to be here;" Would not a glimpse of heaven transport any holy soul, even those who now lie in tears and fears, overwhelmed with doubts and troubles? When they are groping after God and groaning on their knees, feeling more of His frowns than His love, if they were to have such a sight as this, what a change it would bring upon them! Perhaps you might say that the doubt of their own sincerity could still deprive them of their joy. No; this sight would banish doubts and troubles. It is a communication of love, one that will fully convince those who partake in it.

Without such a miraculous glimpse of glory, God sometimes gives some of His servants a mental illustration—an inward glimpse and taste of heaven that greatly overcomes all fears of pain and death. Many old and recent martyrs have experienced this. It was a remarkable statement from the godly Bishop of St. David's, Mr. Farrar, to his neighbors: "If I stir in the fire, do not believe my doctrine." And accordingly, he did not stir. If he had not received some prophetic inspiration, this could not have been justified; it would have been a presumptuous tempting of God. Mr. Baynam's case was also extraordinary. While in the flames, he called to the papists to witness a miracle, professing to them that in the fire he felt no more pain than if he had been laid on a bed of down or roses.

I am currently reading Melchior Adam's Lives of the German Philosophers, specifically the life of Olympia Fulvia Morata, which concluded with a similar experience. Throughout many ages there has been at least one remarkable woman who excelled men in languages, philosophy, and other human learning. Such a woman was Olympia Fulvia Morata from Ferrara. She married Andreas Gundler, a physician, and moved with him to Germany. On the way, she was convinced of the protection of angels when her young brother fell from a high window onto cragged stones, suffering no more harm than if he had landed on soft ground. In Germany she wrote to Anna Estensis, a Guisian princess: "As soon as, by the singular goodness of God, I departed from Italian idolatry and came with my husband into Germany, it is incredible how God changed my soul, which, being formerly most averse to the divine Scriptures, now delights in them alone. I place in them all my study, labor, care, and mind; and, as much as possible, I despise all the riches, honors, and pleasures that I once admired."

However, the cross soon followed, as was God's usual method. Her husband and she were stripped naked by soldiers, save for the shift next to their bodies, and narrowly escaped with their lives, wandering from place to place with no one daring to take them in, even when she was sick with a fever. Eventually they found some generous hospitality, but shortly thereafter she fell into a mortal illness and died. In her last sickness, after much bodily torment, she smiled pleasantly. Her husband asked her the reason, and she replied, "I saw a certain place filled with a most clear and beautiful light," indicating that she would soon be there, and added, "I am wholly full of joy." She spoke no more until her eyesight began to fail her, at which point she said, "I scarcely know any of you anymore; but everything else around seems to be full of the most beautiful flowers," which were her last words. She had long professed that nothing seemed more desirable to her than to be dissolved and to be with Christ, magnifying His mercies to her throughout her sickness.

Many have joyfully laid down their flesh to go to Christ; what wonder, then, if Peter was reluctant to lose the pleasure of what he saw.

Two things are necessary for great and solid joy: first, the object must be truly and greatly amiable and delectable; and second, the apprehensions of it must be clear and strong. Regarding the first, we have such great and glorious things to delight us that they could feast our souls with constant joy, were it not for the second, which is, alas, much lacking. What man could choose not to be in Peter's rapture continually if he could ascertain heavenly glory in a manner as satisfactory as these sensible things are? If I were lying in prison, or suffering from the torment of colic, stones, or any such disease, and simultaneously had such apprehensions or sight of assured glory, surely the pain would not be able to suppress my joy.

What a mixture, what a discord, there would be in my expressions! Torment would compel my flesh to groan, while the sight of heaven would make me triumph. I cannot help but think how this great discord would illustrate the difference between the spirit and the flesh. What a strange thing it would be to hear the same man, at the same time, crying out in pain with groans while also magnifying the love of God with transporting joy! But we are not yet fit for such joyful apprehensions. Our weak eyes must not see the sun except through the allaying medium of humid air, at a vast distance, and through the crystalline humor and organic parts of the eye. We long to get closer and have clearer apprehensions of the spiritual society and glorious world. We study, we pray, we look up, we groan under our distance, darkness, and unsatisfying conceptions; but it must not be yet. We must be ripened before the shell will break, or the dark womb will deliver us into the glorious light.

Yet Christ granted to His three apostles what we are unworthy of and still unfit for. O happy sight! O happy men! It is incongruous to say, "What would I not give for such a sight?" lest it should resemble the folly of Simon Magus; and I have nothing to give. But it is not inappropriate to say, "What would I not do, and what would I not suffer for such a sight?" Yes, Christ poses such questions to us; O that I had better answered them in the hour of duty and in the hour of temptation! When He asked, "Are you able to drink the cup that I drink, and be baptized with the baptism that I am baptized with?" I have been ready, with James and John, to say, "We are able." But when the trial comes, and they later forsook Him and fled during His suffering, how insufficient is my own strength to fulfill my promise! When He imposed on me the call to deny myself, to take up my cross, and to follow Him, I yielded and covenanted by vow to do it; but it was by the help of the Holy Spirit, which He promised to give me.

I stand, Lord, to my covenant; help me to perform it; and give me, though not His present sight, yet some of Peter's mental apprehensions, and a glimpse, a taste, of that which transported him with delight. Let whoever will take the riches and grandeur of the world; O give me some delightful taste of that which I am made for, redeemed for, and which Your Spirit has long taught me to seek and hope for as my all!

Peter was not weary of the sight of this heavenly apparition. Why should I be weary of the believing contemplation of greater things? Although sight affects us more sensibly than mere believing and thinking, yet these have their happy role and can be effective. And Christ, who thus appeared in glory to Peter, has said, "Blessed are those who have not seen and yet have believed." Peter himself states that those who do not see Christ "rejoice with joy inexpressible and full of glory" in their belief.

O how inexcusable I am for every weary prayer or meditation on such glory, and for yielding to Satan and a backward heart, which have often made me shorten these sweet employments when I had time, opportunity, and need to extend them. What? Weary of communion with Christ! Weary of speaking to my heavenly Father for endless blessedness, on such joyful terms of hope as He has given me! Weary of the thoughts of the city of God, the heavenly society, and work! Weary of stirring divine love and exercising it in divine praise, which are the works of angels and all the heavenly host! Oh, how justly might God be, as it were, weary of me and of my weary services; yes, of the best that I can offer Him, which contains so much to give Him cause for weariness!

Peter did not shy away from this glorious vision; rather, he wished to experience more of it and to remain on the holy mount. When God calls me to a more glorious vision and experience in heaven, will I hesitate and be unwilling to go? Was that mount a better place than heaven? Is not Christ now to be seen in greater glory there? Is the Jerusalem above, the glorious company of saints and angels, not a better and more desirable sight than Moses and Elijah were on the mount? Alas! After we have read, heard, thought, and spoken so much about heaven, and have done and suffered so much for it, how can we still draw back with fear and reluctance to go there? Oh, what lamentable weakness of faith and power of the flesh does this reveal! When I read Peter's words, "It is good for us to be here;" I am saddened that I, who live in a world so close to hell, among the relentless haters of holiness and holy peace, and in a painful, weary body, can only say, with no stronger desire or joy, "It is good to be there." When I see all natural appetites earnestly desiring their proper food, and even animals longing for their beloved companions, how can my holy appetite be so dull and indifferent? Lord, awaken it through the fuller communications of Your Spirit, and save me from this hated, dangerous disease.

But Peter spoke without understanding when he suggested building tabernacles on earth for the enjoyment of what is meant for heaven. Alas! this is our common affliction and folly: we desire Christ in the splendor of His glory, but we want Him here; we would see Moses and Elijah if they would come down to us; we want to possess in the flesh what flesh and blood cannot attain. Oh, if we knew in what land, city, country, or private house we might catch even a glimpse of heavenly glory, how joyfully we would rush to such a dwelling! Merchants seek the most profitable places for trade; the poor inquire about the most fertile and delightful lands for settlement; gentlemen take pleasure in a sweet and beautifully situated home. Yet, if saints on earth could find a place where they could see what Stephen, or Paul, or the apostles saw, and experience a taste of heaven without dying and shedding this body, how desirable that dwelling would seem to them! And yet, alas, how lukewarm are our desires for the time and place where we shall have so much more! We have Christ on earth in the manner and measure that we can handle; we have some communion with heaven, as truly (though not as sensibly) as our eyes have with the sun. God will not deny believers their title, their earnest, and some firstfruits; but when we seek to have everything, or our best, on earth, or that which is meant for heaven, we do not know what we desire or say.

Are we, vile and dirty sinners in the flesh, truly fit for heavenly sights or joys? Or is this world a place for building tabernacles where we may see the Lord and find rest? What! In a world filled with temptations, wickedness, and suffering, where we are daily wrestling for our lives and fighting not merely against flesh and blood, but against principalities and powers, against the rulers of the darkness of this age, against spiritual hosts of wickedness in the heavenly places (Ephesians 6:12)? But that which is of the earth is earthly. Our earthly nature desires earthly happiness; yet when we realize that it is corruptible and fleeting, and that we do not have a continuing city here, both faith and reason urge us to seek the one to come. The unfaithful steward had enough sense to secure another dwelling when he knew he could no longer be a steward here.

God has consistently confounded and humbled me through His marvelous providence whenever I have said, "Soul, take your ease;" and have thought of building tabernacles on earth. This has convinced me that such folly is a significant danger to the soul, from which His mercy has so watchfully saved me. If a little health and comfort, a pleasant home, or cherished company and friends have flattered me into earthly delight and hopes, making me say, "It is good to be here," I have never been long without some pain, a serious illness, a loss or disappointment in friends, or some change, whether personal or public, to remind me that I did not know what I was saying, and that rest and happiness are not found here. Just as industrious ants and bees spend a long time gathering treasures and stocking their hives for winter, only for a contemptuous foot to scatter them, or for the owner of the hive to destroy the other, so too, while I neglected wealth and honor, when I had merely collected the finest books and found joy in my works and friendships, God saw that such pleasure needed a counterbalance. He has taken away books and friends or often driven me away from them and my home to remind me that I have higher aspirations and further to go. Moses and Elijah did not appear to turn earth into heaven and make me think that I was well; they came to invite my soul to their celestial home. When Christ has comforted me through answered prayers, great deliverances, and the wonderful success of my imperfect labors, through comforting friends and public mercies, it was not to make my condition pleasant and keep my desires from heaven, but to draw them there through such foretaste. Contentment with our condition, without seeking more of the world, is a great duty; but to be content with the world or anything on earth, without more holiness and communion with God, and without a share in heavenly perfection, is a grievous and harmful sin.

But, alas! it is a far worse mistake than Peter's that deceives most people. They say, just like he did, "it is good for us to be here," until melancholy or misery makes them intolerable to themselves. It is not because they have glimpsed heaven on earth or tasted the sweetness of holy fellowship and work, but because their bodies are healthy, their purses are full, their appetites are satisfied, and those beneath them obey and honor them. This is all the heaven they desire; to leave it is the death they dread.

They will not heed God or the common experiences of humanity that expose their folly until the night comes when their souls are required of them. Then, to whom will all their treasure belong?

Yet it was an even greater folly on Peter's part to think of building tabernacles for Christ, Moses, and Elijah, and to desire to fix heavenly beings on earth. If you offered the humblest saint in heaven an earthly kingdom in exchange for their condition, how disdainfully they would refuse it! My kingdom is not of this world; nor would Moses and Elijah trade their lot for that of Alexander or Caesar.

We are easily tempted by trifles that seem weighty while we are taken up with the flesh—like toys to children. But once we are delivered and behold celestial glory, our understanding will be changed.

We now fear the dark journey to that world of light. We are reluctant to strip off the rags of the flesh and leave behind a known, though dirty and decaying, home. But once we reach heaven, we would be unwilling to return to earth and be clothed so coarsely again.

When we are there, no worldly treasure will lure us back into this corruptible body until God transforms it into a spiritual, incorruptible one. Friends whom we passionately mourned at death would not then trade their company for our company, their abode for this wicked world, or their work for the best of ours on earth. It is no wonder that departed souls do not commonly appear to their friends; most apparitions are of devils or of miserable souls to whom it is no loss or condescension.

If I were once in heaven, could I possibly want to return to a world filled with madness and chaos—living among those blinded by pride and rage, and among those who call themselves Christians but whose god is their belly, who glory in their shame, and who set their minds only on earthly things? Would I choose to be among those who hate and persecute the regenerate, and all who will not take their mark and become as mad and wicked as they are?

Would I wish to groan in pain here again, to be weary in this frail body, and still more burdened with a feeble, sinful soul—weak in faith, cold in love, doubtful in hope, and imperfect in duty? Would I face the grave again, trembling at death as if it were now strange to heavenly bliss?

Lazarus will not leave Abraham's bosom for the rich man's wealth and earthly pleasures, not even to warn his indulgent brothers. Had Peter truly seen heaven as he witnessed the glory on the mount, he would never have suggested that Christ, Moses, and Elijah should remain here; they possess a far better home.

But this glorious appearance was brief—like the passing display of God's back parts shown to Moses. A cloud soon came, separating the company and ending the delightful vision. When Christians taste an extraordinary sense of God's love or a sweet foretaste of promised happiness, they must not expect that this is ordinary or perpetual.

When a fervent prayer is answered in an extraordinary way, when a sacrament is enriched with unusual drops of heavenly sweetness, or when a holy discourse or meditation lifts us higher than before, we must not assume this will be our constant nourishment. Times of fasting and of sober duty also have their place. Moses did not remain forever on Mount Horeb, nor on Mount Nebo or Pisgah, from which he saw the promised land.

God's children do not always laugh and sing; along with seasons of grace there will be times of suffering and tears. How suddenly the lark that had soared out of sight, singing in the higher air, comes down to the earth. A rich, continual diet is not best for those with many corruptions to be healed; cordials cannot be our only medicine. Unreasonable expectations of greater or more sustained joys than we are fit for harm both God and ourselves. We may and must desire more, but those desires should look up to heaven, where they can be satisfied.

The joy of the spectators turned to fear when they entered the cloud. No wonder: the change was sudden and dramatic—from a vision of the kingdom of God in power to a dark, obscuring cloud. Moments before they seemed almost in heaven; now they did not know where they were. It was a shift from glorious light to a kind of prison of obscurity.

Such changes are what we endure here. The same soul that recently tasted transporting joy may now lie in terror, barely resisting temptations to despair. The person who was confident of God's love may quickly find themselves doubting it, even denying it in sin. One who had clear evidence of sincerity may conclude it was all hypocrisy.

The same soul that once triumphed in love may cry, "O miserable man that I am!" The one who magnified the grace of Christ may lament that the day of grace has passed—especially if the tempter gains advantage through a melancholy body, or if the soul is cast into renewed guilt by some wounding sin, or into impatient discontent with its circumstances.

There is stability in the essentials of holiness; eternal life begins here. But the degrees of grace, the exercise of it, the consistency and integrity of our obedience, and consequently our comforts, are sadly mutable.

Just as all worldly things change for the ungodly, so the degrees of grace vary for the godly. Expecting nothing but joy from God, or expecting more than we are fit for, magnifies our disappointments and pain. None are cast lower into terror and almost despair than those who have been most overwhelmed with joy. Meanwhile, other Christians who live consistently enjoy a steady, constant, holy peace—even without such ecstatic experiences.

The cloud separated the group; Moses and Elijah were no longer seen, nor the visible glory of Christ. Yet Christ was not separated from them; His ordinary presence still remained. He does not abandon the soul when extraordinary joys depart. A soul does not lose His saving grace or the presence of His Spirit simply because it loses a sense of heavenly delight.

Desire shows love to Him and to His holiness, and He never forsakes those who love Him. As long as the soul breathes after Christ—seeking more communion with God, aware of its imperfections, longing for perfection, and resolved to wait for increased faith and holiness by the means Christ has appointed—it is not forsaken. Christ, by His Spirit, dwells and works within that soul.

The soul may enter into a cloud, and Christ may seem hidden and lost, but the cloud will vanish and He will appear. He will seek us first, that we may find Him. If He appears to us in humiliation and as crucified—humbling us and crucifying us to the world and the flesh, with their affections and lusts—and causes us to seek first His kingdom and righteousness, He will raise us higher and show us His glory when grace, conquest, and perseverance have prepared us.

We live in a cloudy world and body, and our sins add an even thicker cloud between God's face and us. But as God is God and heaven is heaven, so Christ is Christ and grace is grace—true even when we do not see it, even when we fear we are lost and imagine ourselves in outer darkness. At sunrise, all our darkness, doubts, and fears will vanish.

"And a voice came out of the cloud, saying, 'This is My beloved Son. Hear Him!'" (Luke 9:15) If I had heard such a testimony from heaven, would it not have lifted my faith above all doubts and unbelief? The voice that thus acknowledged Christ and His word would embolden me to trust all His promises and bind me to obey His precepts.

God's love is effective and communicative; just as His life and light beget life and light, so His love begets love. Christ, who is called His beloved Son, most fully reveals that love. No one loves us as the Father and His beloved Son do—the very source and essence of love.

Should I regard such a God and such a Savior with cold or little love? It is as unreasonable to flee from God or Christ for fear that He lacks love, as it is to flee from the sun for fear it lacks heat or light. Oh, how unruly and stubborn the corrupted human soul is!

Divine Revelation and the Truth of Christianity

When we consider God's judgment and our dependence on Him for all hopes of soul and body, we are apt to fear that He does not have sufficient love and mercy to assure us. We trust some friends with our lives and souls if they were in power over us; yet we can hardly trust infinite love itself to comfort us in pain or death.

And yet, to cure this distrust, Christ has manifested His love by the greatest miracles—His incarnation, life, works, death, resurrection, intercession, and the exaltation of human nature in Him above angels. The greatness of this incomprehensible love can make it hard for dark and guilty sinners to believe it, whether it is offered through ordinary means or through the most extraordinary effects.

Just as Christ is called the Son of God, so are all His members called sons. We share that title to partake in the same comforts. He is God's only Son by eternal generation and by the hypostatic union through His miraculous conception; but through Him we become sons by regeneration and adoption.

Should we not trust the love of such a Father and desire the presence and pleasure of such a Father? If Manoah's wife could say, "If the LORD had desired to kill us, He would not have accepted a burnt offering and a grain offering from our hands," I may say, if He would have damned me or forsaken my departing soul, He would not have adopted me or made and called me His son. Christ was made His incarnate Son so that we might be made His adopted sons; we are adopted for the sake and by the grace of Christ, His natural Son.

The command "Hear Him!" is directed against Moses and Elijah in two senses. First: hear Him whom the law and the prophets foreshadowed and pointed to—the One they served and instructed us to receive. Second: hear Him as superior to Moses and the prophets, since His coming and covenant supersede the law of Moses; as a greater light He eclipses the lesser. He has revealed more and has revealed it more clearly. Life and immortality are more fully brought to light by Him; His gospel is the heart of the Holy Scriptures, and we use the Old Testament primarily as witnesses to Christ.

And whom shall we hear so willingly and obediently as Christ? Abraham did not send Dives' brothers to the king or to the high priest to learn what religion they should choose or how to escape hell's torments; they were to hear Moses and the prophets. But God has sent us a better Teacher from heaven and commanded us to hear Him.

Moses was faithful in God's house as a servant; Christ is faithful as a Son. His authority is above that of kings and high priests, who now have no power apart from Him. Therefore none can stand against Him or His laws; commands that contradict Him are null to conscience. The examples in Daniel 3 and 4, and the example of the apostles, teach us whether God or man must be obeyed first.

This is why the Bible is more necessary to be searched and learned than statute books or canons. If men were to be heard before Christ — or as necessarily as He is — why do we not have law-preachers every Lord's Day to expound statutes and canons to the people? Why are people not catechized from the book of canons or law just as they are from the Bible?

Surely, if we must hear Christ and His gospel before priests or princes, or even before our dearest friends, how much more should we hear Him before our fleshly lusts and appetites, before a profane and foolish scoffer, and before the temptations of the devil? Oh, had we listened to Christ's warnings when we followed the tempter and the flesh, how safely we might have lived and how comfortably we might have died!

But this word, "Hear Him!" is as comforting as it is obligatory. Hear Him, sinner, when He calls you to repent and turn to God. Hear Him when He calls you to Himself, to take Him as your Lord and Savior, to believe and trust Him for pardon and salvation. Hear Him when He says, "Come to Me, all you who labor and are heavy laden, and I will give you rest. If anyone thirsts, let him come to Me and drink. Whoever desires, let him take the water of life freely." Hear Him when He commands, and hear Him when He promises. Hear Him before worldly wise men when He teaches us the way to God. Hear Him, for He knows what He says. Hear Him, for He is true, faithful, and infallible. Hear Him, for He is the Son of God, the greatest messenger that God has ever sent. Hear Him, for He came in the flesh to teach us intimately. No one else in the world has made known the things of God as He has, and no one can do it. Hear Him, for He means us no harm; He is our dearest Friend and love itself, speaking only for our salvation and promising only what He will fulfill. Yes, hear Him, for every soul who will not hear Him will be utterly destroyed from among the people.

Hear Him, therefore, if He contradicts your fleshly appetite; hear Him whether the great or the small, any or all, are against it. Hear Him if He sets you to the hardest work or calls you to the greatest suffering. Hear Him if He calls you to deny yourself, take up your cross, and follow Him, forsaking all in hope of a reward in heaven. Hear Him if He calls you to lay down your life, for no one loses by following Him.

Hear Him now in the day of grace, and He will hear you in the day of your extremity — in the day of danger, sickness, death, and judgment, when the world forsakes you and no other hearing can help you.

"But I did not see this vision; had I seen it myself, it would have satisfied me and resolved all my doubts." The answer is that God intends the ministry and testimony of men to be a means by which we believe. Faith, not sight, must be the ordinary way of our salvation. Otherwise Christ would have had to show Himself, with His miracles, resurrection, and ascension, to every person who must believe in Him. He would have had to be visible at once in every kingdom, parish, and place on earth, and continue so until the end of the world. He would have had to die, rise, and ascend millions of times in every place. Those who demand such conditions of their Lawgiver before they will believe must be saved without Him and against Him if they can. That is more unreasonable than telling God you will not believe in heaven or hell unless you see them. God wants us to live and be saved by believing, not by sight. He will use man to instruct and save man, and not send angels with every message.

Why, then, did Christ show this vision to only three of His disciples? He is not obligated to explain why. Still, we can see that a vision of heavenly glory is not something to be ordinarily expected on earth. Why did God show the back parts of His glory to none but Moses, not even to Aaron? Why did He speak to Moses only in the bush and on the mount? Why did He translate none to heaven without dying except Enoch and Elijah? Why did He save only Noah and seven others with him in the ark? These events are not ordinary occurrences, nor were they meant to be common to many.

This shows that even among His twelve apostles Christ made distinctions and preferred some over others. Although He did not place anyone in governing authority over the rest, some were more qualified and were esteemed and used by Him accordingly. Peter is called first and appears to have been more prominent because of his frequent speaking and familiarity with Christ, and by his speeches and miracles after the resurrection. Yet the faction that claimed, "I am of Paul," or "I am of Cephas," was rebuked as carnal; that shows how far Christ was from directing the churches to resolve all differences by obeying Peter as their supreme ruler. James and John are called the Sons of Thunder; they had some more eminent qualifications than the rest, so that James was the first martyred apostle, and John was the disciple whom Jesus especially loved. Ministers of the same office may differ greatly in gifts and grace, in labor and success, in God's acceptance and reward, and in the church's just esteem and love. Not all pastors are like Cyprian,

Basil, Gregory Nazianzen, Chrysostom, or Augustine. The rest ought not envy the preference given to Peter, James, and John. Andrew seems to have been Peter's elder brother and to have known Christ before him, just as Aaron was elder to Moses, yet he must allow God to choose whom He will give preeminence.

Why did these three apostles not tell anyone about this vision until after Christ's resurrection? Because Christ forbade them. This fits His method of revelation. He intended to make Himself known to the world gradually, more by His works than by mere words. These works were to be completed and presented together as His convincing witness to the world. The chief of these were His resurrection, ascension, and the sending down of the Holy Spirit. Only then could the apostles declare, "Jesus is risen, ascended, and has given us the seal of the Spirit; therefore He is the Son of God." Christ first preached repentance like John the Baptist; next He taught that the kingdom of God through the Messiah had come and was among them; then He taught them to believe that His word was sent from God and was true. He taught holiness, love, and righteousness toward men, and performed miracles to convince them that what He said deserved their belief. Yet before His resurrection the apostles did not understand many articles of our creed. They did not know that Christ was to die for sin and redeem the world by His sacrifice, nor that He was to rise, ascend, reign, and intercede in glory. Nevertheless, they were in a state of grace and life, similar to believers before Christ's incarnation. Surely no more is required of the nations that cannot hear the gospel.

The resurrection was the beginning of the true gospel state and kingdom; everything before was preparatory. Then, by the Spirit, Christianity was established in its settled form and became a known and unchangeable reality.

It greatly strengthens our faith that Christ's kingdom was not established primarily by His personal presence, preaching, and persuasion, but by the Holy Spirit working through His apostles and disciples after He ascended into heaven.

How can we be sure these three men told us nothing but the truth? The answer appears elsewhere. The Spirit by which they spoke and acted was both Christ's witness and theirs. They healed the sick, raised the dead, spoke in languages they had never learned, and preached and recorded the holy doctrine entrusted to them by Christ—the doctrine itself containing evidence of its divine origin and their truthfulness. Christ has vindicated this doctrine, then and now, by the sanctifying power of the same Spirit upon millions of souls.

How holy a doctrine Peter himself delivered, as confirmed by his vision! "For we did not follow cunningly devised fables when we made known to you the power and coming of our Lord Jesus Christ, but were eyewitnesses of His majesty. For He received from God the Father honor and glory when such a voice came to Him from the Excellent Glory: 'This is My beloved Son, in whom I am well pleased.' And we heard this voice which came from heaven when we were with Him on the holy mountain." (2 Peter 1:16-18). The words "in whom I am well pleased" are found only here and in Matthew; Mark and Luke omit them, indicating that the evangelists did not attempt to recount everything said and done, but only what seemed necessary for their purpose.

And now, what remains, O my soul, but that you take in the proper impression of this vision of the glory of Jesus and His saints, and that you joyfully obey this heavenly voice, and hear the beloved Son of God, in whom the Father is well pleased?

I. As those of us born in another age and land must learn what Christ said through the transmission and certain testimony of those who heard Him—through infallible tradition by action, word, and record—so even the glorious vision itself may be partially conveyed to our imagination by their infallible account. An embodied soul is accustomed to a mixed way of knowing through imagined ideas received by the senses, and it desires a similar understanding of separated souls, other spirits, their glorious state, place, and work. It is often left unsatisfied without it. Since Christ has partially condescended to this our culpable weakness, do not neglect the benefit of His condescension. Let this clear description of the heavenly sight be to you as if you had been one of the three witnesses, until you can say, "I almost see the face of Christ shining like the sun, and His clothes whiter than snow; and Moses and Elijah (no doubt, in some degree of glory) standing with Him." I almost hear them discussing Christ's death and man's redemption; and through this sight I partly conceive of the unseen heavenly company and state. I almost see the cloud receiving them after Peter had been overwhelmed by the vision; and I can almost feel his joyful rapture, ready to say, as if I had been with him, "it is good for us to be here." I almost hear the heavenly voice, "This is My beloved Son. Hear Him!" And shall I still doubt the existence of the celestial society and glory? If I had once seen that, what a profound impression it would have left on my heart regarding the difference between earth and heaven, man and God, flesh and spirit, sin and duty! How gratefully I would have reflected on the work of redemption and sanctification!

Why should I not place myself in the position of those who witnessed all of Christ's miracles, who saw Him risen and ascending into heaven? Or at least in the position of ordinary Christians who witnessed the wonders performed by those who reported these events? I can form a pleasing image of some distant, happy country described by a traveler, even though I have never seen it. My reason can partially deduce what great things are if I see lesser examples of the same kind or something similar. A candle reveals something by which we can conceive of the greatest flame. Even grace and gracious actions give some insight into the state of glory; but the sight on the mount conveyed it far more vividly.

Do not think, then, that heavenly contemplation is impossible or merely a dream, as if it had no conceivable subject matter to work upon. The visible things of earth are but shadows, cobwebs, bubbles, shows, mummeries, and masks. It is the love of them, and the rejoicing and trusting in them, that constitutes the real dream and folly. Our heavenly thoughts, hopes, and pursuits are far more significant compared to these than the sun is to a glow-worm, or the world to a molehill, or governing an empire to the movements of a fly. Can I make much of these almost-nothing things and yet make almost nothing of the active, glorious, unseen world? Can I doubt and stumble in my meditations about it, as if I had no substance to grasp? If invisibility to mortals were a cause for doubt, then God Himself, who is everything to men and angels, would be as if He were no God to us; heaven would be as if it were no heaven; Christ as if He were no Christ; and our souls, which are our true selves, would seem as nothing to themselves. All men would be as no men to us, and we would converse only with carcasses and clothes.

Lord, shine into this soul with such a heavenly, powerful, quickening light that I may have more vivid and living conceptions of that which is all my hope and life. Do not leave me to rely only on art and empty ideas. Make it natural for me to love You and long for You.

You teach the young to seek their mother for food and shelter — both human infants and animals. Grace is not a brutish principle; it works through reason. Yet it also has its own nature and inclining power, and it moves toward its origin as toward its end. Do not let my soul lack that holy sense and appetite which the divine, heavenly nature contains.

Let me not place more trust in my own sight and senses than in the sight and faithfulness of my God and Redeemer. I am not so foolish as to live as if this earth were no larger than the small part I can see. Let me not be even more foolish and think of the vast, glorious regions, their blessed inhabitants, and the dwelling-places of justified souls as if they lacked substance or certainty.

Let me engage in heavenly fellowship here, delight the believing soul with joy, and be stirred to earnest desire to "depart and to be with Christ."

Therefore, hear—and hear with trust and joy—the tidings and promises of Him whom the voice from heaven commanded us to hear. He is the glorified Lord of heaven and earth; all things are under His power.

He has told us nothing but what He knows, and promised nothing but what He is able and willing to give. There are two kinds of things He asks us to trust Him for: those given through express, specific promises, and those promised in a more general way and only known to us generally.

We may know specifically that He will receive our departing souls, justify them in judgment, raise the dead, and fulfill all the particular promises made to us. And we know, in general, that we have a heavenly city and inheritance. We shall see God and be with Christ in everlasting happiness, loving and praising God with joy in the perfected, glorious church of Christ.

Therefore we must explicitly believe all this. Yet we know little distinctly about the nature and operations of spirits and separated souls in formal terms. Much about their place, state, and mode of action and enjoyment remains unclear to us, though none of it is unclear to Christ. Here, then, an implicit trust should both restrain our selfish, overly bold inquiries and soothe and comfort the soul, as if we knew everything ourselves.

O my soul, detest and mortify your selfish trust and your unbelieving desire to possess the knowledge of good and evil for yourself. That was the sin that first corrupted human nature and brought calamity into the world.

God has given you enough to learn; know that, and you know enough. If more were possible, it would be a perplexity and a snare—he who increases such knowledge would increase sorrow. When it is both unprofitable and impossible, what a sin and folly it is to waste time, tire the mind, and deceive ourselves in long, troublesome searches for it. Then to murmur against God and the holy Scriptures, and die with sad, distrustful fears because we do not attain it, is shameful.

We should have understood that this knowledge belongs to Christ and the heavenly society, not to sinful mortals here. Without it we have all that is necessary to live and die in holiness, safety, peace, and joy—if we will but trust Him who knows for us. Christ perfectly knows what spirits are, how they act, whether they have any corporeal organ or vehicle, the difference between Enoch and Elijah and those who left their bodies here, what a resurrection will add to souls, how it will be accomplished, and when. He knows what is meant by the thousand years' previous reign, who will dwell in the new earth, and how it will be renewed.

He knows all the dark passages of Scripture and providence perfectly. He understands why God leaves the vast majority of the world in Satan's slavery, darkness, and wickedness, and why He chooses so few for true holiness. He knows why men are not made as He commands them to be, and why He allows even serious Christians to experience so much weakness, error, scandal, and division. All these difficulties are fully known to Christ.

It is not the child but the father who must know what food and clothing the child should have; it is the physician who must know the ingredients of his medicines and why.

Lord, open my eyes to see what You have revealed, and help me willingly close them to everything else. Teach me to believe and trust You for both kinds of knowledge: not to waver at Your sealed promises, nor selfishly to desire specific knowledge that does not belong to me, as if I could rely on myself and my own understanding rather than on Yours.

Lord, teach me to follow You in the dark as quietly and confidently as in the light, holding the general assurance of Your promise of happiness. I do not understand the mystery of Your conception and incarnation, nor the workings of Your Spirit on souls. It is no surprise that much of the resurrection and the unseen world is beyond my grasp; still more so, that Your infinite majesty is incomprehensible to me.

How little do the creatures around me know of my thoughts or of me!

I have no adequate knowledge of any one thing in the world, but I know that many things remain unknown. Blessed be that love and grace that has given me a glorified Head in heaven, who knows for me what I do not understand.

Hear and trust Him, O my soul. He has told you that we shall be with Him where He is and shall behold His glory; that a crown of salvation is laid up for us, and that we shall reign with Him when we have conquered and suffered with Him. He has commanded us to live in joyful hope of our exceeding, eternal, heavenly reward, and at our death to commit our spirits into His hand.

Receive us, Lord, according to Your promises. Amen.

www.ingramcontent.com/pod-product-compliance
Lightning Source LLC
LaVergne TN
LVHW041620060526
838200LV00040B/1355